Re-Creating Ourselves

Ja Paula

in solidarity

Molara Ogundipe-Leslie

Re-Creating Ourselves:
African Women & Critical Transformations

Molara Ogundipẹ-Leslie

Africa World Press, Inc.
P.O. Box 1892
Trenton, New Jersey 08607

Africa World Press, Inc.

P.O. Box 1892

Trenton, NJ 08607

Copyright © 1994 Molara Ogundipe-Leslie

First Printing 1994

All rights reserved. No part of this publication may be reproduced, stored in a retrieval system or transmitted in any form or by any means electronic, mechanical, photocopying, recording or otherwise without the prior written permission of the publisher.

Book design: Jonathan Gullery
Book Cover Design: Carles J. Juzang
Book Cover Photograph: Armet Francis
> from *Children of the Black Triangle*
> (Africa World Press, Inc. 1989)

Library of Congress Cataloging-in-Publication Data

Ogundipe-Leslie, Molara.
    Re-creating ourselves : African women & critical transformations /
    Molara Ogundipe-Leslie.
        p. cm.
    Includes bibliographical references.
    ISBN 0-86543-411-5. -- ISBN 0-86543-412-3 (pbk.)
    1. Women--Africa--Social conditions. 2. Women--Nigeria--Social
    conditions. 3. Feminism--Africa. 4. Feminism--Nigeria. I. Title.
HQ1787.038 1994
305.42'096--dc20   93-43967
                                                              CIP

Contents

Part II: Practice

Dedication

To both of them who gave us the examples

for my mother always, my pathfinder and First Lady
the brainy one; grace and generosity personified
ace teacher, leader and promoter of people and causes
Chief Mrs. Grace Tayo Ogundipe
ọmọ ạsi wọn l'owo tọketọkẹ
ọmọ asii beere
ọmọ okẹ mẹta ko d'owo

and her partner, that handsome fun-person
of laughter and wisdom playfully rendered
mystic yet household "impressionist"
charmer yet visionary
the late Right Revd. Chief L. M. O. Ogundipe
who loved to say:

"Raise your mind to high things. Think on the plane of
the Infinite Consciousness."

Foreword

What does empowerment mean to us as black women of Africa and her diaspora? It means social recognition and dignity just as, most of all, it means space to speak, act, and live with joy and responsibility as it has always meant for our ever-so responsible foremothers wherever they were in history. Our work, writings and exhortations as women in various forms and media show that we want to end our silences and speak our truths as we know them. We wish to have power which positively promotes Life in all its forms; power to remove from our path any thing, person or structure which threatens to limit our potential for full human growth as the other half of Life's gendered reality; power to collapse all screens which threaten to obscure our women's eyes from the beauties of the world.

—Mọlara Ogundipẹ-Leslie

Preface

On Transformational Discourses and Hearing Women's Voices

"Find(ing) A Light-Filled Place"

by
Carole E. Boyce Davies

The struggle to produce and to be heard is commonly experienced among women in academic and other social contexts.
The detractions and subversions are myriad. There is rejection,
condescension and derision;[1] there are institutional trials and
abuse;[2] there are personal attacks, distortions and attempts at
minimization. 'Molara Ogundipe-Leslie is a scholar and feminist activist who can bear witness to these myriad attempts at
silencing. But to her credit, she has sustained a critical voice
and as a result we are able now to see, in one place, the products of those years of relentless critical insight and its expression.

There is the tendency in Western academic contexts, borne
of U.S. and European hegemony, to assume that what is said
in Euro-American universities is *only what has been said* or *only
what matters*. As well, the ways that research is conducted, the
subject positions and locations of those conducting the
research, and the types of questions engaged are often set, in
the West. Thus, the context for the reception of scholarly products as well as their very nature and the primary themes of
scholarly inquiry, as well as the results, are often pre-deter-
mined. As a result, the incredible output and intellectual contributions, by scholars from other parts of the world, often in

advance, of questions raised in the West, generally get relegated in Western theoretical formulations, to the "unsaid" or
more precisely the "unheard."

'Molara Ogundipe-Leslie is one of those women's voices
which have been speaking, both critically and creatively on the
issues of gender, politics, social transformation for at least three
decades. Her terrain has been both in and outside the Western
academic/publishing contexts. She is one of those scholars who
brings with her an impressive range of credentials from years
of teaching at the university level, public lectures, publication
to organization, activist work and practical applications at the
governmental, national, continental African, and international
level. For example, she served on the Editorial Board of the
highly regarded *Guardian* newspaper in Nigeria for which she
wrote a weekly essay, and was from 1987-1989 the National
Director of Social Mobilization in the Federal Government of
Nigeria with the specific responsibility for political and cultural
education of women in anticipation of civilian rule.

She has been founding member of women's groups such as
WIN (Women in Nigeria), a women's research and activist
group and AAWORD (Association of African Women for
Research and Development) an African women's research
organization. She has also in the past held both research,
administrative and creative positions and lectureships at a
variety of universities in Nigeria and around the world. A
number of the essays in this collection document that
activist/intellectual work.

Because of the inherently male-oriented nature of African critical discourse and its politics, supported with the "politics of
citation" otherwise known as the "politics of exclusion" in the
academy, African women's voices, like 'Molara Ogundipe-
Leslie's, have not been accorded the same kind of audience as
have many of their male counterparts. Even those men with
less information of value to transmit are accorded some hearing by virtue of their subject position in phallocratic order. But
these are also the days of scholars, (male and female) working
on women but avidly hostile to feminist inquiry and to women,
or disregarding the ground breaking scholarship and activism

of women before them; of Women's Studies and related institutions still maintaining its politics of subordination in relation to work from the non-Western world; of some male scholars seeking to work on gender now for opportunistic reasons and not for any commitment to fair play.

For these and other reasons, it is of radical importance to have access to the works of one of the leading feminist/critical thinkers from Africa. With the contributions of works such as this one, scholars in women's studies and African studies in particular can no longer claim not to be informed. In fact its thematic focus on "critical transformations" speaks to the need for transformational discourses, to now be recognized as a new and central discourse in the academy.

The academic backdrop against which work of this nature is produced is represented by two signifying sketches which follow:

(1) A well known Africanist meets one of his former students whom he had not seen since graduate school and who was now a scholar in her own right. Meeting anew as professionals in the corridors of an African Studies meeting, he discovers that her field of research was women, and says *privately* to her "Oh no, you are too bright to just work on women!"

(2) Another even more well known Africanist in response to a perceived challenge to his "manifest destiny" and right to write on women without seriously studying the field, says publicly in a central forum, that the study of women is too important to be left just to women.

Re-creating Ourselves is about women, therefore about the world in its diversity of problematics, oppressions, representations, lives. It is the product of a variety of intellectual desires. It resists those uninformed and inherently biased views as expressed above. It demonstrates the long-standing intellectual and activist work which goes into the development of a feminist critical practice for black women. It recognizes the condition of women as central and legitimate subjects for seri-

ous examination. This is a much needed text in the context of
African literature, women's studies, literary studies in general, culture, politics, critical thought, social action and so on. It
is an important contribution to the range of debates on gender
issues from an African feminist scholar who has done the work
and knows what she is talking about. A few earlier essays like
"Not Spinning on the Axis of Maleness," "African Women,
Culture and Another Development," and "The Female Writer
and Her Commitment" have been indispensable texts in the
teaching of African literature and Black Women's Writings,
repeatedly cited by countless scholars. Producing this text,
therefore, is an academic milestone in the field of Africana
Women's Studies since we are now able to have access to these
critical writings in one place.

Re-creating Ourselves will prove to be an invaluable research
source for students and scholars in the field. It examines African
women from the point of view of an African woman who has
done the work and can speak from an informed place. It pro-
vides information and ways of articulating feminist positions
that another generation of younger scholars need to re-engage.
For example, students in my Black Women's Writing course,
after reading Ogundipe-Leslie's "Not Spinning on the Axis of
Maleness" and noting the way she handled an antifeminist,
reactionary critique, said for example, "She taught me, among
other things, that there are some things for which we cannot
afford any sympathy whatsoever, like an unfounded argument."[3] In hearing Ogundipe-Leslie's words then, we find the
bridge between her critical mind and writing, across which students of feminist inquiry and general readers can gain access
to some of the bases of African/feminist critique.

Those of us who contributed essays to the collection Ngambika.
Studies of Women in African Literature[4] operated then out of a
sense of new beginnings and therefore of incompleteness. We
began (in the context of the U.S. academy) to articulate some
issues that had to do with gender and African literary criticism.
In many ways, we lamented the absence of scholars like 'Molara
Ogundipe-Leslie from the centers of African critical discourses
but knew that we were both raising and responding to

antiphonal calls from the disparate geographical locations of Africa and the diaspora as we awaited points of intersection.

Mindful of the danger of "speaking for others,"[5] we attempted to speak with our sisters, (many of us also as African women) and raise questions for which we knew there were answers and pre-texts and what I have identified elsewhere as a continuum of "unheard articulations"[6] in which the production of women occupies a central space.

Ogundipe-Leslie's work, then brings forward some of those prior articulations and pre-texts which provide paths to new knowledge. In that same way then, it is a resounding response to many of the earlier "calls." What we are witnessing here is another breaking through this wall of "strategic non-hearing." Even so this is only a fraction of 'Molara Ogundipe-Leslie's work, a vast output unavailable in one place, which had to be assembled, meticulously in order to present a selection of the wide range of ideas she articulates. Those who work in the Western academies and/or operate out of strategic exclusions based on "not knowing" or "false knowing" will now be able to interact with considerably more knowledge and information of the African feminist practices and ideas of this scholar.

In an Ethiopian restaurant in Atlanta, during yet another African Studies meeting, a small group of African scholars including the now gone Joe Kubayanda, 'Molara Ogundipe Leslie and this writer, spoke, among other things, of the need to identify, articulate and advance "Transformational Discourses" as a theoretical perspective and as an area of linking intellectual and activist work. Although that discussion remained unfinished for that moment, we see now some of the ways in which it is being pursued. It is therefore critical to address how the transformational has been articulated in various attempts to dismantle oppressive modes of intellectual pursuit, disengage from politics of dominance and violence and affirm the right to ask for new, transformed and more egalitarian modes of being. Audre Lorde, for example in her essay, "The Transformation of Silence into Language and Action"[7] was already signaling the need for the articulation of the "transformational." A number of scholars in different ways, throughout history, have been calling for "transformed worlds."

Transformational discourses then can be assigned to those discourses which both challenge and re-recreate, which seek to begin anew on different and more humane grounds, which combine intellectual work with activism and creativity. Transformational discourses then speak as well to curricula transformation, as well as transformations in consciousness; the transformation of epistemological and pedagogical bases of those responsible for the futures of countless minds in and outside of academic contexts. Transformational discourses reject on principle the "discriminatory paradigm" which operates on the basis that discrimination is a given and that each group must therefore negotiate its way out of discrimination and prove itself worthy of serious consideration. They resist the variety of oppressive practices in existence in our world and seek to transform them, move one from positions of limitation to positions of action.

As you read the work of 'Molara Ogundipe-Leslie, in this text, you are reading one important manifestation of how she identifies the transformational. But, providing alternative insight into the discourse of the transformative, in the closing verse of a poem, she says,

> We are mad
> who seek to find a light-filled place
> resisting well
> who seek to dance in its green and gold
> to hug in the joy with which we know
> the spirits of grace do melt
> into the spirits of life[8]

Within the context of hegemonic discourses which normalize their insanities and illegitimacies and seek to maintain their power, those who resist well, are not "mad." Rather they often occupy the "wild space" outside of the margins of dominance. We remember as well that it is in the nature of oppression to define all those who resist as "mad." It is this space of resistance and transformation which dares to demand clarity, joy, freedom and the creation of "new worlds"[9] of being. *Recreating Ourselves*, therefore shows the critical mind of 'Molara Ogundipe-Leslie, in process as she engages and explores, with confidence, a variety of timely issues of relevance to Africans, women, critical thinkers and those who resist "global violences" and ask for transformed worlds. It dances strongly in the "green and gold" of new life and certain brilliance.

Notes

1. See Ama Ata Aidoo, "To Be a Woman," in *Sisterhood is Global* ed. Robin Morgan (Garden City, New York: Anchor Books, 1984): 258-265 which incisively addresses the obstacles in the path of the African woman as academic.
2. Witness the experiences of Anita Hill, Lani Guinier and other black women academics in the United States. For further discussion, Nellie Y. McKay's "A Troubled Peace: Black Women in the Halls of the White Academy," in Glynis Carr, ed., *"Turning the Century": Feminist Theory in the 1990's* Lewisburg, Bucknell University Press, 1992, pp. 21-37.
3. Student response paper in Black Women's Writing courses, March 14, 1993
4. Trenton, New Jersey: Africa World Press, 1986.
5. See Linda Alcoff's "The Problem of Speaking for Others" in *Cultural Critique* 20, Winter, 1991-1992, pp. 5-32.
6. *Women's Studies International Forum* 14:4(1991):249-263.
7. In *Sister Outsider*, Freedom, CA., The Crossing Press, 1984, pp. 40-44.
8. "Because We are Mad (song to a black sister in Chicago)" in *Voices. Canadian Writers of African Descent*, edited by Ayanna Black (Toronto, Harper Perennial, 1992, p. 5.
9. A forthcoming 2-volume work, *Moving Beyond Boundaries* (London Pluto Press), edited by Ogundipe-Leslie and Davis demonstrates this point further.

Introduction

Moving the Mountains, Making the Links

In the lead essay to this volume of essays, I theorise that African women have six mountains on their back, over and above the four mountains proposed by Chairman Mao for Chinese women. From this concept of mountains, I have drawn the title of my introduction which proposes to show which mountains African women need to move and are moving. I also attempt to link their struggles in the various topographies where the mountains are being assailed.

These essays represent a harvest of over two decades of theorising, writing and organising in Nigeria and abroad around the issues of women and transformations which I consider critical to their lives and their continent of Africa. The word "critical" is being used in the sense of discriminating, evaluative and analytical; "engaged" and perhaps not "neutral" since most African women and myself are emotionally and spiritually committed to the wellbeing of their continent.

Added to the senses of "careful judgement" or "judicious evaluation" in "critical," which I have evoked, are the sense of a crisis and that of "being at a turning point or points," of "reaching specially important junctures." In many ways and particularly sociologically, historically and in terms of values, Africa is at a critical juncture, awaiting and demanding transformations.

What are some of these critical transformations that are required and necessary? Primarily, and at a very basic level, Africa needs economic transformation geared towards the interests of its populations. But African perspectives on this need are often ignored or suppressed. Africa needs to be recognized and re-introduced into discourses of world affairs, history and culture. Africa is always that place which gets left out, forgotten and omitted in global discourses. Take a note of that and try to look for Africa in newspapers, anthologies, essay collections and books which claim to be globally inclusive. The African person is that person who does not have a "self," who gets represented or spoken for by others. At the creative level, travellers and settlers in Africa become the spokespersons for the indigenous peoples. Where Africa comes up at all, it is either white South Africa, or "English Kenya" (as a New Jersey high school teacher said to me in April, 1993) or Arab Africa. The black indigenous African is the international "dirty secret." He/She is that person who cannot participate in world discourse or action on his/her own behalf. In this problematic, we can imagine where the indigenous woman would be. Reading about Africa's place and role in world history from the beginnings of time should be part of the requisite education of every foreigner—for the sake of world peace.

An attitude, residual from 19th century racism and hegemonic, colonial times, still persists towards the indigenous black African (read "negro"; if the secret be unmasked). It is that attitude which makes indigenous Africans (constructed as "negroes" privately) left out of world discourses and disqualified from speaking for themselves or from being recognised in the gathering of the world's peoples as minds and agents of culture and history. This absence of indigenous Africans (indigenous as pre-Arab invasions of the 7th century A.D.) is at the heart of the discourses on voice and voicelessness which at the present moment suffuse scholarship and creativity in and about the African world.

Literary scholars in various perceptive ways have traced the absence of Africans from texts since the early days of European expansion and hegemony; from Elizabethan times where Othello's blackness is "Moorish" not African; where scholars and theatre practitioners still debate Othello's Africanness; where not only Caliban's mother is absent[1] but also Caliban's mate[2], that is, the archetypal helpmeet and woman owner of the land which is invaded and expropriated by Prospero and Miranda in Shakespeare's *The Tempest*. In a world constituted by surviving colonial visions and terminology into "people" (read: white) and "natives" (read: all other peoples)[3], the black woman's absence is ever central and taken for granted. At the heart of the discursive storms around voice and voicelessness, therefore, are African women. But who are these African women? And how have they inserted themselves into the critical junctures to activate and participate in the transformations ongoing in Africa? The essays in this book attempt to answer some of these questions as they problematize the questions and reflect the dynamic contexts within which we tried, in the cataclysmic seventies and the more circumspect eighties, to re-vision our lives, re-create ourselves and re-examine received ideas and theories. All hegemonic perspectives and narratives of colonisation went under questioning; methodologies too, as some of us, scholars in Nigeria, warred over "concept and meaning, theory and method"[4], refining Marxist theory with African history, sociology and experience.

> "Shall we say this war consumes the heart and enervates the soul? Shall we will the war, as we must, to clarify and guide us only? And shall we note the blue-eyed inertia, the glazed-eye indifference from passing weariness? . . . The passing weariness, born of tension and relax, the tension and relax which is the certain rhythm of life?"[5]

African women were re-discovering themselves again, re-creating themselves and their lives in various social arena as the essays herein show. Through theory and practice, we tried to re-discover African women in the academy as speaker and spoken about, as critic and creator. We pursued women's episteme in society through research and activism. Through writing and organising women, we tried to uncover and learn from how we know what we know and how we create what we do create socially and ideationally.

These essays have therefore been collected in two sections: theory and practice. While the first part features essays written in and about the world of thought, the second part describes my experiences with other women and men with whom we organised for critical transformations—in the home/families and the workplace; in spirituality (radical theology) and materiality (political economy). The stories behind each of these essays deserve to be told, and they would form enough material for another book. Suffice it to say that I shall probably do that in another text in order not to delay you from getting to the material behind these covers. The first two essays were written for AAWORD conferences in Dakar and Algiers respectively, the first being commissioned as a keynote address for the 1981 conference in Dakar. AAWORD (Association of African Women for Research and Development/in French, AFARD: Association des Femmes Africaines pour les Recherches et Developpement) was our special baby, a pan-African organisation we decided upon at the 1975 Wellesley Conference whose proceedings became the volume: *Woman and National Development: the Complexities of Change* (Chicago, University of Chicago Press, 1977). As early as 1975, the third world women (or AALA, my acronym for Africa, Asia and Latin America) at the conference disagreed with the intellectual and social attitudes and positions of the Euro-American feminists and gender scholars. We quickly caucused and after several meetings, produced a position paper which I was delegated to read. Has the necessity of AALA women resisting Western gender scholars changed since then? Have we in fact learned anything? Are we, as feminists and gender scholars, educable, if after three decades, AALA women still have cause to complain about issues of race, class and gender, not to mention other mediations which I mention in the following essays? Or perhaps some of us simply prefer to remain not educable?

The initial meeting of what became AAWORD/AFARD took place in Wellesley with the presence of Bolanle Awe, Nawal el Sadaawi, Marie-Angelique Savane, Filomena Steady, Achola Pala, Dina Osman, Niara Sudarkasa and myself among others. After follow-up planning meetings in Lusaka, Zambia, and Dakar, Senegal, we formalised the organisation as AAWORD/AFARD in 1977. It may be noticed that I keep referring to "African women" in my introduction here even though

4

I have written all the essays. This is because I feel very strongly that these writings have emerged from over twenty years of working, organising and networking with other women across my country, continent and world (e.g. the Women for a Meaningful Summit (WMS) with Margarita Papandreou in Greece (now Women for Mutual Security—WMS), the South-South Commission chaired by Julius Nyerere, the Sisterhood is Global Institute which grew out of a workshop at Stonybrook that accompanied the launching of the *Sisterhood* text;[6] and women in Nigeria, Britain, Canada, Africa and her diaspora.

Many of us women who constitute these networks, from India to Norway, from Rio de Janeiro to New Zealand have become firm friends and colleagues who keep meeting, mixing and sharing our dreams, thoughts and energies. My essay "Women in Nigeria" was commissioned by the founding conference of *Women in Nigeria*, an association which came to being at that conference. All participants at that 1982 conference wanted the organisation and willed it into being; therefore it was not the brainchild of any one person. I remember the excitement of those days; my travel to that conference in Zaria, Northern Nigeria with my leg in a cast on which the conferees signed in revolutionary love; the feeling of being at a critical juncture of transformation where we had brought to being a progressive organisation of women and men—yes, male feminists.

WIN became linked to AAWORD from which we had learned not to make the old organisational errors. We insisted on a non-hierarchical constitution, our executive comprising all secretaries. Our first publication, *Women in Nigeria Today* (London, Zed Books, 1985) was edited by a collective, again to prevent cults of personality and the promotion of individualism and bourgeois careerism. Those were earnest days. Who says women are not also "in" to power and dominance, egoistic autocracy and self interest?

The remaining three essays in the first section on **Theory** are about literature and literary theory. "The Female Writer and her Commitment," now somewhat of a classic, is a darling of women's studies departments and literary theorization in African literature from Sweden to South Africa, in a way that has been gratifying. Newer voices are also coming up, again a gratifying experience. As I stated in my keynote address to the Women's Caucus of the African Literature Association at the University of Wisconsin in Madison (1990), African women must also make theory contrary to the inherited prejudice that "Europe is theory, Africa is native informant; Africa is descriptive analysis" (to play with Senghor's schema).

The sections: **Theory and Practice,** are linked by a prose poem written when I was charging around all of the then twenty-two states of Nigeria in a Peugeot 504 (important to name the car since it is a Nigerian vehicular icon) as National Director of a government commission to mobilise women. I learned a lot at that time from the many women of varying social classes and ethnic groups, from the different levels of Nigerian men who are genuinely concerned about the future of Nigeria and Africa. I also learned a great deal about my country as I re-discovered her physical beauty of which I was always convinced. Nigerians should spend their vacations at home, for instance in the temperate climes of the former Gongola or among the beautiful hills and valleys of the Okigwi area or in the lush greenery of the southern coastal states.

The interlude leads appropriately into essays written for practical situations, from the preface to the WIN Document which we presented at the U.N. Decade Conference in Nairobi, Kenya, in 1985, to essays written for various groups to whom I spoke as a social mobilizer at workshops, public lectures and other gatherings. The style in this section becomes polemical, exhortatory and sometimes colloquial. The section also includes five recent essays and one written for a Ghana Conference organised by Ben Turok and the *Journal of African Marxists* in 1985. In that piece, I raise issues of ethics, culture and personal values among Marxists, considerations much neglected in the efforts to re-structure society along newer lines.

Those were years of interjecting practice with theory when we questioned everything and created new visions. We were, of course questioned ourselves, sometimes harshly attacked particularly by those who resented the very mention of Marxism. Criticisms went from the absurd (that Marx was a dead white male) to the psychological (that African Marxists were still in search of the great white father).[7] I have always wondered what being a "dead white male" had to do with anything, considering that mortality is the inevitable fate of all of us and that some of the models of those who evoke that phrase are also dead. Are ideas valuable only in the instant? The critique of the Marxists was often either culturally nationalist (don't use ideas that come from Europe even as you ride European automobiles) or pathologically racist (if the inventor of the idea is white, then the idea must be pernicious). My hope, however, is that we can move beyond a viscerally racist reaction to the source of ideas, from a biological exclusionarism to a critical approach which looks for the relevance of ideas to our experiences, societies and history, and to our project at hand. Believing in culture and not race, I firmly hold that thought and ideas are products and the legacy of the possibilities of the human mind, to be claimed by all humankind.

Culture and cultural studies are, at the moment, receiving attention in the intellectual world. I hold that people's identities are determined by the cultures they carry, not by that nebulous category of race which is a political invention. I discuss this briefly in Chapter 11 (Part II) on "Feminism in an African Context." The area of culture is one where critical transformations must take place. Africans must now pay critical attention to what of their "cultures" must survive and through whom. Who will be the legitimate narrators of African cultures? Exiles, immigrants, part-children of cultural foreigners, some of whom were not raised with the experience of forms of African cultures, or middle class indigenous children who are educated away from their languages? Some Westernised Africans are probably the only cultural types who think they can preserve their cultures by marrying culturally exogamously. Commonsensical people always knew this was bad for cultural survival. Africa is perhaps one of the only places where people marry spouses who do not care to learn their languages (language being a vehicle of culture), who despise the cultures of their marriage partners and identify away from them. We are perhaps the only people (compare Orientals and Jews) who

7

marry spouses who cannot be cultural conduits and who produce children who are completely emotionally alienated from our cultures as we sing paeans to negritude, Africanity, or "culture and heritage." Perhaps more Africans need to develop an attitude of mastering the world rather than entering it through spouses; determining their own vision and setting their own cultural standards rather than imitating, assimilating and vanishing into other cultures.

For the many reconstructions in which Africa has to engage, several of our ruling narratives of culture and epistemology have to be critically reviewed, if not abandoned. Our very view of ourselves, our knowledge of ourselves has to be constantly queried as not coming from what has been told to us, or from what has been constructed on our behalf. Sometimes we now see ourselves through the eyes of the Euro-American "other," in narratives I call "neo-colonial."

There is the "neo-colonial literary narrative" consisting of a paradigm and details which are now *de rigueur* for the African novel: some "tribal" people involved with kolanuts and "weird" rites of passage in some "rural" place, away from their modern variety in "the cities" who are poor (as constantly reiterated), speak some "pidgin," ride around in mammy wagons with quaint and fetching sayings splashed across them, in a country where the political leaders are "incomprehensibly" and "uniquely" corrupt (as only Africans can be corrupt) and the intellectual/writer is in lonely and alienated angst. When shall we get a break from these novelistic clichés? Who sees this Africa? Who speaks of it? When shall we get to see the real Africans as they actually live their lives in the complexity of continuity and change, tragedy and joy, not only in the gleefully, patronizingly reiterated poverty? Are there some Africans who are, in fact, happy to be alive and prefer to live in Africa, even with the hardship which they, of course, want to change on their own terms? Are there Africans who prefer to live in Africa but wish that their political leaders did not negotiate away their lives with such foreign institutions as the World Bank and IMF whose sharp practices and arm-twisting interactions with African governments are not protested by the owners of those same eyes that weep over the poverty of Africa? Unfortunately, despite years of decolonizing research and scholarship, it still needs to be emphasized that paradigms for looking at Africa continue to require re-considerations and re-conceptualizing. Dichotomies of "rural and urban," "tradition and modernity," "elite and people," and others continue to obfuscate knowledge about Africa. Many such analytical simplicities must change; particularly because they are predicated on Eurocentric assumptions. Africans themselves have inadequate self-constructed narratives to abandon and some of these are the narratives of victimhood in which we like to indulge, perhaps to harrow the conscience of Euro-America. We, however, in this manner, do a disservice to our own histories which are more often sagas of proud resistance or intelligent negotiations of and adaptation to imponderables.

One such narrative of victimhood, adopted by and popular among the African intelligentsia, is that of colonisation as the fable of the bible and gun. It sounds touching to say while the "white man" distracted us with the bible, he took away our lands with the gun. Yet, narratives of colonization consist more of interactions of commerce, resistance, negotiations, some conquest, administrative treachery, class collaborations, adaptations and more resistance, not only militarily but culturally.

Nowhere is the re-writing of narratives more mandatory than in discourses on African women. I shall repeat my earlier question here. Who are "African women"? This is neither a trivial question as we shall see; nor is the phrase a truism. I have been saying in my four years of public lectures in North America that there is no such thing as "the African woman." She cannot be essentialised in that way; rather she has to be considered, analysed and studied in the complexity of her existential reality; her classes, cultures, races, and ethnicities among other variables. African women are not a monolithic group of illiterate peasants sporting some twenty to thirty educated women who speak internationally and are discredited for being educated. Social stratification existed in pre-colonial (i.e. pre-nineteenth century) Africa just as there is social stratification, including traditional aristocrats and modern-day bourgeois elements in so-called rural Africa. A finely discriminating approach to African sociology still has to be developed beyond the crudities we now have.

It is important to note that in most Euro-American discourses about women, the term "women" in Europe often refers to "middle class, educated white women" while "women" in Africa refers to "illiterate, peasant, working class or poor women" or perhaps to a dark hole named "women"—a primitive mass that manifests pristine, incomprehensible behaviour in ignorance and speechlessness. The middle class educated African women are not somehow included in this referent of African women; neither are they equivalent to Euro-American women of the middle class. Therefore in discussing Africa, there is usually a "rural Africa" where that pristine, undifferentiated, ahistorical mass of "real" African women inhabit, in which context all theories about "African women" are tested. No one can speak to this process, to this knowledge of this atavistic womanhood, not even African women from the continent themselves, but only Euro-American theorists and experts. In a way, it is ironically true that only these Euro-American experts know about that pristine and primitive "mass" of atavistic African women who can only also transform themselves into people, into history and modernisation only if they heed the policies and ideas of their Euro-American "knowers" and agencies, to whom they are exclusively "knowable."

From the foregoing problematic springs the so-called voicelessness of African women. We neither look for their voices where they utter them nor do we think it worthwhile to listen to their voices. We sometimes substitute our voices for their own and we do not even know when we do this nor are we able to recognise the differences in the mixed or substituted voices. Women of European descent are most prone to these ventriloquisms, frequently calling on African women to play the role of ventriloquists' puppets, speaking to other people's agenda. These are some of the issues burning still between Euro-American and AALA women.

Are African women voiceless or do we fail to look for their voices where we may find them, in the *sites* and forms in which these voices are uttered? One signal example is in the Ivorian movie *Faces of Women* by Desiré Ecaré (1985) in which so-called docile "rural" women, allegedly subjugated by polygamy, amuse themselves about deceiving their husbands as they have extra marital sexual experiences. In what sites do the women express these emotional rebellions? In women's dance games during a very "proper" village festival. We must look for African women's voices in women's spaces and modes such as in ceremonies and worksongs as some scholars like Kofi Agovi, Abu Barry, Helen Mugambi and others are beginning to do. We must look for them in places such as kitchens, watering sites, kinship gatherings, women's political and commercial spaces where women speak, often in the absence of men. It is not only in other modes such as in suicide that women speak, as acceptably argued by Gayatri Spivak;[8] women also speak in words where we do not hear them. They also speak in silences.

Therefore the oral texts of African women must be identified and spoken to just as our attention has been drawn to a definition of voicelessness in the *woman writer's text* as:

"the historical absence of the woman writer's text: the absence of a specifically female position on major issues such as slavery, colonialism, decolonization, women's rights and more direct social and cultural issues."[9]

Thirty years after the earlier texts on the study of African women collected by Denise Paulme,[10] it is still necessary to make corrections about ways of seeing and studying African women. Arguments such as African men occupied the public sphere while women occupied the private (read: domestic) still need to be challenged. Niara Sudarkasa puts it very clearly and correctly when she says "a more appropriate conception (and by that I mean makes more sense of more of the realities of those societies) was to recognise two domains, one occupied by men and another by women—both of which were internally ordered in a hierarchical fashion and both of which provided personnel for domestic and extradomestic (or public) activities. . . . there was considerable overlap between the public and domestic domains in pre-industrial societies."[11]

It is, however, within feminism and its discourses and texts that many issues of conflict abound. While some opponents to feminism tell us that feminism is not relevant to Africa, other scholars, positively declare that the study of women is too important to be left to women. And you wonder where these voices who have now discovered women's causes were when the bodies and careers of feminist women were being splattered on the walls of the academy and the corporate world since the sixties.

African women feminists are being stigmatised as "angry feminists" or "frustrated women." Needless to say, a woman who concerns herself with the negative conditions of African women and social justice for them reveals herself as being "angry about nothing" and secretly sexually frustrated. None of her problems, however, cannot be solved by the indispensable phallus which has the undeniable power to keep her from lesbianism and her other potentially "wayward" ways. "The good African woman" is faithful to her "culture and heritage" and as wife, acts submissive and accepts servitude and emotional abuse.

When trying to include gender issues in the intellectual movements in Nigeria in the seventies, feminists and progressive women received (and still receive) a great deal of flack. At times, I was personally called a "black" white woman by Africans, and a "brown" white woman by certain European friends and colleagues who thought they were naming me to a higher place. In such wise are African women constantly harassed today about "culture," never mind that African men are not themselves fulfilling traditional demands; in marriage, such as burying their fathers-in-law, working on their farms, or working for them in any equivalent way. Without a blind adherence to the "shibboleth" of "culture and heritage," most African women and feminists are "womanist" in Alice Walker's sense of being committed to survival and wholeness of entire peoples, male and female; being not in any way separatist or adversarial to men.[12] African women in general wish to retain certain features of their traditions; those which are positive for women.

In fact, contemporary Africans have to resolve some contradictions between their inherited cultures and their modern conditions of life. We need to critically transform the contradictions between ethnicity and nation, between ethnic cultures which bind us emotionally at the level of family (the most defining area for Africans today) and the level of the state which has little meaning and less emotional significance, often commanding little loyalty. For instance, to whom does the body of a spouse belong in modern Africa today?[13] Does it belong to the birth family or the affinal (marital) family? It is not such a ridiculous question where in most countries in Africa, claims of consanguinity (which determine traditional law and behaviour at the personal level) still override claims of conjugality which are usually derived from Europe or Islam and characterise family laws at the state level.

Privileging conjugality over consanguinity, contrary to African realities, is responsible for misreadings of the statuses of African women and their conditions of life. We have reiterated, seemingly to no avail, that African women are more than wives. To understand their multi-faceted identities beyond wifehood, we must look for their roles and statuses in sites other than that of marriage. The literature on African women, however, continues to focus solely on marriage as evidence for the inferior status of African women. It seems difficult for most outsiders to understand and accept that "African women's relationships with men, within and outside conjugality, are not central to their self-inscription or to an understanding of our stories, lives and desires."[14]

Observing the women in their various sites, paying attention to female bonding which is absent from much of African creative literature written by men would yield a more correct epistemology of women. In consanguineal relationships, women enjoy positions of deference, power and authority beyond gender; other variables being age, seniority as determined by order of birth, wealth and personal standing which is not always calculated by wealth. In some societies, men genuflect to women in many situations. Within marriage itself, statuses are marked by subtle and complex indices such as seniority based on the time of entry into the affinal family and personal achievements; such markers as are incomprehensible or invisible to some analysts. Sudarkasa hits a nodal point when she says "female and male are not so much statuses . . . as they are clusters of statuses for which gender is only one of the defining characteristics. Women and men might be hierarchically related to each other in one or more of their reciprocal statuses, but not in others. Because contradiction, as much as congruence, characterized the status-clusters termed female and male, many African societies did not or could not consistently stratify the categories one against the other, but, rather codified the ambiguities."[15]

Wifehood in itself was a gender, not a sex or biological role (gender being a socially constructed identity), for "it is important to recognise that the terms *husband* and *wife* connote certain clusters of affinal relations, and in woman marriage (technically a woman marrying another woman) the principles concerned emphasise certain jural relations."[16] The female husband is a *pater*, to the children of her wife for whom she finds a sexual husband. All women married into a woman's birth family on her father's side (her patrilineage) are her wives, in some societies. Women's roles within kinship systems are not always determined by their sex. A woman can be codified as husband to her mother, her own siblings and women married into her patrilineage. Ifi Amadiume has carried further the discourses of the statuses of African women within consanguineal relations, showing how a woman can paradoxically be a male daughter and a female husband.[17] She is a male daughter in her father's house and a female husband to the women married into her father's lineage.

Other discourses of African women which need to change are those which insist on issues of polygamy and female circumcision (almost gleefully) over and above the other experiences of African women, while paying no equivalent attention or valuation to the violence done to women's bodies in Western cosmetic surgery for the same reason (pleasuring men); they totally ignore women's roles in other non-sexual domains. Is there some secret war against the myth of the superior sexual vitality of African women? In my view, coitus is given far too much attention in the discussion and appreciation of women's rights and conditions by some Western women; otherwise, how does one find surrogate motherhood less objectionable than polygyny? But then, certain readers of African culture seem very committed to narratives of victimhood about African women despite the women's own different value systems which, in the final result, certainly give the women concerned a stronger and prouder sense of self and autonomy, self-reliance, dignity and the ability to manage life better than the women who pity them.

Some gender issues are not yet receiving the intellectual attention they should if we are to be comprehensive in our research and knowledge of women. As Seble Dawit mentioned at a symposium on "Gender Violence and Human Rights of Women in Africa" at Rutgers University, Africa has not yet given voice to her sexuality;[18] too many silences persist in the area of human sexuality in Africa. Sexual orientation is certainly one area that has not been opened up for research or discussion. In some countries of Africa, the death penalty awaits gay people; in others, the state does not persecute them. The experiences of sexual orientation in traditional arrangements require discovery still. It would seem, however, that some of the themes of female bonding, the search for female community and love between women so strong in lesbian literature already receive their expression in African societies, past and present, where non-sexual female bonding, community support and network exist as defining and basic characteristics.[19] Women in Africa have also always known the option of making *de facto* families, consisting only of themselves and their children, even within polygyny. More women in contemporary Africa are opting for motherhood without wifehood or independent wifehoods in matrilocal and polygynous arrangements as in the novel, *One is Enough* (1981) by Flora Nwapa.

Speaking of human sexuality in general, gender violence is another area of silence. African women tend to be protected by their larger families in the occurrence of violence within marriage through the possibility of the return of the bride wealth or the withdrawal of the woman by her male relatives who can also do a physical counterstrike of vengeance on the abusive husband. It can be argued that African kinship systems provided the abused woman the family and community support which feminist movements tried to give to Euro-American women through shelters for battered women. Police certainly give little protection in Africa as elsewhere. Unfortunately, African women in abusive situations are beginning to lose some of the protection they enjoyed from male relatives due to the nuclearization and Westernization of African families.

Finally, it must be indicated that patriarchy as understood and theorised in my work does not yield a simplistic paradigm of all women ranged against all men. African complex kinship structures and the day-to-day negotiations of our lives through gender, sex, and male and female relational experiences make us realise that patriarchy not only includes women but gains some of its force and effectiveness from the active participation of women too. We see a female patriarch in the Zimbabwean novel of Tsitsi Dangarembga.[20] We know of other African women more powerful in patriarchy than her Tete. Patriarchy takes different and complex forms in differing societies. We continue to examine critically our cultures and experiences as we transform them.

Mọlara Ogundipẹ-Leslie
Rutgers University, 1993

Notes

1. Abena Busia, "Silencing Sycorax: on African Colonial Discourse and the Unvoiced Female," *Cultural Critique* 14 (Winter 1989-90), 81-104.
2. Maryse Conde, *La paroles des femmes: Essais sur les romancieres des Antilles des langues francaises* (Paris: Harmattan, 1979). Also cited in Sylvia Wynter, "Afterword: Beyond Miranda's Meanings: Un/silencing the 'Demonic Ground' of Caliban's 'Woman'," ed.

Carol Boyce Davies *Out of the Kumbla*, (Trenton, N.J.: Africa World P, 1990) 355-72.

3. A Canadian woman professor once asked me in Toronto whether my dress was something worn by native Nigerians. Another European in Calgary said an archaeologist was at that time doing research on "native" Nigerians. You wonder "who are the *native* Nigerians" and who the "non-native"? Why is it necessary to qualify Nigeria by "native"? Take note of the use of "native" from now on, when you read.

4. Molara Ogundipe-Leslie, "Letter to a Loved Comrade, A Prose Poem," *Sew the Old Days* (Ibadan: Evans P, 1985) 26.

5. Ogundipe-Leslie, 26.

6. Robin Morgan, ed., *Sisterhood is Global* (London and New York: Doubleday, 1984). See my chapter on Nigeria, "Not Spinning on the Axis of Maleness," 498-504.

7. Conversations with Ayi Kwei Armah.

8. Gayatri Spivak, "Can the Subaltern Speak?" *Marxism and the Interpretation of Culture*, eds. Cary Nelson and Lawrence Grossberg (Urbana: U of Illinois P, 1988), 271-313.

9. Carole Boyce Davies and Elaine Fido, *Out of the Kumbla* (Trenton: Africa World P, 1990), 1.

10. Denise Paulme, ed., *Women of Tropical Africa*, trans. H. M. Wright (Berkeley: U of California P, 1963).

11. Niara Sudarkasa, "The 'Status of Women' in Indigenous African Societies," *Women in Africa and the African Diaspora*, eds. Terborg-Penn, Harley and Rushing (Washington, D.C: Howard UP, 1987), 28. This essay is highly recommended as a basic text on indigenous African women, conceptually and particularly on West African women.

12. Alice Walker, *In Search of Our Mothers' Gardens* (New York: Harcourt, 1983), xi.

13. Such questions will arise and drama such as surrounded burying Otieno in Kenya will continue to arise until Africans resolve conflicts in their emotional realities, resulting from contradictions between ethnicity and nation—ethnic culture and national culture. See Patricia Stamp, "Burying Otieno," *Signs* 16.4 (Summer 1991) 808-45 for a feminist perspective which still requires indigenous African feminist interventions. Otieno, a Kenyan Kikuyu, died and his wife, a Luo, had to resort to state legislation to contest the cultural claims of her in-laws concerning the burial remains.

14. Conversation with Kagendo Murungi, participant in The Colloquium on Women's Studies, the Laurie New Jersey Chair in Women Studies, 1992-93, Douglass College, Rutgers University.

Re-creating Ourselves

15. Sudarkasa, 27.
16. Sudarkasa, 31.
17. Ifi Amadiume, *Male Daughters, Female Husbands* (London: Zed Books, 1987).
18. Symposium on Gender Violence and Human Rights of Women in Africa, Paul Robeson Center, Rutgers University, April 7, 1993. Panelists: Nahid Toubia (Sudan), Asma ben Halim (Sudan), Seble Dawit (Ethiopia), and Molara Ogundipe-Leslie (Nigeria); moderator, Abena Busia (Ghana).
19. For descriptions of the emotional characters of lesbians, see for instance the writings of the poet, Audre Lorde; and Rosemary Curb and Nancy Manahan, *Lesbian Nuns: Breaking the Silence* (Tallahassee, Florida: The Naiad P, 1985).
20. Tsitsi Dangarembga, *Nervous Conditions* (Seattle: The Seal P, 1988).

18

PART I

THEORY

1. African Women, Culture and Another Development

"Just as men have a right to food, they also have a social right to speak, to know, to understand the meaning of their work, to take part in public affairs and to defend their beliefs.

The right to education, to expression, to information and to the management of production are all rights which articulate the same need of socialisation.

It is therefore a perversion to imagine that the discussion on development can be limited to what is called the satisfaction of basic material needs. When peasants or workers are excluded from all responsibilities in the production system, when scientific research is subjected to profit, when education patterns are imposed that make school children or students strangers to their own culture and more instruments to the production process, when protest is reduced to silence by force and political prisoners are tortured, can it be thought that these practices do not hinder the goals of development and that they do not inflict an injury on society?"[1]

The idea of "development" has been a much-touted word in the last two decades, universally considered necessary by the industrialised countries who have pushed the idea on to Third World countries who may or may not know what "development" means, why it is necessary and what it may cost in material or social terms. It was, in fact, an ideology, and very often the official ideology in countries with very different social and economic forms of organisation and with different political color. Distilling the main features of development in an essay on "The Cultural Dimension of Development," J.C. Sanchez Arnau says ideology was

> 1) based on a mechanistic and linear conception of history which assumes that every society must go through the same stages of 'development' until it reaches the stage in which the economic apparatus continually ensures to the population an income level similar to that of those countries at present considered as 'developed;'
> 2) based on an ethnocentric approach which assumes that the basic goal of any society is to achieve the same values characterising the 'so-called developed' societies: spirit of enterprise, the profit-motive, competition, material security, and especially endeavours to achieve the possession of certain goods and services typical of highly industrialised societies. Therefore, those countries or societies which have not already achieved these goals or which do not share them, are not considered 'different' but instead 'primitive,' 'traditional,' 'under-developed' or in the best cases, 'developing' countries or societies;
> 3) 'development' is also based on an essentially economic approach, since it considers that the adequate management of the instruments of economic policy is in itself sufficient to maintain any country on the road to achieving these goals, and ultimately reaching them. Thus it globally ignores what we call her 'culture,' i.e. the collection of values, aspirations, beliefs, patterns of behaviour and inter-personal relations, established or predominating, within a given social group or society...

Development has thus essentially become a mechanism to transfer culture from industrialised to Third World countries, from the 'centre' to the 'periphery,' playing a similar role as previously played by the ideology of 'progress' in the nineteenth century in Latin America and the Middle East or by colonisation in Africa. In this way, societies, bereft of adequate economic means, have adopted or try to adopt a lifestyle only accessible to limited numbers of their population, mortgaging their economic future and losing their cultural inheritance.[2]

"Development" cannot only be criticized for its features stated above, its "cultural" imperialism and ethnocentrism, but also for ignoring the social cost of its effect of upheaval on individual and collective lives and its interruption of — or interference with — the internal and natural dynamics of evolution in the societies into which it has been introduced.

Supposedly, it is in reaction to the failure of the practice of "development" thus far, that the concept of "Another Development" has been introduced. The 1975 Dag Hammarskjold Report, *What Now*, which encapsulates and inculcates the concept of "Another Development," is a brave and admirable document which would be even more useful if it could attain the cooperation and "good faith" of the industrialised countries to achieve its stated objectives. One of the best notions in *What Now* is the recognition of the need to "decolonize" the U.N. as a pre-requisite to any affirmative action. There is need to not only "decolonize" the U.N. but also necessarily trim its unwieldy, expensive and resultantly inefficient administrative structure. In addition, *What Now* positively calls for an approach to development which recognizes cultural specificities in societies and demands an endogenous and "participatory" approach. In sum, "Another Development" claims to be "totally-man-centred." It is *need-oriented*, being geared to the satisfaction of man's needs, both material and non-material; *endogenous* — stemming from the heart of each society, which defines in sovereignty its values and the vision of its future; *self-reliant* — relying on the strength and resources of the society which pursues it, rooted at the local level in the practice of each community; *ecologically sound* — utilizing rationally available resources in a harmonious relation with the environment; *based on structural transformation* — originating in the realization of the conditions for self-management and participation in decision-making by all.[3]

These are large claims and large hopes. How does woman fit into these schemes and conceptions; and how do the African

women in particular fit in? The first criticism that can be made
of *What Now* is that the language of its expression is "totally
man-centred." The initial quote at the top of this essay also illus-
trates the point. English-speaking feminists have pointed out
and reiterated the need to "humanize" the very language of
discourse, to "de-masculinize" it and find androgynous and
generic terms to discuss what concerns and affects both men
and women in society. This question of a "man-oriented" language is not so trivial when we consider that scholars in the
social sciences of history, sociology, anthropology, law etc., have
regularly and frequently totally excluded women from their
studies; and how "development" agents have also neglected
women in the effectuating of their so-called "development"
schemes.

Secondly, in *What Now,* there seems to be a primordial concern with ecology and eco-systems. The problems of ecology
and what happens to eco-systems are priorities in Third World
countries; but they should not be named before the very serious problems of socio-economics are mentioned; in particular,
the problems of colonialism and neo-colonialism in their multi-
faceted forms.

Thirdly, the argument about OPEC and Indochina can evoke
a cynical attitude in the Third World reader. *What Now* argues
that two elements give a political dimension to the hope for
change. Firstly, the power of OPEC countries to extort economic
demands and affect economic policy — secondly, the example
given to the whole world by Indochina that peasants with a
will for independence could organize and free themselves from
"formidable military and technological power that the world
has known."[4] Thus, the interest in development is not just
humanistic but based on naked self-interest and the fear of
stranglehold on the West by previously powerless and scorned
Third World nations. Third World radicals would argue that
Third World nations should, in fact, sharpen such tools for lev-
ering the *international economic order;* they should use this potential for power which is based on a structure of dependence of
the West or the Third World.[5] Wilmot argues cogently in this
chapter how, in fact, the real causes of the economic crisis in the

West predate the formation of OPEC in 1960; they precede the steep rises in the price of oil since the end of 1973. He argues that the real causes of the crisis is to be found in the structures of the Western economies, primarily that of the United States of America, and in the economic and political decisions taken by governments in the West.

Despite *What Now's* view of OPEC as significant because it represents a historical reversal, as historic as Vasco da Gama's arrival on the coast of West Africa which opens the present historic period of conquest of Africa, the document *What Now* does rightly situate the sources of the crisis of development. The crisis does lie in the poverty of the masses of the Third World, as well as that of others, whose needs, even the most basic — food, habitat, health and education — are not met. And this situation cannot be properly understood, much less transformed, unless it is seen as a whole. In the final analysis, the crises are the result of a system of exploitation which profits a power structure based largely in the industrialized world, although not without annexes in the Third World; ruling *elites* of most countries are both accomplices and rivals at the same time.[6] The drama of a Third World elite group exploiting its own country and competing nastily with its industrialised economic partners and *collaborators in oppression* can be exemplified by Nigeria, in particular, among other neo-colonial countries. Informative studies of the Nigerian example have been made.[7]

The condition of the African woman is situated within this global socio-economic reality. Her condition is one of living in neo-colonial or colonized countries such as South Africa and enduring the repercussions of such a reality. Before an analysis is made of her condition, a definition of culture will be made. Culture will be seen in its broad, comprehensive and total meaning; not as a conglomeration of superficial aspects of life such as dance, dress, hairstyles and naked women. Culture is defined here as the total product of a people's "being" and "consciousness" which emerges from their grappling with nature and living with other humans in a collective group. Thus *"their culture is itself a product and a reflection of history built on the two relations with nature and with other men."*[8] Culture, for the present writer, is the total self-expression of a people in the two relations basic to human existence in society: the relations between generic man and nature and the relations between person and person in that society. (The reader may note that this writer is trying to avoid masculine references; a very difficult feat in English!)

The very effort of defining culture is itself fraught with problems. In an effort to give a materialistic definition, a definition usually accepted in Western Marxist thought, one is pulled up short by the awareness that other cultures reject the notion that the human relation to nature is one aimed at mastering, controlling or exploiting her. *What Now* itself bemoans this exploitive attitude which now threatens eco-systems with the exhaustion of renewable sources. A Cherokee Indian has written about the Amerindian relation to nature which is one of harmony and the submergence of the human self to other living things.

> All our lives are directed towards 'tuning in' to the rest of nature. There are ceremonies for all sorts of phenomenon... What we are really doing is trying to get ourselves into certain rhythms of certain moods. When I dance 'the Wolf Dance,' I am able to put myself in a completely different place than where I normally am. I see myself and the world through different eyes for a moment, and I partake in someone else's (the wolf's) rhythm and power. But it is reciprocal. I also give my rhythm to those animals or events. In other words, I tune in.[9]

Mr. Durham is of the Wolf clan. There is no word for "clan" in Cherokee, he says. He is, more correctly, simply a wolf himself and the Cherokees believe that the animals are the elders of human beings. Thus human beings have to learn from animals as they have to learn from nature in general. Oriental commentators have also written widely on their view of life which is essentially different from that of the post-Renaissance West. The Asiatics see all human behaviour as geared not towards the exploitation of nature and the acquisition of material goods but towards *"the search for truth, as a means of self-realisation and self-control, not as a means of bringing anything under domination, including nature."*[10] Africans can be said to live in harmony with nature, to use the material world for the satisfaction of basic human, emotional and psychological needs. Such basically divergent cultural views and objectives should be quite relevant to the theoreticians of *What Now* in their implementation of one of their objectives — the satisfaction of basic human needs identified as food, health, shelter and education. But most Africans would tend to ask, then what? "We get all these fine things, yes, but to what objective?" It would be to use these things to attain human basic emotional needs in the social realm. There are very deep cultural differences between Europe and Africa regarding the how and why of life.

Considering the wide scope of the definition of culture here, obviously this paper cannot intend to deal with all its aspects. Here we will confine ourselves to the super-structural aspects of culture — the non-material products of culture. We will consider the products of consciousness such as ideas, institutions, social patterns and the arts — and even here — we can only glance at these issues.

The Woman's Condition in Africa: The Six Mountains on her Back

A brief glance at women all over the world today shows that women are oppressed. A brief glance suggests that "educational attainments," "participation rates," "occupational structure," private and public laws, family planning systems, technological advance and, above all, socio-cultural attitudes are all weighted against them.

Across distance and boundaries in history and society, women have been placed on pedestals as goddesses, but imprisoned within domestic injustice (custom has been nothing but a tyrant hidden in every home). They have been romanticised in literature and lyrics, but commercialised in life.[11] They have been owned, used and worked as horses, even today.

But what is the specific condition of the women in Africa?

This is a broad subject which needs on-going research. It is now well-known that Third World women adopt different postures. This is how AAWORD-AFARD (Association of African Women for Research and Development) was born. I want to initiate a discussion with a take-off from a statement of Mao-Tse Tung. Mao is quoted to have said that a Chinese man had three mountains on his back: the first was the oppression from outside, because China was colonized; the second was the feudal oppression of two thousand years of authoritarianism and the third was his backwardness; but a woman had four mountains — the fourth being man.[12] One might say that the African woman has six mountains on her back: one is oppression from outside (colonialism and neocolonialism?), the second is from traditional structures, feudal, slave-based, communal etc., the third is her backwardness (neo-colonialism?); the fourth is man; the fifth is her color, her race; and the sixth is herself. We shall attempt to discuss these in their cultural significance.

1. Oppression from outside: Foreign Intrusions

The African woman lives in, or comes from, a continent that has been subjected to nearly five hundred years of assault, battery and mastery of various kinds. These historical experiences have taken their toll and left their mark. They can be dated from the historical arrival of Vasco da Gama in the fourteen hundreds, beginning with the mercantile trade with Europe which soon broadened into the trade in slaves only, followed by the integration of Africa into the *full capitalist system* in the nineteenth century, (to borrow phrases from Samir Amin's periodicisation in *Underdevelopment and Dependence in Black Africa: Origins and Contemporary Forms*). Then followed the period of political or structural integration within capitalism which was colonisation. The economic and political integration of Africa into capitalism has been studied by several brilliant scholars such as George Padmore, Kwame Nkrumah, Samir Amin, Walter Rodney for instance, so the details need not delay us here. We may, however, look at the cultural outcome of these historical experiences.

The introduction of new economic activities such as slavery, the slave trade and the growing of national sole "cash crops" (as opposed to food crops) must have thrown the total pattern of production in African societies into severe crisis. The resultant social upheaval must have affected the position and roles of women within the production processes and the relations of production. More research into the role of women in pre-capitalist economic formations in Africa needs to be done. Her role in production and her relation to the economic surplus of those economic formations needs to be studied. The woman's social and economic place in the colonial period is more accessible to knowledge since the period is nearer; still, studies need to be done to reveal the actual nature of the woman's predicament at that time and to collate such information for availability. Both men and women, with the intrusion of the West, were pushed into dependent economies resulting in the pauperization and the "proletarianization" of the whole continent. Whole societies became geared to the upholding of foreign metropolitan economies, committed to the expatriation of their own surpluses to the countries of the colonizing powers. Women in the labor process became the "proletariat" of the proletariats, becoming more subordinated in the new socio-economic scheme, and often losing their old and meaningful roles within the older production processes.

Women became more marginalised in the production process, for the cash crops became the main crop, leading to new economic arrangements between men and women and new attitudes of male social and economic superiority. These economic changes in Africa following the intrusion of the West were inextricably linked to political changes in society which, again, affected cultural attitudes towards women. The creation of a new class of subordinates — missionaries, clerks, police and soldiers changed social aspirations in society. The traditional political structures were either completely abandoned or so distorted as to sweep away any female participation in the handling of local power and administration.

The British simply swept aside previous female political structure in society, replacing them with completely male structures and positions. Modern societies have now inherited these male-dominated structures and, with them, the hardened attitudes of male superiority and female exclusion from public affairs which had been introduced by the colonial systems. The colonial systems negatively encouraged or brought to the fore the traditional ideologies of patriarchy or male superiority which originally existed in African societies. The cultural outcome of these political transformations in Africa is manifold. Women are "naturally" excluded from public affairs; they are viewed as unable to hold positions of responsibility, rule men or even be visible when serious matters of state and society are being discussed. Women are viewed to need tutelage before they can be politically active; politics is considered the absolute realm of men; women are not considered fit for political positions in modern African nation-states, though their enthusiasm and campaign work are exploited by their various political parties.[13]

Thus colonialism has brought out the basic sexist tendencies in precapitalist Africa. It has calcified existing ones and introduced others. It has also thrown up new roles for women which are creating conflicts since men are not yet able to adapt to them, nor are they rid of old attitudes and expectations. The effect of colonization on the total continent has myriad forms, not the least being the feelings of inferiority and dependency which have been created in both men and women. Famous studies have been done on the psychology of the oppressed and its characteristic dependency complex (Frantz Fanon, Albert Memmi, etc.). Fanon described psychological oppression as the worst form of oppression. Its continuing impact on the psyche of African men and women is, sadly, very significant. The feelings of inferiority affect the economic and political behaviour of Africans, denuding them of creativity, self-reliance or productivity. There is no desire or confidence to be productive or creative; rather the ruling elites only consume and spread their values to the rest of their societies. The dominant ideas of a society are the ideas of its ruling class. The ruling elites feel totally dependent on industrialised countries in material, intellectual and emotional terms. They can do nothing but imitate Europe even in ideas, generating none themselves but simply applying to their own societies ideas and practices which were not conceived for their societies. Within this cultural universe of Third World dependency, the "elite" woman is the dependent of the dependent, being pulled along in the whirligig of neocolonial meaningless behaviour. Like her male counterparts, she imitates everything European, and despises her traditional culture and race while she fails to understand her own true needs.

Colonization has also affected the legal structures of African societies, introducing nineteenth century European ideas of patriarchy. Women lost inherited special rights and became more subordinated. Similarly, Islam disrupted traditional societies politically and legally, creating new oppressed and subjugated status and roles for women. Consequently, women have contemporary legal battles to fight for their rights, in particular within family law — marriage, divorce, the sharing of property within marriage, inheritance, the possession of her own body and children among other issues.

In the religious cultures of societies, colonization introduced Christianity which destroyed the old religions or subverted them, as did Islam. With the introduction of new patriarchal religious values, women sometimes lost their important and high positions in the old religions. Christianity is itself a very male-dominated religion. So male-dominated is it now that women have to fight for leadership roles within Christianity, and the very idea of female leadership in Islam is inconceivable.

In the artistic cultures of African societies, Western intrusion destroyed the forms of creativity and indeed the very urge to create in those forms. Women had been active in the pre-colonial artistic world: in rituals, music, dance, visual and plastic arts. More research needs to be done into this area to identify the nature and social significance of women's roles in the field of the arts. Many of these arts were destroyed with colonization, Christianity and Islam, followed by the creation of economic and emotional voids which led to an increasing population of unemployed women. Unemployment leads to other social problems such as prostitution, vagrancy, mass proletarianization, lack of self-respect and self-worth, etc.

It is clear that foreign intrusions into Africa have had wide-ranging and cataclysmic effects on her societies and cultures. Fuller research into specific aspects of the colonial impact on women, in particular in the field of culture is advisable. Foreign historical intrusions have certainly created cultural changes in the social realm, affecting the self-definition of women, the relationships of individuals to each other, the notions of female inferiority, etc. Colonization and Westernization, with their attendant capitalism, have introduced capitalist values such as greed, acquisitiveness, autonomy and individualism which, in turn, have affected human relationships just as the synchronous introduction of wage labor has undermined pre-capitalist structures of human relations. The capitalist system of production itself draws women out of the home into low-wage slavery, encouraging the subordination of women, financial disabilities and low female self-esteem.

Whatever studies we make of women in Africa, we should be aware of the need to "periodize" African history adequately. It is also necessary to recognize various social and historical categories which would affect our analysis of women's positions in Africa. We need to see problems in their class perspectives in both present day and past economic formations. In present day Africa, we should bear in mind that problems differ from society to society, depending on their ethnic history and specific relation to capital and neo-colonialism. Thus women's problems in Nigeria, a neo-colonial country, differs from those of South Africa, still a colonized country. The newly liberated areas of Africa such as Angola, Mozambique and Zimbabwe have their own unique problems. The revolutionary societies, in their own place, again have unique problems of "realising" the social revolution after the armed struggles as in Guinea Bassau, where women claim they are fighting two colonialisms; the second being men.[14] Another variable in our cultural studies should be religion — the various cultural effects of Islam, Christianity and the traditional religions on women's positions in Africa.

Obviously, this paper cannot encompass such a massive work which would need to be farmed out to researchers. But under whatever scheme the research takes place, as methodology I would like to suggest that the research proceed from the material bases of the societies to the superstructural, so as to yield information about the social and living reality of the societies wherein the women are situated. It is apropos to quote a historian in Nigeria regarding the kind of reconstruction and study of African societies needed.

An organisational principle of the study of Africa may well focus on

> the production process itself and in this case a categorization such as pre-capitalist may be more in keeping with the actual material environment [vis-a-vis the pre-mercantile Africa]. The focus on the environment, in a sense that goes beyond routine ecological description, may well focus on the productive capacity of the areas in question and would make more possible the analysis of superstructural forms and institutions such as the State. It would also encourage a focus on issues that are crucial and would divert attention from peripheral issues to matters of more importance. A focus on the productive forces at any specific period would in fact discourage static analysis and a situation where explanations tend to be frivolous and superficial. There is need for focus on production relations as manifested in forms of authority, the distribution of rights over labor power, the technical organization of labor and work relationship and all are to be seen as integrally related to the amount of cultivable land available [or other forces of production], the type of tools to which there is access, the means of subsistence and more generally the application and availability of labor. No in-depth analysis of superstructural forms such as the state and political institutions [or the role and position of and attitudes to women] is possible unless in the context of the latter. Any meaningful reconstruction of the past should take full cognizance of the inter-relationship between the 'economic structure' as a whole and 'the superstructural' reflexes.[15]

2. The Heritage of Tradition: the Second Mountain

This second mountain on the African woman's back is built

of structures and attitudes inherited from indigenous history and sociological realities. African women are weighed down by superstructural forms deriving from the pre-colonial past. In most African societies, whether patrilineal or matrilineal, gender hierarchy, male supremacy or sex asymmetry (or whatever term we choose to use) was known and taken for granted. Even in matrilineal societies, women were still subordinate to men, considered as second in place to men; the only difference being that inheritance and authority pass through the women to the male of the line. Men are still dominant in private and public life. The ideology that men are naturally superior to women in essence and in all areas, affects the modern day organization of societal structures. This ideology prolongs the attitudes of negative discrimination against women.

In traditional society, there was the division of labor based on sex with an attendant contempt for women's work. Men would not serve food at the revolutionary meeting in Guinea Bissau, so Cabral had to dignify this "women's work" by appointing women in charge of food as members of Revolutionary Councils.[16] Such an attitude is certainly a carry-over from the past. Not only was women's work condemned by men, it was often poorly regarded when not totally unpaid. In modern neo-colonial Africa, therefore, men tend to take lightly the labor of their female counterparts in the business and educational professions, considering women's jobs as hobbies and wondering what women do which makes them so tired at the end of the day. Proletarian and peasant women are known to work all day and longer than men. Such attitudes towards women's work lead to discriminatory behaviour in employment practices. In addition, women are considered the best hands for the most menial of jobs so that they are employed to do the most back-wracking agricultural labor and other servile jobs in factories and urban life. There is a tendency in Nigeria today to use women in the building trade jobs, to carry cement, water and do other taxing jobs and be paid less than men who occupy better paid managerial and skilled positions on the construction sites.[17]

From the traditional past also come notions of the physical

control of woman's body and its products. Under this issue come purdah, genital mutilation, the lack of control over her body's biology or its products such as children who are viewed to belong to the man's family. She is but a beast that produces the man's children on his behalf. These aspects of the oppression of women in Africa are very important to African women though they tend not to wish to emphasize the quest for sexual freedom and promiscuity which preoccupy the Western feminist. Nonetheless, the African male fears the attainment of equal sexual freedom for women. Some men also argue that genital mutilation was not wicked or sadistic in intent since it was a societal or parental effort to do the best they thought fit for their daughters. Nonetheless, backward (in the sense of unscientific), painful and undemocratic practices should be stopped. A child's body should not be mutilated without her consent.

Attitudinal forms, too many to enumerate, have certainly been inherited from the traditional past. These attitudes derive from the socio-economic formations in existence at the time and have lasted into the modern period in the fields of law, politics, religion, education, philosophy of life, etc. Serious work has to be done to educate whole populations out of these attitudes and notions. Outmoded structures such as the legal (as in marriage) and the political also need to be eradicated.

3. The Other Mountains

The backwardness of the African woman is the third mountain on her back; men, the fourth; race, the fifth and herself, the sixth. We can only comment briefly on these aspects of female culture in Africa. Her backwardness is a product of colonization and neo-colonialism, comprising poverty, ignorance, and the lack of a scientific attitude to experience and nature. Her race is important since the international economic order is divided along race and class lines, with the industrialized countries in the North of the North-South dialogue, notably White or approved White, like the Japanese. In the whole of the world, race is an important variable of imperialism and neo-colonialism. Race affects the economics and politics of North-South interaction. Within Africa herself, race problems are basic to any understanding of the societies of Eastern and Southern Africa. Special problems exist, for example, in education where a special effort has to be made to fight racist ideology, as seen in the Black Consciousness Movement of Steve Biko or the various and special educational programmes in Mozambique, Zimbabwe and other newly liberated areas.[18]

The woman has to throw off the fifth mountain on her back which is man, who is steeped in his centuries-old attitudes of patriarchy which he does not wish to abandon because male domination is advantageous to him. Not even the most politically progressive men are completely free from patriarchal attitudes and feelings of male superiority. Thus it is up to women to combat their social disabilities; to fight for their own fundamental and democratic rights, without waiting for the happy day when men will willingly share power and privilege with them — a day that will never come. The liberation of women in society is not simply about sexual freedom as most men tend to think and fear, but about the larger problem of the redistribution of privilege, power and property between the rich and poor, encompassing the smaller problem of the redistribution of power, property and privilege between men and women.

The sixth mountain on woman's back — herself — is the most important. Women are shackled by their own negative self-image, by centuries of the interiorization of the ideologies of patriarchy and gender hierarchy. Their own reactions to objective problems therefore are often self-defeating and self-crippling. Woman reacts with fear, dependency complexes and attitudes to please and cajole where more self-assertive actions are needed. It is clear that programs are needed to educate women about their positions, the true causes of their plight, and possible modalities for effecting change. Both men and women need "conscientisation." This is an area where the U.N. and other bodies can be very useful in providing and funding schemes to raise the consciousness of whole populations.

4. What is to be done?

What Now obviously feels that the satisfaction of basic needs identified as food, habitat, health education, is a pre-requisite for women. The achievement of these objectives is rightly seen as dependent on basic structural transformations of societies. These transformations can only be achieved by the endogenous struggles of the people of various and specific societies. There is not much the U.N. can do about this political requirement. The question not clearly asked in *What Now* and other theoritizations on changes in the Third World is "what kind of political organization will best achieve the most satisfactory social existence?" *What Now* seems to envision some grand ideal where the industrialized countries are forced to abandon, re-furbish, or reconstruct capitalism and imperialism! Industrialized countries are to be subsumed into some all-encompassing world government which is powered by the belief that we must all work together, share and share alike or we sink. Well! Some Third World countries are convinced that socialism is the only key to a more just society; that under that political regime, the "woman question" will be given adequate and specific attention as it has been in most socialist countries, though the questions have not been solved in these countries. But State recognition of the problem of women is already a step in the right direction.

There are those who feel that the solution to the oppression of women in society turns on two issues: education and the provision of employment for women. It is felt that employment guarantees the economic independence which leads to other forms of social and spiritual independence. Ahooja-Patel has suggested discrimination in favour of women in national and international policies, while new national policies of equal opportunity are provided. Discrimination in favour of women can be defended on the grounds that women have an unequal start in society in all areas of work and life. In addition, they are discriminated against and are at a disadvantage in all societies throughout the world — only their problems take different manifestations. The idea of discrimination in favour of women needs serious discussion since the blanket law of no discrimination on the grounds of sex can back-fire against women as in the famous Bakke case in America, regarding affirmative action for Blacks. In fact, men now use the slogan of "no-discrimination" to discriminate against women, to ignore their problems where such legislation exists.

It is, however, known to all that there can be a wide divergence between law in the books and social practices. In all societies, industrialized and Third World, women are excluded from public affairs despite incidental or cosmetic cases like Mrs. Thatcher, Mrs. Golda Meir, Mrs. Bandaraike, Mrs. Jean Kirkpatrick or the few Ministers of States, Permanent Secretaries and other government functionaries in African countries. Discrimination does not always spring from legislation but from practices originating in the psychological and cultural environment.[19]

※

So what is to be done about African women, culture and another development? Some suggestions and comments will be made:

1) First the basic social and cultural needs must be met in the concerned societies. Most development theories recognize this, but the question is how?

2) *What Now* identifies the eradication of poverty as a pre-requisite. But the eradication of poverty is not solely dependent on the increase both in food production in the Third World at local, national and regional levels and in the purchasing power of those countries.[20] The continuing poverty, *the underdeveloping* of Third World countries, is more basically tied to the sharp economic practices of the industrialized countries and their Third World collaborators in the ruling classes.

3) Thus, *What Now's* recommendation of the transformation of social, economic and political structure (p.15) is a basic requirement. This transformation, however, can only be achieved by the populations of the countries concerned.

4) Meanwhile, to attain the basic needs of women, there must be a battle against poverty and the exploitation of women in society. Women must be able to control and benefit from the products of their labor, which need to be better valued

and compensated.
5) Thus, there needs to be re-education on sex roles in whole nations. External and internal policies, schemes and projects could be set up to achieve such massive raising of consciousness.
6) On this issue, the improvement of public information already cited as an important objective in *Another Development* will be very useful.[21] The use of media — radio, television, printed matter will be effective and this is where foreign bodies and funds can be of great use. Educational policies in nations also have to be geared towards this cultural need: to change oppressive and discriminatory attitudes towards women. Education must be seen as a force to liberate and inculcate positive values, particularly regarding women.
7) Finally women in the arts in Africa need encouragement and financial assistance. Women artists in Western modes are relatively few in African societies and successful ones are even fewer. In the modern artistic expressions such as the novel, the film, written poetry, secular theatre and painting, women artists are still fewer. Not only do educational possibilities militate against women, women are often hard put to find capital to back their own projects or to develop themselves. This is another area in which "Another Development" agencies can be useful in setting up a foundation specifically for the training and assistance of women artists, and for the support of research into the issues concerning African women and culture.

Notes

1. The 1975 Dag Hammarskjold Report, What Now, p. 27.
2. Arnau: 3-4,5.
3. Sterky: Development Dialogue, 1978: 1, 4-5.
4. Sterky: op. cit., 5-6.
5. Wilmot: 119-120.
6. What Now: 5.
7. Williams, 1976; Turner, 1978; Y. Bala Usman, 1982.
8. Ngugi wa Thiongo: 2.
9. Durham: 15-16.

10. Rajni Kothari: 81.
11. Ahooja-Patel: 83.
12. Ahooja-Patel: 85.
13. Ogundipe-Leslie: 17-19
14. Urdang: 1975.
15. Thomas Emeagwali, 1982.
16. Urdang: 215.
17. Zack-Williams, 1982.
18. Van de Merve *et al.*, Ngugi wa Thiongo: *Development Dialogue*, 1978: 2.
19. Ahooja-Patel, 1977.
20. *What Now*: 16.
21. *What Now*: 17.

Bibliography

Ahooja-Patel, Krishna, Another Development for Women, in Nerfin, Marc. ed., *Another Development : Approaches and Strategies* (The Dag Hammasrkjold Foundation, Uppsala, 1977), 66–89.
Samir Amin, *Underdevelopment and Dependence in Black Africa* in Cohen & Daniel eds., *op. cit.*, 28–44.
Juan Carlos Sanchez Arnau, The Cultural Dimension of Development, in *Development Seeds of Change*, (Culture, The Forgotten Dimension), 1981 3/4, 3–4; 5.
Cohen & Daniel eds., *Political Economy of Africa, Selected Readings* London/ New York: Longman, 1981
Development Dialogue (1978 : 2), Special issue on *Another Development and Education.*
Jimmie Durham, Eloheh or the Council of the Universe, in *Development*, 1981: 3/4.
Gloria Thomas Emeagwali, *Political Institutions in Pre-Nineteenth Century Nigeria : Some Observations on the Groundwork of Nigerian History*, Paper presented at the Annual Congress of the Historical Society of Nigeria, Port Harcourt, Nigeria, 13–17 April, 1982.
Rajni Konthari, The Cultural Roots of Another Development, in *Development*, 1981 : 3/4.
Ngugi wa Thiongo, *Education for a National Culture*, Paper presented at the Seminar on Education in Zimbabwe, — Past, Present and Future, held at the University of Zimbabwe, 27 August–7 September 1981.
Ogundipe, Chief (Mrs.) G.T., *The Ordination of Women* (Methodist Church of Nigeria, Literature Bureau, 1977).
Ogundipe-Leslie, Omolara, *Women in Nigeria*, Paper presented at the National Seminar on Women in Nigeria, Dept. of Sociology, Ahmadu Bello University, Zaria, May 27–28, 1982.

Rodney, Walter, *How Europe Underdeveloped Africa* (London, Bogle L'Ouverture Publications, 1972).

Samir Amin, *Underdevelopment and Dependence in Black Africa* in Cohen & Daniel eds., *op. cit.*, 28–44.

Goran Sterky, Towards Another Development in Health, in *Introductory Remarks, Development Dialogue*, 1978, 1, 4–5.

Terisa Turner, Commercial Capitalism in Nigeria: The Pattern of Competition, in Cohen & Daniel eds. *Political Economy of Africa* (London: Longman, 1981) 155–163.

Stephanie Urdang, Fighting Two Colonialisms: The Women's Struggle in Guinea-Bissau, in Cohen & Daniel eds., *op. cit.*, 213–220.

Y. Bala Usman, Behind the Smokescreen : The Real Causes of the Current Economic Crisis [in Nigeria : my insertion] Public Lecture by Y.B. Usman, Secretary to the Government of Kaduna State organized by the Kaduna State Council of the Nigerian Labour Congress, Kaduna, 30th April, 1982. To be found in *Who is Responsible? : The Nigerian Workers and the Current Economic Crisis : May Day Speeches and Statements*, 1982 (publication of the PRP National Research Directorate, Kaduna, Nigeria)

Williams, Gavin, *Nigeria, Economy and Society*, (London: Rex Collings, 1976).

Wilmot, Patrick F., *In Search of Nationhood: The Theory and Practice of Nationalism in Africa*, (Lagos/Ibadan, Lantern Books, 1979).

Van der Merve et al., *African Perspectives on South Africa*, (London: Rex Collings, 1968). See sections on *Dignity and Consciousness* and *Education*

A.B. Zack-Williams, *Female Labour and Exploitation within African Social Formations: Some Theoretical Issues.* (2) *Women in Construction in Jos*, Papers presented at the National Seminar on Women in Nigeria, Dept. of Sociology, Ahmadu Bello University, Zaria, May 27–28, 1982.

What Now: 17.

2. Studying Women Through Literature: Thesis on Rural Women in Africa*

I. The Uses of Literature for Sociology

In the contemporary concern with women's studies, much intellectual energy and time have been devoted to expressing the inadequacy of the tools of research-concepts, terminologies and methodologies of looking at the position of women. As a result, many calls have been made for a variety of research methods, particularly innovative ones (Zeidensteinn ed. 404: Wellesley Editorial Committee, 1977). Calls have been made for the use of interdisciplinary team-approaches of men and women and the use of life histories but seldom are calls made for the use of imaginative literature as a data source for the study of women and society. Christine Obbo (1980 : 51) mentions novels in her useful and highly researched book but does not use them for analysis. The data-source closest to imaginative literature suggested has been life-histories, i.e. biographies. But the uses of imaginative literature for sociology or the study of society are manifold and need to be emphasised and exploited. The neglect of literature for the study of society is true not only for women's studies in general, but for rural women in particular.

What could be the uses of literature for the study of society? How can we have sociology through literature? The subject under discussion here is not the sociology of literature; that is a separate intellectual activity within literary criticism which

First presented at the AAWORD Conference on *Rural Women in Africa*, Algeria, 1981. Published in *Women and Rural Development in Africa*, (AAWORD Collective eds., Senegal, 1986.)

treats such issues as the sociology of the authors, their reader-
ship, the mechanics of book publication, the marketing of books
and so forth. Nor is the subject here the analysis of literary
sources. Rather, it is sociology through literature, to borrow a
phrase of Lewis Coser's, quoted by Jean Rockwell (1974; p. ix).
Hence, the subject here is more the use of literature in the systematic study of society (Rockwell, *op. cit.*). Why should literature be thus employed? Literature, though imaginative, can
be used for a systematic study of society for various reasons
which will follow.

Literature by its nature reflects or mirrors society but not in
any simple, naturalistic or one-dimensional way which the
words "reflect" or "mirror" often evoke. The relation of literature to society is more complex and dialectical than common
usage usually presupposes.

On a very primary level, literature can be said to mirror or
reflect society, providing a reliable image of a number of hard,
social facts. In this light, literature can be viewed as a social document, a record of existing facts of life in the society. Literature
has been used throughout human history by disciplines of the
social sciences such as history, anthropology and sociology. In
fact, African literature was so much explored in such an anthropological manner early in this century and in the early history of
African literature in European languages, as to arouse the resentment of Africans. Nonetheless, literature can be used to document social facts and realities in our study of women and society.

On a secondary and more profound level, literature can
reflect society in the sense of embodying and revealing that
which pleases that society. What pleases can then be subjected
to analysis to reveal other factors; namely, aesthetic tastes, ethical values, norms and so on.

The present writer would agree with Rockwell that literature
neither reflects nor arises from society; but rather it is an integral
part of it and should be recognised as being as much so as any
institution, the family for instance, or the state, (Rockwell, vii).

The reflectionist theory of literature has been much discussed
in Marxist aesthetics. However, the crude and mechanistic
notions of reflectionism have been rejected by the best Marxist

critics, including Marx himself, and by others such as Engels, Lukacs, Brecht, and Jameson. Marxist theoreticians have articulated the views that art is not a simple reflection of reality like a mirror or a photographic plate; that the artistic consciousness is a creative intervention into a world rather than a mere reflection of it; that artistic creation is a deflection, a changing and a transformation of reality *in accordance with the peculiar laws of art.*(Eagleton. 48–54).

Further, the use of the literary imagination within religious consciousness and its ritual enactments should convince us of the profound ability of literature to reveal the values of a society. Religion, which can be seen as the essence of the transcendental values which society claims to value most highly (or, according to Durkheim, the essence of society itself), presents these values consistently in the form of fiction. Much of the content of all religions is *stories of the deeds of the gods.*

From the example of religion, we may proceed to discuss the function of literature as a transmittor of norms and values in society. Literature, as is generally known and accepted, can play a didactic role, while it is also diversionary — providing entertainment. Therefore, the role of forms of literature in the socialisation of the individual cannot be underplayed. We are all aware of the didactic function of the literature of initial socialisation which comes in the form of children's rhymes, folktales, fables, fairy tales, etc.

That literature can function this way in society is proven by the reaction of ruling powers in society to literature through censorship, the reception of protest literature (Rockwell: 42), the persecution of authors and other forms of social control imposed on literary activity. Such repressive social measures certainly indicate that societal powers recognise the importance and force of literature in influencing norms and values. Thus we can read back from literature to perceive the outlines of the society which produced it. We can look for the viable models of a society in her literature. With respect to Africa, we may look for what were considered viable models of the family, the virtuous person, the good life, the exemplary woman, etc. Because these forms of literature can reveal the values of the society which produced them, they should be a source of data-collection in our study of society and the woman within that society.

A. On the Limits of Literature for the Study of Society

Counter-arguments are sometimes made against the use of literature for sociology; that art itself is a doing; as *poesis*, it is a falsification of reality; that literature being artistic, imaginative, invented and fictive, cannot be scientific and reliable; and that the truth of art is mediated by the artist and her vision and therefore is only subjective; that certain forms of art are even more sociologically unreliable than others because of their very subjective character (for instance, poetry).

These arguments can be countered in a discussion of the nature and role of art and the artist.

B. On the Nature and Role of Art and the Artist

Rather than being a falsification of reality, art is a form of cognition for the artist and the consumer of the work of art. The artist objectifies her intellectual and sensuous perception of reality. Herein lies the truth of the charge that the artist mediates with her vision, the subjective and objective reality for herself and the consumer or reader. However, art is not a falsification of reality by the artist but a necessary and particular ordering of reality; necessary because absolute reality cannot be apprehended, as it is complex, infinite, (some would say chaotic), and composed of discrete and ever-changing entities and events. In fact, it has been argued that second-hand information about reality has been presented to and by the human species in the forms of narrative fiction: History, Law, Religion, Epic Poetry, the Novel, the Drama, and the statements of politicians and journalists. In one sense, therefore, everything is fiction; in another sense, fiction is reality (Rockwell : viii).

Art is often considered unreliable by those who consider artistic objects the product of gratuitous and playful activity. Many modern artists themselves defiantly declare this. Others feel art is unreliable because it is the product of the most radical individuality; still others feel that art exists in a completely autonomous aesthetic sphere which escapes all conditioning (Vasquez : 112). But, as Vasquez rightly points out, the relationship of art and society cannot be denied; for art itself is a social phenomenon: first, because the artist, however unique her primary experience might be, is a social being; second, because her work, however deeply marked by her primary experience and however unique and unrepeatable its objectification or form might be, is always a bridge, a connecting link between the artist and other members of society; third, because her work of art affects other people —contributes to the reaffirmation or devaluation of their ideas, goals or values — and is a social force which, with its emotional or ideological weight, shakes or moves people. Nobody remains the same after having been deeply moved by a true work of art (Vasquez 112-113).

Because, despite the artist's intention, her work inevitably reflects her sense of herself as a concrete human being, living in a given social situation, it is necessary that attention be paid to the sociology of the author herself in the use of literature for a systematic study of society. It is on this issue that artist-mediation becomes most pertinent.

C. On the Sociology of the Author

In considering the sociology of the author, it is necessary to pay attention to the artist herself and elicit information on how she situates herself in social and historical terms. We must note the contemporary attitude of society toward art, and the artist's own attitude toward society and art — whether it be one of harmony and agreement, evasion or retreat, protest or rebellion. The class of the artist should also be noted for analysis. It has been argued that creators of imaginative literature are bound by the values of their social groupings. Further, the writer's level and kind of education and, needless to say sex and gender, should also be analytical factors.

Historically, the artist has been working in a capitalist world where the very act of writing itself is alienated and isolated labour. More concretely, the facts of writing in a capitalist world, and of art as alienated labour, affect the products of African artists. The writers create and the publishers laugh all the way to the bank. Very often, the publishers dictate what they want through various forms of financial duress : they dictate the themes and characters they want, the kind of Africans they wish to see depicted, and even the genre of novels, that is, romances or adventure stories, protest or reformist novels as opposed to violently revolutionary novels. The image of the African woman can thus fall victim to the politics of alienated labour.

African writers are, in fact, caught in a double-faced fastness. Not only are they writing in a capitalist universe, they are writing in a colonial and neo-colonial one with all its attendant problems. Not only are they fighting the values of the ruling elite in their country, they are also fighting foreign influences. Yet as mentally colonised and alienated persons, they are often unconsciously judging their society by Western standards and imposing foreign values while at the same time trying to sell their indigenous values, their Africanity, to the West. For these reasons, they are writing in a foreign language, talking to the West while claiming to forge the uncreated consciousness of their race. And it is this African image presented by the African writer that is ironically the view of the Western world of Africa. Within the context of the above, the image of the rural woman in African literature should be appropriately situated.

II. Myths and Pitfalls to be Avoided in the Study of the Rural Woman in Africa

This section of the paper will discuss myths about the rural African woman and the pitfalls to be avoided in research. The section will be presented in the form of theses.

A. The Myths of the "Traditional" Woman

There is an elite view of the traditional woman which fossilises rural women in time and space. In Ayi Kwei Armah's words, there is an attempt to fix something that is moving. The archetype of this kind of illusory woman is Lawino in Okot's p'Bitek's *Song of Lawino*. She is the traditional woman who speaks like a child at the sight of machines like railways, aeroplanes or clocks. They are iron snakes, iron birds, etc. This mythical rural African woman is helpless before change and imported ideas. She is unable to integrate them into her consciousness as an adult. Naturally, she is imagined as awaiting the elite group of artists and non-artists to liberate her.

B. The Myth of the Uncreative Rural Woman

Most African imaginative writers, either by omission or commission, portray rural women as uncreative. Bound by tradition and culture (both vague concepts), she is constantly depicted as closed to or frightened by new ideas, limited to her narrow world, interested only in what affects her in her small environment, i.e., her hearth and the market. The women in Chinua Achebe's novels and others can be said to exemplify this variety of the uncreative rural woman.

C. The Myth of Linear Development from Rural Bondage

Deriving from the myth of a linear progress from primitivity to development which bedevils the social sciences and Western scholarship in general, is another myth: the linear development of rural women from rural bondage to the sophisticated, urban Westernised and thus free women. From this notion arises false urban characters who seem to have no roots in the countryside. Cyprian Ekwensi's *People of the City* is an example; so is Clara in Achebe's *No Longer at Ease*.

From the myth of linear developmment springs the tendency to create false oppositions in character and concerns between rural and urban women : Clementina and Lawino in *Song of Lawino* and Sidi and Lakunle's views in Soyinka's *The Lion and the Jewel*. Christine Obbo, in her study of rural women in East Africa shows that the novels of the sixties depict a rural-urban dichotomy which is a false division of the East African woman's reality. Yet this concept is central to contemporary Western social science. Obbo says town and village women viewed the rural and urban areas as warp and woof of the same cloth and not as an either/or situation. When the economic opportunities and personal options became restricted in the rural areas, the urban areas represented an *expanded* spectrum of opportunities, rather than a totally different set of circumstances (Obbo: 68).

D. The Myth that the "Traditional" Woman wants to Stay "Traditional"

The so-called traditional woman, who is herself a reified entity, is supposed to want to stay traditional but for the pernicious influences from the city, the West and from rotten African females with imported ideas. This concept is enhanced by male wish-fulfilment that women desire to be repositories of culture and tradition. Women who desire change are demonised as bad women while their attempts to cope with the changing world and new situation are seen by men as a problem, a betrayal of traditions which only results in a confusion of women's roles. Women must act as mediators between the past and present, while men see themselves as mediators between the present and future (Obbo : 143). Only the most progressive African male writers such as Sembene Ousmane, Ngugi wa Thiong'o, Alex la Guma and Nuruddin Farah, try to avoid this pitfall. Even these writers are being shown to be basically phallogocentric in recent research in African literature. (Stratton, 1990).

Ironically, it is the same writers who peddle the myth of woman as the pot of culture who also function under a second myth — namely, that the best thing that could happen to an autochthonous African rural woman is to make her *rite de passage* from rural bondage to Western sophistication. Such contradictions spring form the confused cultural mentality of the writer himself who has a dual attitude toward his own past as he has a dual one towards the West; and indeed, a dual one towards the woman whom he respects as a mother but despises and abuses as a sexual being. Such writers, and they are many, are victims of the self-division and cultural schizophrenia that contact with the West has forced upon Africans in addition to their male desire for the unconditional love of the mother from their sexual partners.

E. The Myth of the Submissive "Traditional" Woman

The rural woman is often depicted as subordinate, dependent and passive. In many novels she does nothing except to endlessly serve food and kolanuts to men and then get beaten up by them for her pains. She is full of complexes, feels inferior and is wholly dependent on the man materially. Thus, in such novels, we never see rural women participate in the production process of their society, whether it is farming, fishing or herding. An example is John Munonye's *Oil Man of Obange* which is about the palm oil industry in rural Ibo land where women are depicted as contributing nothing. Yet, in agricutural societies, women are engaged in production at various levels. One novel that shows an Ashanti woman engaged in farming and in fact controlling her production unit as an owner-farmer is *A Woman in her Prime* by Asare Konadu. The author, however, was obviously not writing a roman-a-these. Typically, the blurb-writer writes: "Pokuwaa, *though a woman,* has become a successful farmer," thereby showing ignorance of Ashanti culture.

The rural woman is supposed to live in mortal terror of men, an assumption that the studies of Perdita Huston and Christine Obbo disprove. Dependent and unproductive, the rural woman is supposed to be satisfied with what men bring her materially and fight only to secure benefits through them. Of course, as a repository of the mythical culture, she is not interested in money, which is of the devil and the white man. However, Obbo shows how both rural women and men want economic autonomy and how the women resort to hard work, urban migration and manipulation to achieve better social conditions for themselves. Rural women revealed to Obbo that they, too, want power, wealth and status. For the male African writer to perceive this, he has to see that these legitimate human desires of women do not threaten the male world or render women "uncontrollable" — a pejorative term in this usage.

In fact, rural women who have never heard of the Women's Movement in the West and probably will never hear of it, have created their own patterns for emancipation and, in the process, are spearheading social change for better or for worse.

Some women unconditionally question male supremacy and the associated myths of the inevitability of marriage, the undesirability of illegitimate children and the general problem that women's place is assumed to be subordinate and dependent upon men, whether they are fathers, brothers or husbands (Obbo : 4). As Filomena Steady rightly opines in her introductory essay, because the African woman's role is paramount in production, and because true feminism is impossible without intensive involvement in production, it can be stated without much equivocation that the black woman is to a large extent the original feminist (Steady : 36). Very few writers show this self-assertive and self-reliant aspect of the woman's role in Africa. When shown, it is by female writers such as Ama Ata Aidoo of Ghana, or Flora Nwapa and Buchi Emecheta of Nigeria. There are, of course, a few male exceptions.

In fact, the associated myth that rural women do not desire autonomy of individuality, having no knowledge of these concepts, is false. The attitude of the rural woman is, more truly, a complex one. While having no desire for the atomistic individualism of the Western variety, she does have a sense of herself as a person, a sense of her own individuality albeit that this sense of self is ensconsed in a group reality. It appears that rural women wish to assert their individuality and humanity within a group context, in harmony with other related individuals, and not in the lonely isolation of the cash-nexus. Even when she migrates to the cities, she does not break her familial and social bonds. It is the duty of researchers to delineate the dialectics of the individual-group nature of the rural woman's identity. We need to discover the values held by the rural woman herself. How does she see herself fulfilled ? What are her definitions of self, womanhood, manhood, creativity and freedom?

F. The Myths Around Marriage in Rural Life

Numerous are the persistent myths about marriage in Africa; thus a need exists to debunk these before progress in research can be made.

One of the most persistent myths is that polygamy is the greatest form of oppression from which the African woman suffers. Other aspects of the myth are that the polygynous form of marriage is on the wane as we move towards modernity and Westernisation and that the existence of polygyny is proof of the chattel status of the African woman. These views derive from a lack of understanding of the structures and motivating forces in African societies. Polygamy is not always oppressive to the woman. It has its economic role in guaranteeing women the autonomy and human dignity they need. As recently as September 1981, one researcher of polygamy and family planning, found that men and women even now consciously choose to enter polygynous marriages for various reasons of culture, economic status, prestige, desire for offspring and for sexual gratification (Brown : 322-323). She concludes that polygyny, rather than being on the wane, continues to be a legitimate and desirable form of marriage in sub-Saharan Africa.

Few of our African writers have been able to debunk the myths surrounding polygyny. One serious failure lies in their inability to present polygyny in its serious relation to production instead of as some form of sensational pornography or as an institution deliberately designed to humiliate women. The complementarity of male/female roles in the pre-colonial economy is often not appreciated. Okeyo's monogram on, "African Women in Rural Development" is an informative pointer to what needs to be done in this respect (Okeyo : December 1976). Our creative writers need to situate women concretely in the political economy of their societies.

The nature of man-woman relationships in rural society is another controversial point. It is often noted that the absence of overdependent emotional relations between rural men and women, makes it possible for women to be more self-reliant and enterprising. Others would carry this point further to say that there were no romantic relations between men and women in pre-colonial Africa or even today in the rural areas. Our writers have tended not to deal much with romantic love, although, Buchi Emechata does so in *The Joys of Motherhood* (1979). It seems to me, however, that romantic love existed traditionally and continues to exist. The point is that it was not a priority for the organization of society and its members, as it was not even in Europe before the 20th Century. It is my thesis that personal sexual love relations were considered secondary to the effective exploitation of the material reality of society and to the spiritual and physical continuity of the life of the group. We may recall that this was also the case in Europe before the rise of capitalism and the glorification of the individual and his emotions. Romantic love and money are still not always coincident in certain social classes in Euro-America.

Another area that should yield rewards is the socio-economic definition of womanhood in African societies. The definition of womanhood in African societies is not always biological or sexual. There are socio-economic points and levels where women cease to be seen as women but are ritually and officially designated as men. The concept of womanhood as social and economic dependency must therefore be re-examined.

The above theses and considerations should assist our approaches to the study of women in Africa in general, and rural women, in particular.

References

1. Achebe, Chinua (Nigeria). *Things Fall Apart* (Novel). London: Heinemann, 1958. *No Longer at Ease* (Novel). London: Heinemann, 1988. *Arrow of God* (Novel). Garden City, NY: Anchor Books, 1989, c1974. *A Man of the People* (Novel). Garden City, NY: Anchor Books, 1967.
2. Aidoo, Ama Ata (Ghana). *No Sweetness Here* (short stories). New York: Doubleday, 1971. *Anowa* (Book). Burnt Mill, Harlow, Essex, England: Longman, 1987, c1985.
3. Aniebo, L. N. C. (Nigeria). *The Journey Within* (Novel) deals with love and personal relationships. London: Heinemann Educational, 1978.
4. Beti, Mongo (Cameroon). *Mission to Kala* (Novel). London: Heinemann Educational, 1964, c1958. *Perpetua and the Habit of Unhappiness* (Novel). London: Heinemann Educational, 1978.
5. Brown, Judith E. "Polygyny and Family Planning in Sub-Saharan Africa." *Studies in Family Planning* Aug./Sep. 1981: 322-325.
6. Eagleton, Terry. *Marxism and Literary Criticism*. London: Methuen & Co. Ltd., 1976.

7. Ekwensi, Cyprian (Nigeria). *People of the City* (Novel). London: Heinemann, 1983. *Jagua Nana* (Novel). London: Heinemann, 1979, c1961.
8. Emecheta, Buchi (Nigeria). *The Joys of Motherhood* (Novel). London: Heinemann, 1979.
9. Farah, Nurrudin. *From a Crooked Rib* (Novel) for an image of a pastoral, Islamic woman of Somalia. London: Heinemann, 1970.
10. Head, Bessie (South Africa). *Maru* (Novel). New York: McCall Publishing Co., 1971. *A Question of Power* (Novel). London: Heinemann, 1974. *When Rainclouds Gather* (Novel). London: Heinemann, 1987, c1968.
11. Huston, Perdita. *Message From the Village*. New York: Epoch B. Foundation, 1978.
12. Konadu, Asare (Ghana, Ashanti). *A Woman in Her Prime* (Novel). London: Heinemann, 1976.
13. Little, Kenneth. *The Sociology of Urban Women's Image in African Literature*. London: MacMillan, 1980.
14. Lukacs, Gregory. *The Meaning of Contemporary Realism*. London: Merlin Press, 1963.
15. Marx, Karl and Frederich Engels. *On Literature and Art*. Moscow: Progress Publishers, 1976.
16. Munonye, John (Nigeria). *The Oil Man of Obange*. (Novel).
17. Thiong'o Ngugi wa (Kenya). *Weep Not, Child* (Novel). London: Heinemann, 1976, c1964. *The River Between* (Novel). London: Heinemann, 1975, c1965. *A Grain of Wheat* (Novel). London: Heinemann, 1968. *Petals of Blood* (Novel). New York: Dutton, 1978, c1977. *The Devil on the Cross* (Novel). London: Heinemann, 1987, c1982.
18. Thiong'o Ngugi wa with Mugo Micere. *The Trial of Dedan Kimathi*. London: Heinemann, 1977, c1976.
19. Nwapa, Flora (Nigeria). *Flora* (Novel). London: Heinemann, 1978. *Idu* (Novel). London: Heinemann Educational, 1970. *One is Enough* (Novel). Enugu, Nigeria: Tana Press, c1981.
20. Obbo, Christine. *African Women in Rural Development: The Struggle for Economic Independence*. London: Zed Press, 1980.
21. P'Bitek Okot (Uganda). *Song of Lawino* (long poem). Nairobi: East African Publishing House, 1966.
22. Ousmane, Sembene (Senegal). *Xala* (Novel). Westport, CT: L. Hill & Co., 1976, c1974. *Tribal Scars* (short stories).
23. Oyono, Ferdinand (Cameroon). *Houseboy* (Novel). London: Heinemann, 1966.
24. Pala, O. Achola. "African Women in Rural Development: Research Trends and Priorities." OLC Paper no.12. December, 1976.

25. Rockwell, Joan. *Fact in Fiction: The Uses of Literature in the Systematic Study of Society.* London: Routledge and Kegan Paul, 1974.
26. Steady, Filomina ed. *The Black Women Cross-Culturally.* Cambridge: Schenkam Publishing Co. Inc., 1981.
27. Soyinka, Wole (Nigeria). *The Lion and the Jewel* (play). London: Oxford University Press, 1963.
28. Stratton, Florence. "Periodic Embodiments: a Ubiquitous Trope in African Men's Writing." *Research in African Literatures.* 21.1 (Spring, 1990).
29. Vasques, Adolfo Sanchez. *Art and Society: Essays in Marxist Aesthetics.* Monthly Review Press, 1973.
30. Wellesley Editorial ed. *Women and National Development: The Complexities of Change.* Chicago and London: University of Chicago Press, 1977.
31. Zeidenstein, Sondra ed. "Learning About Rural Women." *Studies in Family Planning.* Nov./Dec., 1979. (A special issue, with articles by Kameme Okonjo, Achola Pala Okeyo, Marsha Safia, Hanna Papanek.)

3. The Female Writer and her Commitment[1]

Does the female writer have any particular commitment as a female? What could this possibly be? We shall try to answer this question through a discussion of issues surrounding her commitment. We shall also consider only creative writers.

Feminists have posited that the woman writer has two major responsibilities: first to tell about being a woman; secondly, to describe reality from a woman's view, a woman's perspective. These two postulations immediately give rise to other questions. What is a woman? What is being a woman and what is the nature of womanhood? These may sound like obvious and ridiculous truisms but we will soon find that the concept of a woman is complex and differs from society to society. Men of careless thought are prone to say: "Oh, we know what a woman is! She is a being with breasts and female genitalia," but this conception is only one aspect of womanhood.

True, the biological identity of a woman counts and is real. But woman, contrary to what some, maybe most men think, is more than "a biological aperture" as Anais Nin said.[2] Woman's biology is indeed an important and necessary aspect of her but it is not all she is and it should not be used to limit her. Not only has woman's biology been made her destiny over the ages, it has given rise to stereotypic notions of the nature of women. Mary Ellman has written about these stereotypes in her book, *Thinking About Women*.[3] Her list of imputed female attributes includes formlessness, passivity, instability, confinement, piety, materiality, spirituality, irrationality, compliancy; and two incorrigible figures: the shrew and the witch. Orthodox or mainstream American literary criticism can boast of works on female stereotypes not necessarily by feminists. The eminent critic, Leslie Fiedler, discusses the female nature while he interprets a few works by women in his *Love and Death in the American Novel.*[4] In this work, he adds images of the woman as the Rose and the Lily to the list of classic American female stereotypes in literature. Other classic stereotypes in American literature are the *Earth Mother,* and the *Great American Bitch.*

What are our own female stereotypes in African literature? It would be a worthwhile literary activity to begin to identify them. A brief attempt here will show that we already have the stereotyping of women in African literature. There is the figure of the "sweet mother," the all-accepting creature of fecundity and self-sacrifice. This figure is often conflated with Mother Africa, with eternal and abstract Beauty and with inspiration, artistic or otherwise as in much francophone poetry, particularly that of Leopold Sedar Senghor and David Diop. The figure of Beauty is not unrelated to the stereotype of the woman as the passionate and sensual lover. Much African poetry concerns itself with the eroticism of the African woman to the extent that it can be argued that many male writers conceive of women only as phallic receptacles. This writer once had to do a radio programme on the image of women in Africa through poetry. Searching through the anthology, *Poems of Black Africa,*[5] she found only the image of woman as lover; a great deal of this poetry was about the love of women, not love in its larger sense but sexual, physical love. There was little about the deeper aspects of love such as loyalty, care, kindness, or nurturing. The woman was mainly conceived of as mother or "erotic lover." The mother stereotype leads to the limiting of a woman's potential in society. How this affects the female writer will be seen later. The falseness of the myth of motherhood has been demonstrated by Buchi Emecheta in her *Joys of Motherhood* (1979). The way African writers enthuse about motherhood, one wonders if there are no women who hate childbirth or have undeveloped maternal instincts.

In addition to the mother and *houri* stereotype of the African woman, we may consider the stereotypes of the "sophisticated" city girl and the rural woman. The two are often contrasted in order to dramatize the conflict of modernity and traditionalism. Both figures are often shallow, exaggerated and false. The sophisticated woman is shown as completely divorced from life in the country or from relatives and friends who are not living in her city or sharing her night life. Very often she is a prostitute,[6] an early and recurrent figure in African literature since Abdoulaye Sadji's *Maimouna, la petite fille noire* (1953) and Cyprian Ekwensi's *Jagua Nana* (1961). The "sophisticated" woman, like Okot p'Bitek's Clementina, co-wife of Lawino, in *Song of Lawino* (1966) is an unreal being. Counterpoised to this "city girl" is the rural woman, another mirage, the "pot of culture" who is static as history passes her by, who wants the old ways of life, who speaks like a lobotomized idiot about "iron snakes" (railways) and "our husband." This naive-sounding woman who does not want change and is happy with no innovation does not exist in the African countryside. Lawino is one such. She is one such impossible and unlikely image of the rural woman.

In fact, this writer would like to submit that *Song of Lawino* is one of the most critically neglected works in African literature. Overwhelmed by the book's lyricism and the startling use of fresh images, we all enthused over the work on its appearance. But it can be very seriously faulted, as I hope to show later, in another place, for its total conception of existence, culture, African history and the needs of modern Africa. It should be faulted for its unhistorical view of culture, its simplification of Acholi culture and its philosophical yearning for "a state of nature" that does not adequately describe Acholi culture or indeed most African cultures. It is the mission-educated man's vision of Africa. But what rural woman can be as "dumb" as Lawino! What rural woman can react, see and speak like Lawino, the wife of a university lecturer in Makerere or Nairobi who nevertheless talks like an idiot about modern things, reacts so naively to a clock and longs for the village verities that Okot also fondly longs for! The figure of Lawino is a displacement from the mind of a male, Westernized writer just as Okot's *Malaya* is a man's view of how a prostitute thinks, speaks or dreams.

Unfortunately, it is not only African male writers who are guilty of this kind of mythification of the rural woman. One feels the same way about the rural woman in Ama Ata Aidoo's *No Sweetness Here* (1970). For after all the felicities and elegance of her narrative style and her just social perceptions, one wonders whether the rural woman actually speaks and thinks so naively and limitedly; so childishly. Is the rendering not the educated person's view of what the rural person sees, notes, values, and cares about? The truth is that the rural woman wants change and innovation. She wants power, wealth and status like the men. She wants to ride a car rather than walk; use plastics or metal instead of calabashes; use a gas or electric stove instead of firewood, despite all our middle-class nostalgia for that past. After all, we only need these ways of life on our postcards and Christmas cards to send abroad to our oh-so-intellectual friends. We do not have to live in a smoke filled hut! And it seems that the African male needs this myth to buoy up his conservatism and his yearning for that pre-colonial patriarchal past where he was definitely king as father, husband and ruler. The myth of the unchanging, naive rural woman seems to coincide with the actual social practice and tendency of men to discourage change and innovation in women's lives. In an anthropological study of East African women and their struggle for economic independence which often takes the form of hard work, transactional manipulation and urban migration, Christine Obbo concludes that:

> even though the world is changing all about them, it seems that women's own attempts to cope with the new situations they find themselves in are regarded as a `problem' by men, and a betrayal of traditions which are often confused with women's roles. Women must act as mediators between the past and the present, while men see themselves as mediators between the present and future. This seems to be part of the reason behind opposition to female migration. The forces of urbanization and international influence have imposed rapid changes upon East African societies, yet men expect women to be politically conservative and non-innovative. Socially, women are accused of 'going too far' when they adopt new practices

usually emanating ultimately from the capitals of the metropolitan countries.[7]

One of the commitments of the female writer should be to the correction of these false images of the woman in Africa. To do this, she herself must know the reality of the African woman, must know the truth about African women and womanhood. I have said earlier that the concept of a woman is a complex one. Womanhood does not only relate to gender, because situations exist where women adopt other gender roles (although sometimes only after menopause) as with women in the armies of Dahomey in the eighteenth and nineteenth centuries; women who marry wives in Igboland and lord it over the husbands of their acquired wives and women who are called "men" when they attain certain levels of economic and social independence. Among the Enuani Western Igbo, women who are professionally liberated, such as owners of theater troupes or poets, and women who are financially independent and strong in character are named "men."[8] In that society, the concept of a woman varies, depending on the institution within which she is being considered; political, marital, professional or economic. The female writer must tell us about being a woman in the real complex sense of the term.

On the biological level, she must tell us about being a woman: what the facts of menstruation, pregnancy, childbirth and menopause contribute to the woman's personality and the way she feels and knows her world. Do women's bodies affect their senses, their use of imagery, their personal writing styles? Debates on these considerations have taken place in European literary criticism involving women such as Charlotte Bronte, George Eliot, Virginia Woolf, George Sand and Anais Nin among others. Male writers have also had their own "phallic" or "phallocratique" contributions to make. We need to know the African female writers' views more directly. Male African writers have, from time to time, given their artistic reactions to female experiences such as menstruation, sexual love and childbirth among others, but a female writer's view would be more authentic. The theme of childlessness has been explored by

African female writers so much that one would wish they would seek other themes.[9] But much remains to be said in the area of female biological experience. Even the sensitive and beautiful *So Long a Letter* (1981) by Mariama Bâ does not explore the personal, physical areas of the women's relationships to their loves. There, Bâ becomes very abstract and poetic, almost mystical. What did Ramatoulaye feel to be sexually abandoned by Moudou? How did she feel at night? "How did Aissatou survive in New York?" as the critic Femi Ojo-Ade, has asked?[10] But to enquire about the female biological experience is not to posit that there is a feminine nature, immanent and recurrent, that can be used to identify all females and thus pigeonhole them as has been done in history. Simone de Beauvoir as early as 1953 in the history of radical feminism gave short shrift to this notion in her long and laboriously scientific discussion of the woman as the second sex.[11] She argues that it is absurd to speak of "woman" in general as of the "eternal man." She submits that there is no feminine nature, only a feminine situation that has in many respects remained constant through the centuries and that largely determines the character of its victims. The notion of "femininity" (to be distinguished from "femaleness" - my insertion) is a fiction invented by men, assented to by women untrained in the rigours of logical thought or conscious of the advantages to be gained from compliance with masculine fantasies. To quote Patricia Spack's summary of Simone de Beauvoir's position:

> Their assent traps them in the prison of repetition and immanence which limits woman's possibilities. Man reserves for himself the terrors and triumphs of transcendence; he offers woman safety, the temptations of passivity and acceptance; he tells her that passivity and acceptance are her nature. Simone de Beauvoir tells her that is a lie, that her nature is complicated and various, that she must escape, liberate herself, shape her own future, deny the myths that confine her.[12]

The socialization of women is certainly very important here. The European notion of femininity is even less applicable to Africa where women have adopted all kinds of roles not considered feminine in Europe. The wife of Amos Tutuola's Palm-Wine Drinkard is one of the best and most correct images of the Yoruba woman of all classes: a courageous, resourceful woman who dares situations with her husband, who works at anything and willingly changes roles with him, where the need arises. To restate, what then is the commitment of the African female writer in view of the above? The female writer should be committed in three ways: as a writer, as a woman and as a Third World person; and her biological womanhood is implicated in all three. As a writer, she has to be committed to her art, seeking to do justice to it at the highest levels of expertise. She should be committed to her vision, whatever it is, which means she has to be willing to stand or fall by that vision. She must tell her own truth, and write what she wishes to write. But she must be certain that what she is telling is the truth and nothing but - albeit her own truth. Most African female writers are committed to their art by being conscious craftswomen, though their skill varies in quality from person to person. For formal ingenuity, we could name: Bessie Head, Ama Ata Aidoo, Mariama Bâ in the genre of fiction; Efua Sutherland, Aidoo, `Zulu Sofola and Micere Mugo in drama and poetry. One is struck by the paucity of female poets. (Are there genres that are particularly attractive to and malleable by women?) There were English critics and writers who believed that fiction was the proper genre for a woman writer. George Henry Lewis, the "consort" of George Eliot, certainly believed that. But there are even fewer African playwrights — about five. Why is this? Could it be that being a playwright implies production; working in a theater, after hours, at all hours, in the company of men? Such a profession would be a source of insecurity for some husbands. I have known a male playwright who withdrew his actress wife from the theater!

Committed to their art African female writers definitely are. But being committed to their womanhood is another matter and a problematic one. Being committed to one's womanhood would necessitate taking up the tasks discussed earlier in this essay. It would mean delineating the experience of women as women, telling what it is to be a woman, destroying male stereotypes of women. But many of the African female writers like to declare that they are not feminists, as if it were a crime to be feminist. These denials come from unlikely writers such as Bessie Head,[13] Buchi Emecheta, [14] even Mariama Bâ.[15] I would put this down to the successful intimidation of African women by men over the issues of women's liberation and feminism. Male ridicule, aggression and backlash have resulted in making women apologetic and have given the term "feminist" a bad name. Yet, nothing could be more feminist than the writings of these women writers, in their concern for and deep understanding of the experiences and fates of women in society.

That the female writer should be committed to her Third World reality and status may lead to disagreements. Being aware of oneself as a Third World person implies being politically conscious, offering readers perspectives on and perceptions of colonialism, imperialism and neo-colonialism as they affect and shape our lives and historical destinies. Most apolitical writers and critics would balk at this and claim their illusory freedoms, their "Hyde Park Corner" freedom, as an Egyptian writer and activist, Nawal el Saadawy calls it. They would argue that they need not be forced to be political. But any true intelligence in Africa must note the circumscription of our lives here by the reality of imperialism and neo-colonialism. Perhaps only Ama Ata Aidoo and Micere Mugo can be said to be thus politically conscious. Yet, in spite of the fact that most of the writers would not speak about political economy, they do tend to believe in art for a purpose, in tendentious art, so to speak. Statements have been made, in their various interviews, about the educative nature of art, while the term "education" is itself used in various and broad senses; in the directly educational manner of Efua Sutherland's plays for children; as the education of sensibility and ethical awareness in the writings of Bessie Head; as the education of Africans about their traditional culture and their present-day problems in the works of 'Zulu Sofola, Mariama Bâ, Aminata Sow Fall, Grace Ogot and Rebeka Njau, to name a few. Flora Nwapa and Buchi Emecheta certainly wish to educate us about the woman's realm of experience, while the women writers of Southern Africa - Angola, Mozambique and South Africa - of which nine have been counted in the works of David Herdeck and of Hans Zell, Carol Bundy and Virginia Coulon, wish to educate us about apartheid and the shaping influences in their strife-torn countries.[16]

This writer feels that the female writers cannot usefully claim to be concerned with various social predicaments in their countries or in Africa without situating their awareness and solutions within the larger global context of imperialism and neo-colonialism. For what is it that makes us so dismally poor? What forced our individuals into such schizophrenic cultural confusion? Why are the national ruling classes so irresponsible, criminal and wasteful? Because they have sold out? To whom? A deep female writer who has anything worthwhile to say must have these insights.

Is there anything that recommends the female writer more particularly to this socially educative role? There is the myth that women are more ethically ferocious than men, and more reliable. (This is why they are always voted to be treasurers in Nigerian organizations!). William Thackeray among other nineteenth-century writers and critics, certainly thought so when he spoke of *the passionate honour of the woman*. Certainly, nineteenth-century European and American women's fiction, (most of which was by women, anyway) was impelled by various kinds of moral impetuses: Jane Austen and the limitations of marriage for the woman; the Brontes and the torments of independent women in society; Mrs Gaskell and her concerns for the working class; Harriet Beecher Stowe and slavery in America; Harriet Martineau and economic and social questions in England; and George Sand and the search for social justice and socialism in France.[17] Does the African female writer have any moral prerogative to point the way to others and educate the spirit? And why? As mothers, more experienced sufferers or more sentient and ethical beings?

Notes

1. Editor's note: An earlier version of this article appeared in *The Guardian* (Lagos), 21 December 1983.
2. Anais Nin, selections in J. Goulianos ed., *By A Woman Writt*, London, Penguin, 1973, 299. Born in Paris in 1903 of Cuban and Danish parents, Anais Nin was taken to the United States by her mother in 1914. She lived in France intermittently in the 1920's and between 1930 and 1940 when she was a member of the Parisian literary circle that included Henry Miller and Lawrence Durell. In 1940 she moved to the United States where she died in 1977. She is famous for her *Diary* which runs into over 150 manuscript volumes. She observes:
'The woman artist has to create something different from man.... She has to sever herself from the myth man creates, from being created by him, she has to struggle with her own cycles, storms, terrors which man does not understand' (Goulianos, 291).
3. Mary Ellman, *Thinking About Women*, New York, Harcourt Brace Jovanovich, 1968.
4. Leslie Fiedler, *Love and Death in the American Novel*, New York, Stein and Day, 1966.
5. Wole Soyinka ed., *Poems of Black Africa*, London: Heinemann, 1975.
6. The use of the prostitute figure has been given a book- length study by Senkoro of Tanzania. See F.E.M.K. Senkoro, *The Prostitute in African Literature* (Dar es Salaam: Dar es Salaam University Press, 1982.) Senkoro identifies backward and progressive uses of the prostitute figure in literature.
7. Christine Obbo, *African Woman: Their Struggle for Economic Independence* (London, Zed Press, 1980), 143.
8. Conversation with Zulu Sofola, female playwright, 29 November 1983.
9. The theme of childlessness has been treated in the following works: Flora Nwapa, *Efuru*, London, Heinemann, 1966; *Idu*, London, Heinemann, 1979; *One is Enough*, Enugu, Tana Press, 1981. Buchi Emecheta, *The Joys of Motherhood*, London, Heinemann, 1979. Ama Ata Aidoo, *Anowa*, London, Longman, 1980. Ifeoma Okoye, *Behind the Clouds*, London, Longman, 1981.
10. Femi Ojo-Ade, 'Female Writers, Male Critics', African Literature Today, 13 (London: Heinemann, 1982), 158-79.
11. Simone de Beauvoir, *The Second Sex* (New York: Knopf, 1953).
12. Patricia Meyer Spacks, *The Female Imagination* (New York, Avon Books, 1976), 17.

13. See the biography of Bessie Head in Hans Zell, Carol Bundy and Virginia Coulon (eds.), *A New Reader's Guide to African Literature* (London, Heinemann), 1983.
14. See biography in *ibid*.
15. See biography in *ibid*.
16. *Ibid.*; D. Herdeck, *African Authors: A Companion To Black African Writing - Volume I: 1300–1973* (Washington D.C., Black Orpheus, 1973). In all, this writer has been able to count thirty-two female writers in these two reference works. Twenty-five write fiction, long and short; five write plays while seven write poetry. Some writers write in more than one genre.
17. For a very informative study of the place and achievement of nineteenth-century women writers, see Ellen Moers, *Literary Women: The Great Writers* (New York: Doubleday, Anchor Books, 1977), in particular Chapter 2, 'The Epic Age: Part of the History of Literary Women' and Chapter 3, 'Women's Literary Traditions and the Individual Talent.'

4. Women in Nigeria*

On The Globality of Sisterhood

This essay begins with a poem[1] by a distinguished male poet friend of mine who is a Professor of English Literature and a Malawian. His poem sprang from the many arguments and discussions we had on women, feminism and politics in Africa and the wider world while he was visiting Nigeria. Although he is Malawian, his poem is pertinent and instructive of some of the basic ideas and attitudes of men in Nigeria and Africa.

Letter to a Feminist Friend

I will not pretend
to see the light
in the rhythm of your paragraphs:
illuminated pages
need not contain
any copy-rights
on history

My world has been raped
looted and squeezed
by Europe and America
and I have been scattered
over three continents
to please Europe and America

* First presented at the founding conference of WIN (Women in Nigeria), Zaria, Nigeria, 1982

And Now

the women of Europe and America
after drinking and carousing
on my sweat
rise up to castigate and
castrate their menfolk
from the cushions of a world
I have built!

Why should they be allowed
to come between us?
You and I were slaves together
uprooted and humiliated together
Rapes and lynchings —
the lash of the overseer
and the lust of the slave-owner
do your friends "in the movement"
understand these things?

The wile of the colonizer,
the juggernaut of apartheid
the massacres of Sharpeville and Langa,
"interrogation" unto death
unreal inquests have
your friends seen these?
like the children of Soweto?

No, no, my sister, my love,
first things first!
Too many gangsters
still stalk this continent
too many pirates
too many looters
far too many
still stalk this land —
every inch of it should be sure

yet inch by inch
day by day we see it ceded
to forces beyond our control.

Where then do we sit
where build our tent
while sorting out
the faults between you and me?
Miracles still happen,
I agree,
and privilege and the underdog
can unite to undo privilege
but sister,
not every yawning of the privileged
amounts to a sacrifice!

When Africa
at home and across the seas
is truly free
there will be a time for me
and time for you
to share the cooking
and change the nappies —
till then,
first things first!

Notice the use of the first person. It is his world that has been
raped. The Promethean persona that endured slavery and the
slave trade, colonialism, imperialism and neo-colonialism, does
not have time for women's rights yet. The world has been built
by *him* and he must attend to the pressing issues of colonialism, imperialism and neo-colonialism.

These attitudes hark back to the important feminist issue of
the representation and understanding of women and their roles
in history ably dealt with by feminists such as Mitchell,
Rowbotham and Firestone among others.

And there is the black/white posing of issues which socialist feminists reject, insisting on the class view of history and human societies. The oppression of women, economic and personal, is not solely a white/black racial confrontation, although the oppression of black women is deeply tied to the variable of race in the history of imperialism. Similarly, some of us, Nigerian women who are Ibadan branch members of AAWORD (Association of African Women for Research and Development) argued this class view in a position paper presented in the group's research workshop in Lusaka, in December 1976. In that paper, we insist that the study of women must be done from class perspectives, taking cognizance of class differences in society, in particular in Africa. Such an approach, we still feel, would yield a true picture of the woman's place in society.[2] The white women in the poem, as wives and relatives of colonizers and as collaborators with colonialism, imperialism and neo-colonial Africa and the United States are not sisters. In fact, we need to keep our minds firmly fixed on what is meant by sisterhood and the globality of sisterhood. Some feminists and activists would reject the term of "sisterhood" outright. Are women oppressed, first as women, or in their roles deriving from their respective relation to the means of production in their various societies? Again, this is another feminist issue which has received much attention from feminist theoreticians. What about aristocratic women within feudalism, or bourgeois women in the ruling classes of capitalism and imperialism? Are they seriously oppressed or oppressed at all, considering they have the money and leisure to soften or remove many of the pains of male domination. In fact, there is greater financial collaboration with the inclusion of women in family rights among families with high levels of capital.

The poem ends on a final note irritatingly typical of male supremacists everywhere: to wit, that other issues exist which are more important and urgent than the liberation of women. Somehow, miraculously, you can liberate a country or society and later, turn your attention to the women of that society — first things first! Note also that the liberation of women is conceived of as the desire of women to reduce men to housekeepers. Since most men despise manual work for feudal and middle-class reasons, women's liberation is feared as an effort by women to "feminize" men, that is, degrade them.[3] In the middle-class of capitalist societies, mental labour is more respected than physical labour; in feudal society, the great man works not at all, but makes others work for him. Hence, women's work is never respected. The poem feels women's liberation is about cooking and nappies. No, women's liberation is about the fundamental human rights of women in all areas of life, public and private.

Women in Nigeria: Problems and Realities

Most Nigerian women of the middle-class whom I know and with whom I have talked, argue that the basic situation of women in Nigeria is not intolerable or appalling because of the economic opportunities women have within the social system. These economic opportunities are not recent or post-colonial but pre-colonial. In fact, colonialism eroded many of the economic avenues women had.[4] Women had been able to engage in farming, fishing, herding, commerce and industrial labour such as pottery, cloth-making and craftwork among other activities alongside their men. These women had the right to keep the financial proceeds of their work and earnings from the sale of products. The economic position, rights and gains of aristocratic African women in pre-capitalist societies are less known. Even in purdah, in Islamic northern Nigeria, where, in the early nineteenth century, Islam took away many of the historically established and strong social rights of the Hausa women driving them indoors, even there, women work in purdah and sell their products through emissaries.

These economic opportunities and the right to work (which the middle-class woman may be fighting for in other societies and in some pockets of post-colonial and post-Christianized Nigeria) have, in fact, always existed. Today, these rights and attitudes have blossomed forth again and women have risen to pluck them, following independence in 1960 and the near cataclysmic change going on now. This deep social change is related to the civil war and the new oil-economy. It is also related to the crisis of being governed by a black national and exploiting ruling class which is subjecting the total population to stress, anxiety, and insecurities of various kinds. Women, in response to the social situation, wish to secure for themselves and their children some financial viability as well as other gains of modernization, such as formal Western education in a society, where all forms of marriage are under crisis, and men may not wish to take complete responsibility for their offspring.

All women in contemporary Nigeria are under the stress of living in a Third-World, neo-colonial nation ruled by an indifferent, oppressive and wasteful black bourgeoisie. The reactions of the women differ from class to class. Women of the urban working class, the urban poor, and the peasantry have definitely differing attitudes. They are more insistent on their right to work, as they very often have to live within polygynous systems, Islamic and traditional. They also tend to ignore the biological and emotional oppressions they have to endure, in the view that men are incorrigibly polygynous and that women are socially impotent to correct them. They insist only on the right to have their children fathered, sexually and financially, while they expect little from men in terms of companionship, personal care and fidelity.

At a symposium organized by the Nigerian Association of University Women in 1974, with market-women of the city of Ibadan on the panel, the trading women revealed interest in problems patently different from our middle-class ones. They were, in fact, contemptuous of some of these problems, in particular, the resentment of polygyny by middle-class and Westernized women. They mainly felt men could not be expected to be loyal to one woman while some outrightly claim they need helpmates in the form of co-wives to assist with housework. They needed younger wives to share, or preferably take over, the chores of kitchen and bed, so they, the older wives, could be freed to concentrate on travel for business reasons.[5] It may be argued that these trading women are victims of false consciousness and social brain-washing, but for them, the old pre-capitalist system exists, works and is respected by them. We may ask if their humanity, dignity, human rights and self-fulfilment are guaranteed within this system. Their only objection was to the rupture or distortion of the older system of marriage where the older wife now is relegated to the background by an uncaring husband or where the younger wife would not keep her lower and deferent place within that system. It is within marriage , however, that the Nigerian woman suffers the most oppression. Illegitimacy was written into the 1979 constitution, making all children born inside and outside a marriage legal. This is surely an underwriting of polygyny in the society. In 1982, there was talk of cancelling the bigamy laws which forbade that the various kinds of marriage possible in the country — Islamic, indigenous and Western ordinance — could be coincident while they forbade that within the Western marriage, one could marry more than one wife legally and officially. Members of women's groups stormed the parliamentary buildings that day to the hilarity of men who, in this country, often and generally react to women's issues with laughter and scorn. It is, however, also known that new forms of polygyny, displaced and new urban varieties, abound in the system today.

The oppression of women within marriage takes various forms. First, the woman loses status by being married because in the indigenous systems, which are still at the base of the society, the woman as daughter or sister has greater status and more rights within her birth lineages. With marriage, she becomes a client or possession; she is voiceless and often rightless in her husband's family except, in some groups, through what accrues to her through children. She also loses much of her personal freedom which she can only gain at prices expensive to herself such as the admittance of other wives or publicly acknowledged girl-friends. She also has to submit to dominance by her husband, or face execration and blame from the total society. She can win, however, by "stooping to conquer," as the generally-held cliché goes in the society. This means accepting subjection in order to "conquer" abstractly.

Men also tend to be less trusting of wives than they are of their own mothers and sisters, a situation which often alienates the wife throughout her marriage, making her a stranger in enemy territory all her life.[6] In fact, men here lean emotionally more on their mothers, sisters and aunts — the womenfolk of their own lineage or kin group than on their own wives. This situation gives some emotional power to women. Consequently, women often take consolation from this fact and help to oppress other women who come into their own lineages as wives. It is generally known that women in their own lineages provide such emotional support for the men that the men cannot function without them. Yet such men will express in acts and words the most blatant notions of male dominance. Such emotional power often satisfies women, to the point of preventing them from wanting to take other more public action or resist the subordination they suffer within their own marriages. In addition to the power female relatives wield within marriage, there exist the pressure and power of peer group values on the husband; values which often confirm male dominance and encourage even recalcitrant and would-be gentle and just husbands in the direction of male supremacy.

The subordination of women within marriage takes various traditional forms though palliated by women's right to work. But the reality of this is that women are overworked. Generally, men do not do housework of any sort or intimate childcare, so the woman struggles on two fronts — in the home and the working place. Consequently, women of the middle-class find that the most important problem they confront now is the problem of house-help. The traditional support systems of grandmothers, siblings, younger relatives and co-wives having been eliminated by new social developments such as compulsory education, urbanization and capitalist atomization of the family, the middle-class woman is, more frequently than not, marooned in her home and struggling with her job and housekeeping. The working-class woman is, of course, more burdened, for often she has to struggle similarly but with less financial wherewithal to solve her problems. She is often more structurally and financially dependent on her husband, particularly if she does only petty retail trading. She is therefore more subject to male domination, while she has some time to care for her own children, especially if she exists within a polygynous marriage where she has to contend for personal and financial attention with other co-wives. Polygyny, not infrequently, leads to the financial neglect of children by a husband too poor to cope with the burden of a large family. So each woman has to care for her own children.

Not least of the biological oppressions women endure within marriage is the compulsion to have children. Childless marriages are blamed on women, as men are never admitted to be sterile or infertile. The anguish of childless women is recorded in many a Nigerian literary narrative, both traditional and modern. One finds that the childlessness of women is a recurrent theme in modern Nigerian women's writing.[7] A childless woman is considered a monstrosity, as is an unmarried woman, spinster, or divorcee. She becomes the butt of jokes, scandal and the quarry of any passing man, married or unmarried. She is often seen by males in the society as an unclaimed and degenerating commodity to be freely exploited in all ways — emotionally, sexually and financially, among other ways.

The greatest strength of women lies in their right and ability to work in addition to their resourcefulness and great capacity for emotional survival. The extended African family probably guarantees this, or contributes enormously to it. The greatest gain made in recent years, particularly since independence in 1960, has been the widening of formal educational opportunities for women, resulting in chances in public life and a gradual change in men's attitudes that women can do as well as men, if not better, when given a chance. As a result, men are more willingly educating their daughters in the Western tradition today.

It can be said that the main areas where women need to struggle now are those of national development and political representation. Abortion is not likely to be legalized soon. When the issue arose in 1981, the greatest opponents were, in fact, middle-class women who adopted very moralistic, even Sunday-school, unscientific attitudes to the need for legalized abortion in the society. Men proved more progressive about the issue. The issue of genital mutilation has not yet seen the light of day in the country. This is probably because not enough is known about its occurrence and the frequency of its incidence. Certainly, basic research for information and action needs to be done on genital mutilation in Nigeria. Since the first version of this essay, much work has been done by Nigerian medical practitioners. Female circumcision is only vaguely known to exist among certain ethnic groups in the country. Within marriage, where this essay argues women are most subordinated, laws exist to protect women's rights.[8] The hitch is that these laws are not always implemented or obeyed. This is due to the pressures of the past and the unwillingness of women to officially and publicly seek redress because of the mental subjection they have integrated into themselves historically. Males also tend to please themselves rather than go through formal legal processes. A male-dominated society guarantees them protection and instant sympathy-even in the law courts.

Nigerian middle-class women have, however, to insist that there cannot be equality without the sharing of responsibilities. There cannot be dignity and the sharing of power without the sharing of burdens of responsibility and power. Women therefore can only claim equality within marriage if they are willing to share the financial and other burdens of marriage. As emotional and financial dependents, they cannot claim equality with the husbands who support them. Strangely enough, though, my discussions with male colleagues over the years reveal that some men would rather shoulder their marital burdens alone in order to be able to give orders to their wives. Power is sweet. In reality, the women have to pitch in on food and school fees since frequently the men do not earn enough. But women still expect certain traditional male gestures of money, cloth and jewellery gifts. All in all, middle-class men do not seem grateful for the contributions to the home made by their wives. They, in fact, resent the contributions, I suppose, because these erode their total "hegemony," their ability to treat their wives as subordinates, slaves or possessions.

Politically, in modern life, the roles of women are negligible, though indigenously, avenues existed for the political participation of women.[9] Dual-sexual political systems very often existed in pre-colonial societies[10] whereafter these systems were either distorted, suppressed or restricted in scope by colonial administrations which excluded women from their new patterns. Indigenously, structures of political participation equivalent or parallel to those for men, existed for women whereby women's voices were heard, their opinions consulted and their participation guaranteed from the familial household to the councils in the larger society. Today, we behave and talk as if it is new for women to have any political voice, role or power.

In today's presidential system, woman's visibility and leadership opportunities are negligible, though the political and personal liberties of women are theoretically and fully guaranteed in the 1979 constitution. In a recent public lecture, the notable Nigerian woman novelist, Flora Nwapa, delineated statistically the scanty number of women in visible positions, despite both the existence of women voters as the majority and the exploitation by political parties of women's enthusiasm to work during the election process.[11] Women are pre-empted from leading political roles by the attitude of men who cannot see women in leadership roles over them. Women were not considered fit to sit among the "fifty" and later forty-nine "wisemen" who drafted the 1979 constitution, despite the large number of professional women in the country. Political parties are alleged to be unwilling to field women candidates. Women are also pre-empted by the lack of capital to conduct campaigns on their own steam if they are not fielded by the male-dominated parties. Women are additionally disadvantaged by their own unwillingness as mothers within a polygynous society to commit themselves totally to the vagaries of public life without the assurance that their children will be supported.

Some women would argue that women withdraw from politics because they are shy of public criticism and would wish to avoid the rough and tumble of politics.[12] Others put the reason down to the lack of dynamism among women and their inability to pull together and exploit their own potential.[13] These sociological observations, whatever their truth, must have their causes sought in social structures and institutions, in particular the structures of oppression which include the effective subjection of women's minds within the society. Women become their own worst enemies and the worst enemies of other women in their effort to please males. This is typical of the psychology of servitude, the constant desire and anxiety to please the master until constant failure produces a dialectical and revolutionary change in the servant. Women also typically engage in self-flagellation, blaming their own oppression on themselves. Mea culpa! So effective has male-domination and patriarchal ideology been within the country.

Can women be organized against the structures of oppression within Nigeria? Are there organized women's movements in the country? Various women's societies exist, such as the Movement for Muslim Women, the Women's Improvement Society, the Nigerian Association of University Women among others, some of which come under the national umbrella of the National Council of Women's Societies, a government-recognized body, and some of which do not.[14] In addition, there are the women's wings of political parties, frequently used only to work for the party without compensation or political recognition for the women members. Women are best organized around definite economic, religious, professional, ethnic or class interests. The most lasting and effective bodies are organized around economic interests with immediate and concrete material and social benefits in view, such as those represented by market women's associations, and credit co-operatives etc. There are also religious interests which are represented by church societies and provide avenues for administrative powers and emotional support for funerals and such mishaps in urban situations where members may need the women's society to act in place of their own more distant families. Not negligible also are the ethnic groups and peer-group associations which attempt to maintain cultural continuity in the city among their members.[15] Class-based middle-class unions such as that of University Women or Old Girls' Associations are the most unstable perhaps because they have no concrete objectives, strategies or gains in view.

Most interviewees admit to difficulty in organizing women. Some of the difficulty, I believe, springs from the overworked nature of women's lives. Married mothers in particular, lack time, which results in an unenduring commitment and a consequent falling-off in participation. Such behaviour should not be explained away by any self-blaming theory of the immanently and intrinsically inconsistent nature of women, as women themselves tend to do. Nigerian women are tired, emotionally neglected, socially stressed, but brave women. The reasons for their organizational behaviour should be sought in objective causes — in social structures which breed various forms of personal, emotional, psychological and institutionalized oppression, some of which are so integrated as to be almost unrecognizable, even by their victims.

Prospects

The future of feminism in this country depends on the raising of the consciousness of women to a greater awareness of their human rights in general and in relation to men, followed by a keener desire to know and act on the various possible modes of ensuring these rights. A certain fatalism, even masochism, about male dominance still prevails in women of all classes. All of them, however, believe that in education as a way out of their differing oppressions. The women all feel Western education will inevitably force men to recognize and acknowledge their equality and abilities. Western education, they feel, will provide the social and economic basis and security from which they can resist subjection and indignities. At this point, resistance is being carried on individually and not through collective and organized action. Bolanle Awe feels that today's women have to be taught to understand the power which men definitely do not want to share.[16] If women actually organized themselves and claimed their places, men would react violently and suppressively, for the male attitude to women is born of a contradictory but explicable fear of, and contempt for women. Chief Mrs. Ebun Oyagbola, the National Minister for Economic Planning, in a recent public statement said that if women proved "arrogant", they would be neglected by the men and made to fail. Women of the urban working class and peasantry who also look so much to education will be radicalized, perforce, and may move into more radical action with men of their class, the more their hopes are disappointed by the national ruling class and the more the national economy degenerates under the stresses of neo-colonial government.[17]

It would seem that this writer is arguing that men are the enemy. No, men are not the enemy. The enemy is the total societal structure which is a jumble of neo-colonial — (that is, primitive capitalist and intermediary consumerist economic formations desperately dependent on international capital) and feudalistic, even slave-holding structures and social attitudes. In fact, other forms of economic formations which are not strictly within the usual Marxist categories of economic formations exist here. As women's liberation is but an aspect of the need to liberate the total society from dehumanization and the loss of fundamental human rights, it is the social system which must change. But men become enemies when they seek to retard, even block, these necessary historical changes for selfish interests in power, when they claim "culture and heritage" as if human societies are not constructed by human beings, when they plead and laugh about the "natural and enduring inferiority of women," when they argue that change is impossible because history is static, which it is not.

I shall end with a stanza from one of my poems which says:

How long shall we speak to them
Of the goldness of mother, of differences without bane
How long shall we say another world lives
Not spinned on the axis of maleness
But rounded and wholed, charting through
Its many runnels its justice
distributive.[18]

Notes

1. Felix Mthali: "Letter to a Feminist Friend". The poem will appear in a volume entitled: *Beyond the Echoes* (unpublished manuscript).
2. Awosika, & Ogundipe-Leslie, M., *Proposals on Research Priorities: A Nigerian Perspective.* Paper presented to the AAWORD/AFARD Lusaka Workshop on "Priorities in Socio-Economic Research on Women", December, 1976.

3. Other reasons can be adduced for the fear by men of women's liberation, a basic one of which is their fear of the loss of their property rights over their women and wives.
4. Sudarkasa, N., *Where Women Work: A Study of Yoruba Women in the Market Place and the Home* (Ann Arbor: Anthropological Paper No. 53, Museum of Anthropology, University of Michigan, 1973).
5. Personal communication during an Interview with Professor Bolanle Awe, Professor of History at the University of Ibadan, leading activist in many Nigerian women's societies, former Commissioner for Education in Oyo State. She was herself present at this symposium. Ibo business women express the same views in Flora Nwapa's latest novel, *One is Enough* (Enugu: Tana Press, 1981.)
6. Nwapa, Flora, *One is Enough* (Enugu: Tana Press, 1981) 30. Note also women's marital problems as dramatized in the work.
7. Nwapa, Flora, *Efuru* (London: Heinemann, 1966), Idu (London: Heinemann, 1970), *One is Enough*, (Enugu: Tana Press, 1981). Emecheta, Buchi, *The Joys of Motherhood*, (London: Heinemann, 1978).
8. See Akande, J., *Law and the Status of Women in Nigeria*, (Unesco Commissioned Monograph, 1979).
9. Paulme, D. *Women of Tropical Africa* (Berkeley: University of California Press, 1971) in particular A.M.D. Lebeuf, "The Role of Women in the Political Organization of African Societies"; Johnson, Samuel, *The History of the Yorubas from the Earliest Times to the beginning of the British Protectorate* (Lagos: C.M.S. Bookshops, 1921, 1966 edition); Awe, Bolanle, "The Position of the Iyalode in the Traditional Political System" in Schlegel, A. (ed.), *Sexual Stratification* (Columbia University press, 1977); Mba, Nina, *Women in Southern Nigerian Political History* (1900-1965) (Ph.D. Dissertation of the University if Ibadan, Ibadan, 1978). Her impressive bibliography will be extremely useful.
10. Okonjo, K. "The Dual-Sex Political System in Operation: Igbo Women and Community Politics in Midwestern Nigeria" in Hafkin, N.J. & Bay, E.G., *Women in Africa* (California: Stanford University Press, 1976).
11. Nwapa, Flora, *"The Role of Women in the Presidential System"* Alumni Lecture, University Alumni Lecture Series, Ibadan, 19 March 1982.
12. Interview with Chief (Mrs) G.T. Ogundipe, mother of the present writer. Retired teacher of trigonometry, elementary mathematics and English in teacher's colleges, wife of a retired Bishop, himself now a traditional chief of agricultural life in his native town of Ago-Iwoye, now deceased. First woman in Nigeria to

attain in the 1930s the Teacher's Grade I Certificate, very presti-
gious at the time and attained by few men in the country.
Currently and for the second time, the Lay President of the
Ibadan Diocese of the Methodist Church of Nigeria, Chief (Mrs.)
G.T. Ogundipe has called for the ordination of women and has
written a booklet to that effect entitled: *The Ordination of Women*
(Ibadan: Methodist Literature Department,1977). As an active
and leading member of many women's societies including business co-operatives, church societies and political party wings,
she has been Deputy National President of the National Council
of Women's Societies and founder of her own recognized group,
The Women's Improvement Society, based in Ibadan. She is a
major figure and sometime president of the Nigeria branch of
the International Women's Alliance, for which organization she
has travelled extensively in Europe, America and Africa. She
toured Nigeria in the 1960's as a leader within the women's
wing of a political party. A traditional chief of all women in economic life, in particular the markets, she sits and deliberates on
the king's councils in her town and her husband's town. To keep
herself busy and in touch with contemporary educational ideas,
she runs a children's day-care centre in her home. She attended
in July 1982 a Conference of the International Women's Alliance
in Helsinki, Finland. Chief (Mrs.) G.T. Ogundipe is seventy-six.
(in 1994, eighty-seven.)
13. Interview with Professor Bolanle Awe, cited above.
14. Interview with Mrs. Adeola Ayoola, current National Social
    Secretary of the Nigerian Association of University Women
    (NAUW), 26 March 1982. She reports how supportive govern-
    ment bodies are of her group and planned women's activities in
    general. Her view is that women members of some organiza-
    tions need to be more committed and consistent.
15. Interview with Professor Bolanle Awe, cited above.
16. Awe, interview cited.
17. Chief (Mrs.) Ebun Oyagbola, *Punch*, 19 March 1982.
18. Molara Ogundipe-Leslie, "On Reading an Archaeological
    Article on Nefertiti's reign and Ancient Egyptian Society". Poem
    in Ogundipe-Leslie, Molara, *Sew the Old Days and other Poems*
    (London & Ibadan: Evans Brothers Publishers, June 1982).

References

1. Adekanye-Adeyokunnu, T., *Women in Nigerian Agriculture*,
   (Unpublished Monograph, Department of Agricultural
   Economics, University of Ibadan, Nigeria, 1982).

2. Akande, J., *Law and Status of the Nigerian Woman*, (Unesco Commissioned Monograph, 1979).
3. Ardener, S., ed., *Perceiving Women* (John Wiley & Sons: N.Y. 1975).
4. Hafkin, N.J. & Bay, E.G., *Women in Africa* (California, Stanford University Press, 1976). Has important essays on the political position of women in some Nigerian groups.
5. Hill, P., *Rural Hausa* (London: Cambridge University Press, 1972).
6. Smith, M., *Baba of Karo* (London: Faber and Faber, 1954). On the socio-economic role of the northern Nigerian woman.
7. Sudarkasa, N., *Where Women Work: A Study of Yoruba Women in the Marketplace and the Home* (Ann Arbor: Anthropological Paper No.53, Museum of Anthropology, University of Michigan, 1973.)

5. The Proletarian Novel in Africa: Problematizing from Iyayi's *Violence**

Violence, a novel by Festus Iyayi is being hailed as the first Nigerian proletarian novel. This description of the novel should be examined before it becomes established in our literary critical vocabulary and taxonomy.

To discuss whether *Violence* is the first Nigerian proletarian novel, we may first ask what we mean by "proletarian". The term is used to refer to the working class; and "working class" does not mean everybody who goes out to work, as the term is often used in Nigerian newspapers! In Marxist political economy, "proletarian" means workers of a specific nature, although this nature is often subjected and still subject to discussion and closer definitions. Of the workers in a society, Marxist analysis stresses the distinction between productive and non-productive workers. The former are exclusively wage-earners, sometimes termed direct producers, whose labour produces value and, especially, the additional or surplus value appropriated by the capitalist and constituting the return on capital (Jake, 1977). It should be noted that only the production of commodities, that is, material goods with an exchange value, can give rise to new surplus value. Thus, productive workers are those who produce such material goods and collectively constitute the working class. Jake argues that non-productive workers who contribute to the accumulation of capital together with the industrial working class, constitute what Marx

---

* I granted permission that this essay be used as an introduction to the Russian edition of the novel, *Violence*.

defined as the proletariat, that is, all the workers whose labour "increases capital."

Now, we may ask if the proletarian exists in Nigeria. Some commentators on, and scholars of, Africa have been known to argue that there are no classes in Africa. Various reasons are given, ranging from a romanticization of indigenous traditional African societies to a covert attempt to subvert socialism in Africa or the desire to maintain the economic status quo. The position that Africa (in the past or present) has no classes has been challenged and dismissed by social scientists and African political theoreticians. Nkrumah, in fact, addresses himself directly to this fallacy, stressing that class structures which exist in other parts of the world exist in Africa (Nkrumah, 1970). He emphasizes that a fierce class struggle has been raging in Africa. Class struggle exists in Africa and *we need to correctly identify* the kinds of classes which do exist and the nature of the class struggle going on in our continent. A useful and intelligent approach is not to seek correlations with classes and class dramas in other societies, but to identify the class specifics of any particular African society. Such useful and original work is what Cabral attempts in his brief essay on the social structures of Guinea Bissau (Cabral, 1969). In avoiding mere imitation of orthodox Marxist terms, Cabral is careful not to use the word "proletarian" but describes the various classes of workers and their relation to productive forces in Guinea. He introduces the term "de-classés" to describe socially dislocated urban dwellers who are orthodoxically considered lumpen-proletarian but who are not so because of the peculiar nature of the African kinship system which guarantees such people room and board in the city. Consequently, they are not as derelict as the European lumpen.

In contemporary Nigeria, we have a society divided into classes with a neo-colonial political economy. Nigeria is neo-colonial because it has an economy dependent on, and exploited by, an external political economy — that of the internationalist capitalist order. Internally, Nigeria has a dependent indigenous bourgeoisie or middle class made up of professionals, bureaucrats and merchants who, through the political process, have been able to accumulate capital and carve out monopolistic advantages for themselves within the neo-colonial political economy, and thereby forming a "bourgeoisie" (Williams in *Gutkind and Waterman*, 1977). Williams notes how the increasing intervention of the state in economic life has caused it to control lucrative contracts and the disposal of monopolistic advantages. This bourgeoisie, as Fanon had said before in the *Wretched of the Earth*, lacks the commitments of a religious, socialist or nationalist character found in the rationalizing, capital-accumulating, surplus-expropriating classes of Britain, Russia, Germany or Japan during the period of industrialization. Dependent on Nigeria's consumerist and dependent bourgeoisie is the equally consumerist and imitative petite-bourgeoisie made up of service people, smaller traders and intellectuals. These have no control of power or the economy, but sell their services and strive to join the bourgeoisie. Lower than this class, is a working class of peasants and "workers" in our definition and the "declassés", the unemployed in town and country. The description of social classes in Nigeria offered here is not complete, but we have a rough schema.

If classes exist in Nigeria, why is Festus Iyayi's *Violence* a proletarian novel? Is it a proletarian novel at all? The novel presents a week in the life of an urban worker and his wife. Idemudia, the protagonist and his wife, Adisa, are school dropouts from the rural areas of Bendel State who go to Benin City to make a living. At first unemployed and declassed, Idemudia lives on his wits in the city, washing cars, and selling his blood to blood banks to make some money for meals. His wife, Adisa, who received more education than he, is jobless and totally dependent on him. Their economic condition has severe effects on their emotional lives as a couple, just as Marx and Engels postulated in the *Communist Manifesto*. In discussing the deleterious effects of capitalism on the institution of the family, they had observed the practical absence of the family among the proletarians and the enforcement on them of various forms of public prostitution (Marx and Engels, 1962). The human and central drama of the novel *Violence*, in fact, turns on the effect of their economic life on their relationship as husband and wife.

On a day of extreme hunger, Idemudia, the husband, goes out to find a job. He finds one, off-loading three trailers of cement, owned by a woman merchant, member of the *bourgeoisie*, a contractor and owner of several hotels, the typical contemporary "Cash Madam" of Nigeria. She is named Queen. Since this strenuous job was done in the rain, Idemudia falls ill and is hospitalized. He later becomes a worker and foreman for the "Cash Madam" on her project to build low-cost housing estates for the government, a contract she achieved by graft and the use of her body and beauty. She also tries to seduce Idemudia in order to break a strike on her building project. The Cash Madam's husband is also a businessman who tried to seduce Adisa, the worker's wife. She, in severe straits to find the hospital fees for her husband, naively falls into the trap of the male bourgeois's clutches. The final scene turns on Idemudia's reaction to the moral dilemma of his wife. The plot therefore has an ironic structure.

The novel, fast-paced and interestingly told, depicts a wider canvas of the social dynamics and reality of Benin society than the brief resume given above. Because the novel treats the experience of an urban worker and his wife and synchronically gives portraits of the lives and situation of other workers, it is a novel about the proletarian rather than a proletarian novel.

It is not a proletarian novel because, firstly, its author is not proletarian. From the little as yet known about the life of the author, a farmer's son and university teacher, he is a petit-bourgeois writing about proletarians and attempting to give a view of life in Nigeria from the point of view of the working class. Secondly, he seeks to identify with the proletarian view through the rhetoric of the novel, as, for instance, when he deals with the nature of social violence in Nigeria. The novel cannot be said to be meant for proletarians because of its style. Its language may not be accessible to the average proletarian though this remains to be seen from the sales pattern achieved by Longman's later.

Most importantly, *Violence* is not proletarian because it does not emanate from a working class culture. Not only is the proletariat, particularly its urban variety, still small in Nigeria, it has no strong awareness of itself as a group and does not yet function effectively as a political force. Nor does the proletariat in Nigeria have a self-created culture which produces its own politically conscious cultural artifacts. There are art-forms and art-products produced by members of the working class for themselves, but *Violence* is not one such, although it may end up being appropriated by the working class because it so sensitively and arrestingly depicts their predicament. *Violence* is a novel which, if started, cannot be laid aside by the reader until finished.

Trotsky, in *Literature and Revolution*, discusses the difficulties the proletariat has in creating a culture of its own. He doubts that this can happen even in a society where the revolution has taken place. In Marxist theory, the period in which a proletarian government is in power is seen as an intermediary period between socialism and communism. During this period, Trotsky feels the proletariat will be too taken up with the problems of restructuring a new society to create a culture of its own.

> ... because the years of social revolution will be years of fierce class struggle in which destruction will occupy more room than new construction. At any rate, the energy of the proletariat itself will be spent mainly in conquering power, in retaining and strengthening it and in applying it to the most urgent needs of existence and of further struggle. The proletariat, however, will reach its highest tension and then fullest manifestation of its class character during the revolutionary period and it will be within such narrow limits that the possibility of planful, cultural reconstruction will be confined.(Trotsky, 1960)

Lenin did try to build a proletarian culture in the period of the revolution and many of the prejudices against Marxist thought and aesthetic theory spring from a misunderstanding of such political actions. Lenin and Stalin, in particular, had political jobs to do and needed to create a particular kind of society. The specific historical practice of Stalin need not be taken as a model for all societies or as the only possible Marxist aesthetic attitude. Lenin, for his part, allowed for the free production of art by the individual artist, although the individualist artist could not be a member of his party. A party is primarily a political machine, Lenin argued, and should not allow divisive or subversive members as he polemically and unashamedly wrote:

> Everyone is free to write and say whatever he likes, without any restrictions. But every voluntary association (including the party) is also free to expel members who use the name of the party to advocate anti-party views. Freedom of speech and the press must be complete. But then freedom of association must be complete too.(Lenin, 1967)

In the same essay he also says that there can be no real and effective "freedom" in a society based on the power of money: "Are you free in relation to your bourgeois publisher, Mr. Writer," he says, "in relation to the bourgeois public which demands that you provide it with pornography in your novels and paintings, and prostitution as a supplement to 'sacred' scenic art."

The point being made here is that Marxist aesthetic theories encompass more than the specific artistic historical activity in the Soviet Union. Mao distinguishes between consciously political art and non-political art and admits that the criteria of art must be of art.

Thus, what can be said to be the achievements of Festus Iyayi in *Violence*? It is the first novel to treat, in a protracted and concentrated way, the life of a Nigerian worker. Not even Cyprian Ekwensi, our urban novelist of the "declasses" and migrant city dwellers, has done this. The Nigerian novel has primarily been concerned with the lives of petty bourgeois protagonists like the authors, the rags-to-riches story, or the encounter of the educated middle class college graduate with the West. An East African critic, Osotsi, has noted how African novelists often choose heroes of the middle class in the ironical present and heroes of the aristocracy in pre-capitalist Africa. Obi Okonkwo is the son of Ozo Okonkwo in Achebe's *No Longer At Ease* (1960). Ezeulu is a priest aristocrat in Igbo society in Achebe's

Arrow of God (1964). The critic identifies this tendency to choose nobly-born heroes as a basic elitism resulting from a commitment to Aristotelian aesthetics of the tragic. "The main characters in our written literature are petty-bourgeois *male* (his emphasis) when they are placed in contemporary African situations (sic). Otherwise they are drawn from the ruling classes of the pre-Westernized African societies"(Seminar Paper, Department of English, University of Nairobi, Kenya, 1980).

The "chap-books"* before Ekwensi dwell a great deal on money-making and the accumulation of wealth in a new urbanized situation but the kind of "hard labour" which is being so pieticized is not clearly portrayed. Though the "chap-books" concern themselves with work, the consciousness that permeates them is more petty-bourgeois than proletarian. So, *Violence* is the first novel about proletarian characters, handled from the world view of the proletarian.

It is effectively written in a realistic mode. It is realist in several ways: namely in the traditional sense of mainstream bourgeois criticism rendered classic by Ian Watt, and in the Marxist sense of critical and socialist realism. Marxist poetics of fiction identify two forms of realism: critical realism and socialist realism. The former is a school and method which originated in the middle of the 19th century and in the Marxist view, includes many artists and writers of the capitalist period who are considered progressive for their critique of the bourgeois order of their time. Critical realists are considered to have revealed the vile nature of bourgeois society, wittingly or unwittingly, and to have played an important part in developing the idea of man's social and spiritual emancipation and in asserting democratic social ideals in the minds of men. Stendhal, Balzac and Dickens, Gogol, Turgenev and Tolstoy are counted among critical realists. In the 20th century, artists such as Charlie Chaplin, Hemingway and Graham Greene are also considered critical realists. The masterpieces of critical realism are considered to have contributed immensely to socialist realism.

An essential distinguishing factor of socialist realism is that workers become the heroes of its artistic products. Socialist realism is an artistic method which presupposes a" truthful," historically concrete reflection of reality taken in its revolutionary development. It originated at the beginning of the 20th century under the conditions of the crisis of capitalism, the upsurge of the proletarian struggle in the Soviet Union and the preparation for the socialist revolution in the country. Seen as a logical continuation and development of the best realist traditions of past art, socialist realism is officially seen as "a new stage in man's artistic progress." The criticisms of Marxist aesthetics spring from this idea of socialist realism and its enactment under Stalin. Unlike critical realism, socialist realism defends a Marxist-Leninist world view and states a decidedly overt partisanship unlike the covert partisanship of bourgeois critical liberalism. The Soviets identify the chief ideological and aesthetic principles of socialist realism as: devotion to communist ideology, service to the people and partisanship, close bonds with the working people's struggle, socialist humanism and internationalism, historical optimism, and the rejection of formalism, subjectivism and naturalist primitiveness. A socialist realist writer is expected to have a thorough knowledge of human life, thoughts and sentiments,.... to be fully responsive to human experiences and to be able to portray them in good artistic form. Socialist realism is considered a powerful instrument for educating people in a communist spirit, and, despite its basis in a Marxist-Leninist world view, it encourages writers to choose various forms and styles consistent with their individual inclinations.

From these definitions, Iyayi's novel can be said to be of both critical and socialist realism. It is socialist realism because it is devoted to the cause of working people and is obviously partisan. It is humanistic in its concern with the human degradation of working people like Idemudia, Adisa and the Jimoh family, by its concern with unemployment and poverty. It is historically optimistic, not in obviously stating that there will be a social change, but in his tender and sensitive depiction of the relationship between the worker and his wife. Their hardships are not allowed to coarsen their lives irretrievably, nor lead to a collapse of their relationship. Rather, their experiences are made to bring them to a higher state of awareness of themselves as human beings, as sufferers from external factors and as lovers caught together in a predicament. The resolution of the lover's drama bespeaks optimism in the author and a hope for the working people. He does not portray workers as bourgeois writers tend to do — as hopelessly depraved hominids. However, this very ending of the novel can be faulted as a weakness. Iyayi leaves the more socially important and dramatic issue of a confrontation between Queen and her workers to end the novel on the nearly sentimental emotional reunion of the lovers. The approaching strike which is building up among the workers and would have crystallized a serious social fact of conflict in Nigerian society, is difused by the ending of the novel. The strike would have given Idemudia a significantly dramatic role to play, as he was caught as foreman between the "Cash Madam" and the proletarian builders. This writer feels that Idemudia is somewhat too saintly a character; that his personality, which expresses no negative reactions to his social oppressors, is somewhat too idealized. Perhaps Iyayi, in making Idemudia express his existential rage against his wife, is making a correct point of social psychology: that the poor and the oppressed tend to express their rage against their immediate and blameless associates, rather than against their true political enemies whom they do not have the political awareness to identify.

Instead of Idemudia's reactions to his social experience, we have authorial intrusions, expatiating, albeit correctly, on the true nature of violence in an underdeveloped and dependent economy like Nigeria (Chapter 15). *Violence is not the violence of striking workers or demonstrating students as the establishment likes to think.* Violence is the material effect of the social actions of the rich on the lives, psyches and personalities of the poor. Although in the hospital, Iyayi uses the narrative device of a play to comment on the social violence in Nigeria, the choice of this method by the author, the issues discussed and the manner of their discussion represent an authorial intrusion.

Finally, the use of the female protagonist, Queen, the "Cash Madam" merits some discussion. This writer queries her use as the major protagonist in the socio-economic drama because it is a false rendering of the reality of the political economy of

Nigeria. Although women are very visible in the comprador activities going on in Nigeria today, they do not represent the major force nor do they have the economic and social power of men in the comprador bourgeoisie.

One wonders why Queen has been chosen as a vehicle for the actions of her class. This writer hopes it is not related to the contemporary trend in Nigerian society and the arts to demonize women, to make them the devils who plague the society. Women are portrayed as the social villains and the source of Nigeria's problems in contemporary plays in the theatre and on the radio, in the newspapers, popular music and even in day-to-day conversation. One hopes Iyayi is not part of this trend. On the other hand, it can be argued that the use of a female character makes interesting reading and allows for a portrayal of the family life of the new intermediary bourgeoisie.

It cannot be argued, as a colleague once did to this writer, that Queen represents a new phenomenon in the society and therefore merits portrayal. This cannot be argued because it is nothing new in southern Nigeria for a woman to be economically strong, independent and wealthy, given the history of merchant princesses and well-to-do women in the society and the precolonial existence of commercially successful women who were also members of the traditional feudal aristocracy. What we see in modern Nigeria is a modernization of the indigenous roles of women in southern Nigeria. The indigenous economic structures which permitted women to be persons of material means have been simply transformed into the newer neo-colonial bourgeois activities of present-day women.

A more interesting proposition is that the use of a female character is an effort by the author to index the dehumanization that capitalism can inflict on the person, if one accepts that the position and nature of women in a society is an index to the humanity of that society. In this regard, one may compare the use of women and Wanja in Ngugi's *Petals of Blood*. Like Ousmane before him and as a revolutionary writer, Ngugi is fighting patriarchal ideology and the oppression of women in Africa through an art work. Ngugi has consciously given Wanja a significant role to play in the novel's structure as well as in the expression of his own ideological stance. And he has gone to greater lengths in this novel than in his earlier novels to explore the psychology of the woman and the meaning of her social experiences in Africa. Ngugi is definitely concerned with the "kingdom of man and woman" which he makes his major male character, Karega seek, recognizing that a society cannot save itself politically or attain human justice if it neglects the fate of its women-folk. Therefore, Robson finds her not merely a vehicle for Ngugi's ideas but also a person possessing a genuine human dimension. The tragedy of her existence is that of many who are exploited and unfulfilled.

Is Iyayi using Queen in *Violence* in such an ideological manner? This writer feels the total canvas of the novel, being too narrow, does not permit one to be clear about the nature of the use of Queen. Of the members of her social bourgeois class, only her husband, Obofun, is given any protracted treatment. And it seems a twist in the social reality of Nigeria to make her more dramatically significant; since her husband has more power, influence and money. She, however, emerges as the more devilish oppressor. Unlike Ngugi, Iyayi does not portray his characters in great enough detail to intimate to us the logic of their employment. One hopes there is no sexism involved in the use of Queen as a she-devil.

To conclude, is Iyayi's *Violence* a proletarian novel? It can be said that it is not a strictly proletarian novel. But perhaps what we need to do is begin a political typology of novels emerging from Africa. We could categorize as follows:

1. Proletarian author and proletarian characters, e.g. Early Ousmane: *The Black Dockworker;*
2. Proletarian author and non-proletarian characters, e.g. local "chap-books" not in Obiechina, op.cit;

---

* Written by indigenous Nigerians, "chap-books" are "proto-novels" which have been named Onitsha market literature. The most substantial research on this genre is by Emmanuel Obiechina. I call these chap-books proto-novels as they precede in from and style the acknowledged novels of the earliest Nigerian writers, Ekwensi, Tutuola and Achebe.

3. Non-proletarian author and proletarian characters e.g. Alex La Guma;
4. Proletarian author with proletarian characters and a proletarian world view. Later Ousmane: *God's Bits of Wood*;
5. Non-proletarian author with proletarian characters and a proletarian world view, e.g. Festus Iyayi;
6. Non-proletarian author with proletarian characters and a non- proletarian world view, e.g. Achebe's *A Man of the People*;
7. Non-proletarian author with non-proletarian characters with a proletarian world view, e.g. Ayi Kwei Armah.

The permutations are obviously not exhausted. Iyayi belongs in the fifth category. (Contributions to a commentary on this typology of African novels will be welcome).

Bibliographic Notes

Amin, Samir and Cohen, R., *Classes and Class Struggle in Africa* (Lagos, Yaba: Afrografika Publishers, 1977).

Cabral, Amilcar *Revolution in Guinea: An African People's Struggle* (London: Stage 1, 1969).

Eagleton, Terry, *Marxism and Literary Criticism* (London: Methuen & Co. Ltd., 1976).

Ehrensaft, Phillip, "The Rise of a Proto-Bourgeoisie in Yorubaland" in Gutkind, Peter C.W. and Waterman, eds., *African Social Studies* (London: Heinemann Educational Books, 1977) 116-124

Gutkind, Peter C.W. and Waterman, Peter, *African Social Studies*: A Radical Reader (London: Heinemann Educational Books 1977).

Iyayi, Festus, *Violence* (London: Longman Drumbeat, 1979).

Jake, P. *How Capitalism Works* (translated by Mary Klopper (New York and London: Monthly Review Press: 1977).

Lenin, V.I., *On Literature and Art* (Moscow: Progress Publishers, 1967).

Lukacs, G., *The Meaning of Contemporary Realism* (London: Merlin Press, 1963).

Marx and Engels: *The Communist Manifesto in Selected Works* Vol.1 (Moscow: Foreign Languages Publishing House, 1962) pp. 34-64.

A Dictionary of Philosophy (Moscow: Progress Publishers 1967).

Ngugi, wa Thiongo, *Petals of Blood* (London: Heinemann, 1977).

Nkrumah, K. *Class Struggle in Africa* (New York: International Publishers, 1970) 7.

Obiechina, E.N. *Onitsha Market Literature* (London: Heinemann, 1972).

Osoba, Segun, "The Nigerian Power Elite, 1952-1965," in Gutkind & Waterman, eds., *op cit.*, 283-295.

Robson,C.B. *Ngugi wa Thiong'o* (London: Macmillan Commonwealth Writers Series, 1979).

Trotsky, Leon, *Literature and Revolution* (Ann Arbour,Michigan· Paperbacks, 1960).

Wallerstein, Immanuel, "Class and Status in Contemporary Africa" in Gutkind & Waterman, eds., *op cit.*, . 277-283.

Watt, Ian *The Rise of the Novel* (Pelican, 1972).

Williams, Gavin, "Class relations in a Neo-Colony: the Case of Nigeria," in Gutkind and Waterman, eds., *op cit.* .283- 295.

Williams, Gavin, "Nigeria: A Political Economy" in Williams, Gavin, ed. *Nigeria: Economy and Society* (London: Rex Collings, 1976).

Williams, Gavin, ed. *Nigeria, Economy and Society* (London: Rex Collings, 1976) see also essays in same volume by Remy, Beer and Williams, and Waterman.

Woddis, Jack, "Is There an African National Bourgeoisie" in Gutkind? Waterman, eds,. *op cit.*,.267-278.

6. The Representation of Women: The Example of Soyinka's *Ake*

To enter the world of *Ake: The Years of Childhood*,* is to enter an enchanted world, Senghor's "Kingdom of Childhood", sometimes charmingly re-created by the adult Soyinka, in some of his best prose to date. One of the most charming features of the work is the image of the boy which comes across — a precocious, mischievous, but clever boy who is only too ready to become physically aggressive in an expression of his, as yet, unreached manhood: a denial of his inevitable youthful weakness. Another element is the child's perspective from which people, things and events are seen and described. Soyinka is able to convey a child's sense of the magic and wonder of life—wonder at the incomprehensible world around him as in the early recapitulations (pp. 1-5), and the magic world of imagined demons and spirits, or "creatures", which people the world of children. Most charming and amusing of all is the child's sense of himself, which Soyinka, the narrator, through his tongue-in-cheek prose, evokes admirably. This sense of self is very meaningful and serious for the child while it is only quixotic to adults; hence the general indulgence of the boy, although this is partly due to his being male and a first-born son. Going to school, being choosy of women when he has not even reached puberty, his concern with his "wife," Mrs. Odufuwa — all these incidents come across humorously from the child's perspective so acute-

* (Rex Collings, 1981)

ly presented in the older Soyinka's mocking tone.

Such passages in the work are best when the older Soyinka's personal view does not intervene, as it does in the later Ogboni scenes. These later scenes sound like the view of the older Soyinka in *The Interpreters* and recent works. Did Soyinka always hold a view of the Ogboni as cruel and awe-inspiring? Does he now carry into adulthood a childhood impression of these societal judicial executives? I think it is a sensational and typically Western approach to underscore and reiterate only the awe-inspiring aspects of what are positive and real roles in Egba traditional administrative structures.

The child's sense of phenomena as disjointed, disparate and incomplete is well conveyed in such scenes as his father's inexplicable and frenetic taking of photographs; the little Soyinka's mystification over mythical words like "Temperature" and "Birthday", or over concepts like "Change". Soyinka conveys well how loved adults appear mythical to children: for instance, Bishop Ajayi Crowther, his mother, (Wild Christian), his retiring father and of course, Daodu, who was a real myth in his lifetime in Yoruba country. As he is depicted in *Ake*, Daodu reminds one of the Forest Father in *A Dance of the Forests*, in the way he strolls, ruminative and brooding, in the school compound, from time to time coming out with brief, wisdom-laden statements *telling the incapable and non-plussed women at their meeting what to do* (p. 178).

My initial reaction was a cry of "male chauvinism again"! But in an interview with Cousin Koye of the book, now Professor Ransome-Kuti (University of Lagos), he confirms that the Rev. Ransome-Kuti was very involved with his wife's activities, read through many of her articles and saw to it that they were flown by special courier to London to appear in *The Daily Worker*. Despite the Rev. Ransome-Kuti's supportiveness, however, it cannot be that the women at the meeting table in *Ake* were completely lost and unable to know what to do.

In fact, histories of the time confirm my initial objection to Soyinka's depiction of the women's activities and Mrs Kuti's role. Mrs Funmilayo Ransome-Kuti was a very politically conscious, sophisticated and able woman. She would have been quite able to guide her group at a meeting. A daughter of educated and wealthy parents, she had studied in England from 1919 to 1923 in the heyday of the British suffragette movement and had been influenced by it. She returned to Nigeria an admirer of Mahatma Ghandi, a confirmed socialist, anti-colonialist and radical feminist. Ironically —but maybe wisely — she used the colonial officers and administrative bodies in Nigeria against her local political enemies, the Alake and the Sole Native Authority of Abeokuta. Mrs Kuti and the women in her group were quite capable of initiating ideas and action.

The child tells his story, particularly in the portion relating to his pranks, in the collective "we" which is typical of children — in particular, Yoruba children. The "we" expresses the strong peer-group sense which is instilled early in the life of many Yoruba children. Also, African children tend to speak individually as "we". In addition, children nearly always play in groups. But significantly, to the reader's disappointment, none of these other children enter into the work or emerge as perceptible and active characters.. Only the little Soyinka is visible. The other children in the book, like Tinu, Femi or the Abiku, appear briefly here and there but only as foils, stills or emblematic figures like the Abiku. Significantly, the child-narrator also sees the cousins and wards as "cousins" and "strays". From whose viewpoint is this? In fact, one of the fictive problems of *Ake* is that of narrative voice — is it the man-child or the older Soyinka who is speaking? The best parts are when the older Soyinka's narrative voice effectively and eloquently emerges from the vision of the man-child's. In seeing his mother's wards as strays, was he estranged from those children and the experience of living with them even in his childhood? Is it a failure of the child to understand the sociological reality of which he is a part; where children normally stay as wards of adults? Despite the narrative "we," there is a striking sense of alienation from the family and other children in the narration. Do we see here the beginnings of the fascination with the "loner" complex which would later yield a whole section of poems on "the lone figure" in *Idanre and Other Poems*?

Soyinka succeeds in recreating the past from a child's perspective by his handling of focus in an almost cinematic but verbal and structural way. It is best exemplified by the first chapter, in particular in the evocation of Bishop Ajayi Crowther (pp. 4-5). In Soyinka's past work, these characteristic techniques, employed in *The Interpreters* and to our chagrin, in *A Dance of The Forests* and in parts of *Idanre* have aroused the cry of "obscurity" and "difficulty" among his readers. But in *Ake* these techniques are perfectly suited to the handling of a child's incomplete, imaginative and often surrealist view of life. But while we enjoy the charming and scenic evocation in Chapter Ten of the parsonage, the old city and the old market at night and the child's memory of the foods and smells, written in vintage prose (which for me is the best portion of the work), some questions about focus and perspective also arise.

Did Soyinka always see his parents as "Essay" and "Wild Christian"? Surely it is the older Soyinka now who dares to be so familiar and teasing? Did he think of them in those names then or is it an emotional, adult Soyinka now projecting backwards and forwards? There is the complex vision of a child speaking at times from his own perspective, being slapped around by someone he calls "Wild Christian." Also, the re-creations of the women's uprising and the dialogues — Kemberi's speeches, for instance — read like pure adult Soyinka. It is the adult Soyinka at work and emergent from behind the child, recreating the speeches and the scenes as something new and his own; in fact, as something totally different from actuality. At such points, the reader is so conscious of Soyinka, the dramatist, at work that an uncomfortable feeling of being manipulated is aroused.

One might be charmed by the recognition of familiar Soyinka, yet the pleasure deriving from this play of writing might be soured by the historical distortion such scenes represent.

The child in *Ake* is portrayed as sensitive (as in his reaction to his sister's death) and naturally loving of justice. Was this love of justice natural or environmental? And we may ask how much of the image of the child in *Ake* is really a recreation of oneself in the image one has of oneself which, I suppose, is the nature of autobiography. For the autobiography, not being a documentary (that in itself cannot be complete) gives us the memory which is an edited, selected, and reworked version of facts and events, battered by time and not as they actually happened. Memory fictionalizes; therefore, one wonders how useful *Ake* will be to the social historian, as the blurb writer claims, considering the high level of fictionalization and incorrect historical ordering in the work. Perhaps the social historian may get some of the feel of the period, but what can she/he make of the actual, historical events? Very little of these appear except in tiny reverberations. One which occurs in *Ake* in some notable proportion — the Women's Movement — is chronologically and factually confused and obscured.

The protest against the Sole Native Authority System and the taxation of women, which spread to other areas of the Western Region took place between 1947 and 1952. Soyinka was thirteen in 1947. Considering how early he started school, must he not have gone to his secondary school, the Government College, Ibadan (GCI) by then? Soyinka was at the Government College, Ibadan, from January 1946 to May 1951 according to two of his school alumni, Professor Olumuyiwa Awe of the Physics Department, Ibadan, and Arts Director, Dapo Adelugba of the Theatre Arts Department. In a longer interview Professor Awe, also Soyinka's classmate, said Wole was always very vocal and irrepressible, and resisted all injustices from seniors, prefects and bigger boys in his own class. He was also very full of his Ake life in conversations with his schoolmates. If he went to the Government College in 1946 and the Women's Movement was in 1947 and after, the closing sections of the book (pp. 222-30) must be out of order chronologically. Mrs Kuti is presented as talking to him about going to Government College after the crises. He himself claims to have been taking entry exams "during the turmoil" (p. 222). But during the turmoil, he must have been in Form Two already. When was he acting as courier? According to Nina Mba,* there were

* Nina Mba, a historian, is one of the most published writers on the Abeokuta Women's Movement. See also Mba, N., *Nigerian Women Mobilised* (Berkeley: South California Press, 1982) and Awe, Bolanle eds., *Nigerian Women in History* (Ibadan: Malthouse Press, 1992).

two forty-eight hour vigils in 1947, one from November 29 to 30, the other from December 8 to 10. We are not sure which one of these vigils Soyinka is describing in *Ake*. In addition, there were five-hour street demonstrations, as on 28 April 1948, where looting and violence were virtually absent. Soyinka was fourteen in 1948. Surely, he must have gone to GCI by then. Atupa-Parlour, the king's favourite wife, is reported in histories of the period to have been rough-handled by members of the Women's Union in 1948.

Perhaps the greatest historical disservice Soyinka does the Women's Movement is to portray it as an unplanned, impulsive, gut reaction to contemporary maladministration. The movement was, in fact, highly organized. The Abeokuta Women's Union had printed *The Constitution, Rules and Regulations for the Women's Union of Abeokuta* (Abeokuta, Bosere Press, 1948). So organized was the union which had diversified to include women's trade unions, common interest associations, and traditional chiefs, that it hired an accountant to prepare a detailed report of the Sole Native Authority's expenditure in order to make their case against that authority. A copy of the report, planned for presentation to the British colonial administration, is to be found among the Ransome-Kuti papers at the University of Ibadan. The movement was politically modern and considered. Its actions did not derive from a rash of spontaneous speeches from women such as Kemberi in *Ake*. The movement used modern methods: petitions, propaganda, the legal process and the press — letters to the editor, articles and press conferences — as well as marches, demonstrations and vigils. Mrs Kuti herself, in her political sophistication not only confronted both the "native" authority and the colonial administration, but also played one group against the other, manipulating the confused and guilt-ridden liberal humanist consciences of the colonial administrators in Nigeria at the same time as she was putting international pressure on the colonial "home" administration in Britain. She had made personal and political friends in the British Labour Party and the Women's International Democratic Federation. She publicized her ideas and movement in Europe in an article in

The Daily Worker (18 August 1947).

It could be argued that a child could not know all this. Precocious as he was, he may have received some intimations. My concern is with the adult artist's responsibility in an auto-biography or any writing left for posterity, and that writing's effect on those who read it. And this particular artist admits his concern with "self-retrieval."

One defense can be made: that this is what he remembers — alas! he remembers that the women could not put their ideas together, chatting like weaverbirds around a table until Forest Father comes strolling by. Essay, for his part, was marionetting — or more contemporaneously, tele-guiding Wild Christian with his notes from a distance(p. 186). That is all that he remembers of how the movement functioned. But since the adult Soyinka is also present in other parts of the book, the adult self could have intervened to give a positive and more correct rendering of the women's doings. It then becomes necessary to publicize the information above for all lovers of *Ake* who may not read African history! One significance of the Soyinka version of the Women's Movement in Abeokuta is the revelation that the roots of his male-chauvinist rendering of society and human endeavour are long and deep. *Ake* is also useful textual material for feminists to demonstrate how adoringly and like a little god an African male child is raised, leading to some of the calloused attitudes of adult male supremacy which obtain in Yoruba society.

To respond to the blurb writer's claim that *Ake* reveals a little-known kind of childhood, it can be said that this kind of childhood is, in fact, standard or stereotypical of the colonial world. Family life in *Ake* is typical, not only in Nigeria but in the Third World, of the people of "the book"* — the church and the missionary school. There exists a common culture among such people across the imperial globe; to wit, the culture of a preoccupation with the Christian faith, of endless prayers, strictness in discipline and sequestration from the local cultural life as with Obi Okonkwo's father in Achebe's *No Longer At*

* Yorubas call literate people *alakowe* "people who write" meaning "people of the book world."

Ease. Often it was the mother who was somehow more in touch with the local culture as a teacher, churchworker or trader. Also typical of this colonial Christian family type was its role as a cultural intermediary exemplified in the cultural angst of Daodu in *Ake*. Certainly, Christianized African readers, even Third World ones, know this kind of childhood. But for whom is the blurb writer writing?

The question of who is writing for whom brings us, appropriately, to the question of the audience of *Ake*, and consequently to the issue of style. The prose is of high quality, subtly interlaced at points with wit and humour which occasionally broaden into admirable and hilarious slapstick, as in the scene of the schoolboys and the stolen chicken. From time to time, however, Nigerianisms slip in; unconscious usages not perhaps intentional and certainly not artistically functional. This is the bane of all writers who live in a second-language situation where local non-English renderings slip into the writer's prose; as for example when the narrator says, "Wild Christian replied him"(p. 209). None the less, the prose is generally so sensitive and moving as to become poetry; yet such poetic moments are controlled and brief "like match-flare in wind's breath." Nowhere in this finely-written work do you find either a purpleness of prose or overwriting.

But these Yoruba intrusions re-open the issues of perspectives in the context of the writer's audience. For whom and what are these intrusions? It seems that Soyinka as a second-language writer is forced to be Janus-faced, as is the fate of any writer riding two emotional horses, talking to two audiences, talking from two mouths in two or several voices (like a Tutuolan character). For the Yoruba reader, these intrusions naturally trigger the pleasure of a recognition of the familiar — writing style, social situation and humour. But for the foreign reader? One is forced to consider why the Yoruba renderings are deemed necessary.

I question why Soyinka does not write in Yoruba and have the work translated if the impulsion to "go Yoruba" at dramatic, crucial or intensely descriptive points is so strong. Is the writer thinking in Yoruba and writing in English, or thinking and writing in English but breaking into Yoruba at points where English emotionally fails him? Or is he thinking and writing in English but using Yoruba at dramatic points for colour? There are other possible permutations, and they all add up to serious problems in the poetics of African writing for all who write in the foreign language.

Significant in this question of audience are the moments when the narrator's voice is obviously directed to a foreign audience — in some detailed and unnecessary description of the familiar and in some stylistically mannered paragraphs. These particular techniques are clearly not meant for the average Nigerian or African reader (whom we cannot stop to identify now), not because such readers are genetically inferior, but because reading tastes and habits are simply not sophisticated enough. This is a simple sociological point.

The enchanted world of *Ake* does get boring. I felt bogged down with too much detail and the trivia of family living. At such times, the reader may feel lost. The obvious narcissism in the whole work, a narcissism which seems to be its whole purpose, also repels in a world of inconsequentialities and insignificant anecdotes. But the book is invaluable for the light it sheds on the sources of some of Soyinka's characters, motifs and later concerns. The cattle-egret critics who trail the writer-cows recognize the sources of poems like *Abiku* and *A First Death-Day;* scenes in *The Interpreters* and *A Dance of the Forests* (in the forest creatures, although Fagunwa and others may have contributed something to the play also); Wild Christian and Amope; the old women in the market and *Madmen and Specialists;* the escaping Ogboni, the miming girls and Iyaloja herself in *Death and The King's Horseman.* It is regrettable that the autobiography says nothing concrete about the formative reading of the little Soyinka — the specific titles of books he read. Since the work harps on Soyinka's concern with books from an early stage and his voracity for them, it would have been appropriate and useful to be told the titles, particularly if the presentation of self and the self's education (in the etymological sense of "e-ducare:" "a leading out") is one of the objectives of the work. Certainly, we cattle-egrets are interested in the nature of the books which perhaps formed the older man and writer.

Despite all my objections and the issues taken up in this essay, I feel that *Ake* is, on the whole, a rewarding and sometimes charming literary experience — an enchanted world of childhood.

7. The Bilingual to Quintulingual Poet in Africa

Very often, foreigners express surprise that one writes in English at all. Americans, in particular, seem to think that language use is related to color. One wonders if there is any thought about their black compatriots who speak English as a mother-tongue. Perhaps it is because many seldom think of their colored population. It appears, however, that people such as the Scandinavians tend to better understand our language dilemma in Africa, in the same way that Asians seem to do, because both groups have had to resolve the situation of living in the modern world with mother-tongues which are not world languages. Asians and most Scandinavians understand the condition of working with foreign, imposed or adopted languages.

Perhaps such understanding comes from belonging to cultures where it is known that language is a cultural artifact and not a genetic, biological or racial (whatever that means) possession. A language is spoken, not because of one's color, but because one is socialized to speak it. Africans seem to know this more than any other peoples, perhaps because of the age of the continent, and centuries of interacting with peoples of varying races and nations, ethnic groups and identities, well before the Arabs or the Europeans entered Africa. Today, most Africans are at least bilingual, if not polylingual to the fifth degree; and so my title.

Why do some of us write in English, which is not our mother-tongue? And what is the experience of writing in English, particularly for a poet? Due to the colonial experience, we gained a facility with English and achieved a proficiency well beyond that in our mother-tongues. The proficiency varies from person to person. Some people are still able to speak their mother-tongue better while they remain fluent in written English; for others, the colonial experience has permanently interfered with their fluency in both the writing and the speaking of the mother-tongue. Still, others end up unable to speak the mother-tongue at all.

I was fortunate to have had a forward-looking mother who felt that children should speak their mother-tongue at home because they will inevitably gain a proficiency in the colonial language from the schools. It was the heyday in their time, the new day of imitating Victorian English families by constantly speaking English at home and calling their parents 'Mummy and Daddy." Mercifully, this was done only in the middle classes. We kept in our home the older Victorian form of "Papa and Mama". You will still find the "mummy/daddy" pattern in most former Anglophone countries today. My own parents' generation could be said to have taken over from the British in more ways than one. My parents were born in 1896 and 1907 respectively; educators both, they continued the traditions of school and church, directly gained from white teachers. Between the 1920s and the 50s, my parents set up and ran many mission schools across Nigeria as far East as Cross River and Ogoja States. My mother was one of the earliest women professors in teachers colleges in Nigeria; she was, for a long time, the highest qualified female teacher in Nigeria, and the first woman to pass the highest exams for teachers in the 30's. The positive impact of our parents' lives and cosmopolitan nature was that we, the children, grew up with the same inclusionary and broad-minded attitudes towards other cultures and a disinclination to think "tribally".

While we were young though, my mother ran the junior section of our mission school where my father was the bishop and superintendent of the schools. Perhaps my mother did this to stay near us while the family was young and to co-operate, as always, with her Romeo, my father. Through all this, we spoke Yoruba, my language, at home and we spoke a particularly refined form of it; that is, without curse words. It took my going outside our home and meeting girls from other social classes, particularly girls with mothers who spoke the mother-tongue only, for me to realize what curserly things my language could do and how altogether bawdy the language could be. Fortunately, the education policy in Nigeria at that time, was to teach every subject in the mother-tongue in the first five years of school. For this reason, the first books I read as a child were in Yoruba; I studied Yoruba all through grade school and high school and graduated with high distinction in it. Still, there were girls who came from the working classes or whose mothers were mother-tongue speakers only, and other girls who belonged to Yoruba sub-ethnic groups (noted for colorful and imagistic Yoruba), who spoke a more beautiful and idiomatic Yoruba than I could have dreamt of speaking at that time. These girls, more linguistically blessed in Yoruba and more adroit in their use of her, did our translation exercises in class with better literary aplomb, rhythm and gusto, striking the rest of us with envy, admiration and joyful laughter. We used to tease those little Yoruba experts in our classes then, calling them "little witches" or "little old women" because you only expected such Yoruba expertise among the elderly.

I can say that I survived the attack on our minds and identity, which the colonial education was, because of the nationalism and natural intelligence or foresight of my parents. Nonetheless, English comes to me more easily in certain situations while Yoruba does in others. A great deal depends on the emotional situation, what I am trying to say and to whom. We have not studied enough the bilingual experience, particularly in its emotional functioning. Situations like living abroad for a long time or marrying a mother-tongue English speaker, (in which case English is spoken for twenty-four hours in the home) can bring the bilingual speaker almost to the point of first language expertise. The language user may find that he or she speaks, even thinks, in English all the time. The same situation may go for the person married across ethnic groups in Africa in a situation where the couple does not or cannot speak a common African language together. A return to a home context or an existence in a mother-tongue setting can, however, make the spouse of a foreigner remain fluent and adept in both languages, in English and the mother-tongue.

In the colonial scheme, getting the best education often meant getting the best alienation, the best aggression on your mind and the best attempt at cultural erasures in your world and psyche. The will to survive and be happy in dignity is perhaps the surest protection we adduced, often unknowingly, against this sometimes insidious, sometimes brutal, onslaught. Many of us were "bad" (read: rebellious) kids. Racially demeaning texts had no meaning at first or were just funny; something to read and laugh hilariously about, tumbling in fun and innocence in the dust or grass; something to forget about thereafter. When racially demeaning texts first begin to mean in our maturation process, then begin to hurt and finally commence to generate intellectual reactions is epistemology. These processes are worthy of our research.

The colonial intention was to produce the nearest imitation of the master culture. Apologists for the colonizers would say that there was no negative intent in the colonial workers; it was only their all too human aspiration to produce what they consider excellent. Research has, however, shown that there was a concerted colonial effort and language policy to create and appropriate faithful and loyal local elites, by seemingly admitting them, through the educational process, into the master class at the metropolitan center. The use of English and the study of English literary studies were to be some of the mechanisms for this cultural and spiritual onslaught. India, Nigeria and Uganda were some of the colonial laboratories for these human experiments. The theoreticians of this intellectual banditry go back to the 17th and 18th centuries in colonial history; to imperialists like Grant, Hastings, Trevelyan and later Lugard, among others.

Now we find that African families are themselves carrying on the heritage of denuding their children of mother-tongue expertise in, I suppose,their bid to enter the international work force, or to share the benefits of belonging easily to a cosmopolitan culture. What does this early apprenticeship do to the African child, however? I hear that recently there were almost ethnic riots in Nigeria at the suggestion of an introduction of a mother-tongue education policy in the early years of school. This was seen as anti-nationalist in the sense of affirming ethnic identities; yet in the process, what happens to the psyche of the child who speaks English from age zero? What does that produce in the individual?

It produces a mental and emotional situation where the person does not think wholly, if at all, in their mother-tongue. It is a situation of informational mixture; a capability only for a situational and positional use of language. We need not speak here of the cultural losses or absences. Let us instead return to my early questions.

Why do some of us write in English? I suppose part of this question has been answered by my long sociological clarification. English comes more naturally in speaking of certain subjects, in certain modes and to certain audiences. A great deal depends on whom you are trying to address, about what and their openness to whatever it is you wish to communicate.

My second question is more interesting for us here. What is the experience of writing in English, particularly for a poet? English has a relational usage, among others, for the bilingual speaker. Cultural signs and usages resonate from the mother-tongue culture depending on the addressed, her situation, and the effect one is trying to have on the hearer or hearers. English can also be used to distance oneself, if you do not like a person or if you wish to emotionally reject a person by interposing a foreign language between yourself and that other party; this could happen with a suitor or a loved one, for instance.

I have always wondered in what language we think our deepest emotions and in what language we naturally express them? Some emotional situations you express in English; in others, you burst out in your head and later, through your mouth in your mother-tongue. In what language do we dream, for instance? And in what language do we make love? An African colleague of mine once laughingly said to me that a person who made love in English was truly colonized! In what language, therefore, do you have an orgasm, if we dare to be truly Rabelaisian or down to earth?! Do you cry out in your mother-tongue or in English, dear bilingual to quintulingual writer! That seems to me like a deep test. In what language do you genuinely cry out to the universe in poetry? In what language do you spill forth the music in your soul to harmonize, integrate or counterpoint it in order to finally dissolve it into the music of which the universe is made, to echo Okigbo, a Nigerian poet?

But, poetic expression is not always an atavistic, pristine and cosmological affair. It also relates simply to the question of audience. Whom do you want to reach and what is the best way of reaching them? Are certain audiences even remotely interested in what you have to say? Is your subject their issue at all?

I have written in Yoruba, my mother-tongue, attempting works in poetry and fiction. I found my voice completely different from when I write in English. I become a different person or persona while the sentiments expressed are different, flowing from another part of me because through language, I am harking back to another philosophical store of knowledge; reaching back to a different view of life, and the meaning of that view of life, in a process which could only percolate that meaning in my use of English. This view of life sometimes has to be forced through your English as you strive with all your linguistic might to avoid sounding merely quaint or exotic because you are speaking from within a living and lived culture, despite all the social science fantasies about vanishing, not evolving cultures. As you write in your mother-tongue, you understand more deeply than theory that how you speak is determined by who you are speaking to and what you are thinking of as you are speaking. Even if you think you are speaking to some vague posterity as many of us writers like to claim, that posterity must have some kind of ears, if no face; and, definitely, a cognitive store to which you must relate.

More deeply than theory too, you realize that language carries its own cultural baggage which you may not necessarily care for, share or believe in anymore. Even simple everyday phrases, conventional turns of language and, more importantly, sentiments, which are considered idiomatic, beautiful or expert are fraught with concepts you no longer accept intellectually. The scramble for an authentic voice which is you as a writer then becomes doubly strenuous and more time-consuming in a situation in which you are hurrying to get heard before mortality intervenes; in a real life drama in which you are running alongside Death against your own temporality. I suppose, finally it is a question of commitment to a particular kind of mode.

If you feel you do not have the existential time nor the interest or commitment to work for the success and acceptance of a new way of using the Yoruba language in a new mode which may not be immediately but only eventually accepted; if you cannot wait to create a new language and build up a new audience, what do you do?

You become a bilingual to quintulingual poet, writing in borrowed tongues, singing to ready-made and familiar audiences. I have used the term "quintulingual," therefore to indicate that Africans often have had to be many-tongued, speaking not only European languages but also several local African languages, in order to interact and communicate, even in their own home setting.

If I were to write a love poem in Yoruba now, I would find myself using accepted and conventional phrases and images which may be far removed from my experience but which images are considered classic and beautiful. My mind would immediately turn to another world.

Listen:

Oko mi, eleyinju ege
adufe mi, aduduyemi
pa'gbo yi mi ka
gbe mi ro
gbe mi leke, gbe mi ro.

It translates as: My husband/ of the balanced eyeballs/ you, whom they struggle over to love/ you, of the befittingly black skin/ make a human fence around me/ hold me upright enduring/ hold me triumphal/ hold me enduring, upright, and

117

stayed— or something to that effect. It is difficult to translate the emotional and aesthetic nuances of the eyeball image; the fencing to protect, a fence made of people standing around you to defend you, and the sense of "ro"-upright and stayed, still and enduring, all impacted in the same word. The husband idea comes in because there is hardly a concept of love outside an approved social union, which is expressed publicly, at least, and approved. The concept of husbanding seems to be the most intimate way in which a woman may convey intimacy which also includes the deep sense of physical husbanding. The word for lover "olufe" is a post-colonial neologism. But who says we can only write in old pre-colonial words? Nonetheless, the post-colonial constructed words tend to sound scribal and emotionally false to me. An in-audience is obviously required for this kind of poetry and a particular kind of audience which may not always be different from the English-reading audience because there are experiential overlaps in multilingual communities.

Perhaps it is the commitment to waiting for one's results and perhaps never getting them; the commitment to forging a new language, literary tradition and audiences which are some of what distinguish the genius from the merely good or great writer—and certainly from the everyday "writer."

Interlude:

Meditations:
A Prose Poem on Nigeria

Racing Through Nigeria: This Land, Our Love

This lovely space of ours. Nigeria. Gongola in my heart.
I remember standing on a farm in Bulawayo, Zimbabwe, looking
across a mountain range. My girl-friend said "behind those
ridges are the remains of Cecil John Rhodes. You need to see
his grave." That man of amazing temerity who collared with
characteristic arrogance, so much of African space.

The ridges in Bulawayo rise and fall in tremendous splendour.
Comparable beauties are here. Here in Yola, Gongola State,
a scene of similarly breath-taking beauty spreads behind my
window. Only here, the hills are greener. Along their feet
and quietly flows a soft river, spotted by green islets. Sleep
well, this land, our Love, I say, after Dennis Brutus.

Driving towards the palace in Yola to see the Lamido. Ranka Dede.
They do not shake hands with women in the palace. Through the old
city with its historic houses of traditional architecture. Lower rooftops
meaning a lower skyline, shading trees, a feeling of healthy space. What
happened to all our trees in traditional landscaping now carelessly cut
down in modern town-planning? In our new world of cement and plastic. These days of aluminum cities, oppressively hot homes and sun-
seared roads.

I mourn the nim trees in Maiduguri with you, Maigain, so callously cut down. They cause a gaping hole in hearts. Racing towards Mubi. Termite castles washed smooth by rain. They point their little spires like tiny cement cathedrals.

Ranges of hills are covered by a slightly blue veil. It is seven o'clock in the evening. The hour of worship. Two hills staring forever at each other like stubborn men. Between them, a passage rises upwards, into the sky like a pathway to heaven. A quiet splendour.

Spots of peasant farms dot the roadside. A bird, elegant like a pelican, tipples across the tar macadam. Gingerly like a thin lady. As the car roars towards her in Peugeot force, she rises on her wings, flying languorously into the savannah. The joys of the savannah are many, gladdening the heart. Only no pelican she; under her thighs are splashes of red colour darkening to black on her back. Do we still know the names of our birds? In our languages? Are they taught in schools?

White small birds fly in air-force formation of six to ten to twelve. Fast flapping wing movements and little anxious faces. Only their tiny beaks are red.

The feel around me is of greenness and fertile lands, arable. A bread or grain basket. What are we waiting for? In Zimbabwe, Mugabe wins a prize for fighting hunger successfully. Here we starve, daily. This land, our love.

I crossed the Benue, the peaceful one. Do you know our people fought the colonists to a heroic end at this now sleepy, peaceful river, flowing now through verdant plains? Do you know the British brought gun-boats here to deprive the Sultan Attahiru of his space? Who says over-running Africa was easy? Not a simple walk-over, it was not; taking Africa or her lovely spaces. Not a simple Bible and gun transfer. Ask the Ndebeles of Zimbabwe. Their kind was never taken or seen again. Only chicanery defeated their heroic hearts. The "Rhodesian" state house stands in contumely over the site of the sacred compound. The sacred home of the king Lobengula. Ranka Dede.

Africa's pain has often been from within. Do you know how many fine young Africans, fine old Africans lost their rights to warring lords? Transported into slavery? How de-populated some areas of Nigeria are by slave-raiding done by these same heroic "last-stand" lords of ours? The colonist's strength was their ability to manipulate our divisiveness; Christian versus Muslim; empire versus clan; slaves versus freeborn.

Seems the same ghosts are here again. Here to haunt and drive us to distraction. Group interests there must be in any polity but are they ends in themselves; pawns for personal lusts to power. Are group interests being marshalled to build a better Nigeria, the product of a good vision for the *whole*? Will 1992 bring with it old injustices and new aggressions, powered by personal lusts in new characters? Are we fighting for "me" or this land we all love precisely or not? This land, our love, must live, not burn again.

Nigeria, 1988

PART II:

PRACTICE

8. Introducing Win: Women in Nigeria

The Organization: Women in Nigeria (WIN)*

Women in Nigeria is an organization which originated from the enthusiasm and interest evoked initially by the First Annual Women in Nigeria Conference, held in 1982. It was at this conference that a group of dedicated women and men from all over Nigeria committed themselves to the task of establishing an organization which would work unceasingly to improve the condition of Nigerian women.

The founding group believed, and the organization still maintains, that the liberation of women cannot be fully achieved outside the context of the liberation of the oppressed and poor majority of the people of Nigeria. However, there are aspects of women's oppression that we can work to alleviate.

Therefore women must organize and fight for their full social and economic rights in the family, in the workplace and in society in general, as a necessary part of the continuing struggle to create and develop a just society for all.

In order to do this we must know clearly and concretely how women's and men's lives are structured by the socio-economic and political conditions in which they live. Thus research, policy-making, the dissemination of information and action are all parts of the organization's objectives.

Women in Nigeria is established, well organized and eager to face and overcome the many problems which women, as a group, face in Nigeria today.

---

* This essay was first published as the introduction to the WIN Document: *The Conditions of Women in Nigeria and Policy Recommendations to 2000 A.D.* (Nigeria, Zaria, 1985), presented to the 1985 U. N. Decade Conference in Nairobi, Kenya.

Why WIN? Why In Nigeria?

It may be asked why an organization such as *Women in Nigeria* is necessary at all, particularly in Nigeria. What is so special about WIN and what makes her necessary in view of the long history of women's resistance, activism and associations in Nigeria?

Indeed, there are fore-running women's organizations in Nigeria just as there are traditions of resistance and activism which go back to pre-colonial times. It needs to be stressed that there were indigenous "feminisms" prior to our contact with Europe, just as there were indigenous modes of rebellion and resistance in the mythified African past. Therefore "feminism" or the fight for women's rights and women's interests is not the result of "contamination" by the West or, a simple imitation, as divisive opponents like to charge. One of the most recurrent charges made to and about Third World women is that they are blind copy-cats of Western European feminists. Many Third World feminists, in awareness of the "divide-and-rule" tactics of their accusers, have replied perceptively that the accusers' ploy is consciously conceived and maintained to confuse women and bind them to their respective men and male systems, and prevent a dangerous comparing of notes and a potentially dangerous unity. The truth is that there have always been, in every culture, indigenous forms of feminism which may take various forms as it does in Nigeria; for example, social harassment and ostracism of males as in the Igbo "sitting on a man" practice; witchcraft, occultism and magic; the exploitation by the wives of sexuality and plain stubbornness. Sometimes, resistance takes the form of different types of anti-social behaviour, including withdrawal into madness. One of our tasks is to explore these indigenous forms of feminist resistance.

WIN follows in the long tradition of organized women's associations and movements. Previously, we have had associations of women and social political activists, as well as plain strugglers who have tried to raise the status of women in the society and the home through various ways in their daily living. They worked through cult groups, women's councils, the market-system, the church, the school, social clubs and family groupings. What is unique about WIN is that it is one of the few organizations, if not the only one, which is consciously organized around a political ideology. WIN is unique in being conscious of the *importance of both class and gender systems* in the struggle to see that women enjoy their fundamental human rights.

WIN is aware that the majority of women, like the majority of men, suffer from the exploitative and oppressive character of Nigerian society; that women suffer additional forms of exploitation and oppression; that women, therefore, suffer double oppression and exploitation — as members of subordinate classes *and* as women. WIN feels it necessary to fight class exploitation and sex subordination together, a conviction which gives WIN its special character. From the class perspective on women's oppression emerges the decision to have both male and female membership, another unique characteristic. We have both female and male members; however, we work, and are willing to work, actively with other women's organizations.

WIN's convictions outlined above presuppose that women are oppressed in Nigeria; this is contrary to the Nigerian male myth that women in Nigeria have no problems, and are particularly blessed socially in contrast to women in other countries. But, as is the case with most human societies, even when those societies are matrilineal, women are subordinated and oppressed. The ideology of patriarchy dominates most societies, patrilineal and matrilineal. Patriarchy is here defined as the belief in the natural superiority of the male gender and thus the necessary and sufficient dominance of the male sex. Everything else in society is defined in relation to male interests, needs and concerns. But patriarchy is not natural and inevitable. Rather, it expresses the concrete economic formation of the society which determines the roles and statuses of persons, and it relegates women to certain positions, roles, and status to an inferior position.

Interacting with gender hierarchy are the systems of class exploitation through which the labour and products of labour of the majority of women and men (peasants and workers) are accumulated and taken over for the benefit of a small minority of rich ruling class men and women. In addition, Nigeria's history and experience of the slave trade, slavery, colonization and imperialism have led to the present structures of under-development and inequality of access to resources which, for most Nigerians, results in poverty and ignorance.

And it is to guarantee the possession of such researched and scientific data that WIN exists. Another unique thrust of WIN is to engage in research, as well as policy-making, the dissemination of information and action. In order to realize our objective of fighting for the full social, economic, and political rights of women in the family, in the workplace and in society in general (as a necessary part of the continuing struggle to create and develop a just society for all), WIN feels we must know clearly and concretely how women's and men's lives are structured by the socio-economic conditions in which they live. WIN will not be satisfied with impressionistic views or visceral opinions about conditions of women in Nigeria.

The WIN Document

The volume represents an exploratory and initial delineation of the status and roles of women in Nigeria — a beginning point of the more in-depth and detailed studies which will follow from the organization. The document is divided into 9 chapters on: 1) Women and work in the rural areas, 2) Women and work in urban areas, 3) Women and education, 4) Women and the law, 5) Women's associations and networks, 6) Women and the media, 7) Women and the family, 8) Women and religion, 9) Women and health. Each chapter analyzes the situation, highlights the disadvantageous realities of women and concludes with a section on policy recommendations for governments and influential bodies. We hope these policy recommendations will be received seriously and will not go the way of most recommendations which end up neglected, unread, or stacked up in file cabinets or on dusty floors in Third World countries.

The chapters in the document are linked by various threads, all meshing to form a composite fabric depicting the positions and lives of the women in Nigeria. On the whole, the chapters reveal that although women make use of opportunities for independent social and economic functioning, from which they gain a sense of fulfilment, Nigerian women are subordinate in status to men as a group, despite other alleviating variables such as age, status, or wealth. Men remain dominant, wield and disburse power. Despite the crucial and basic contributions of women to the economy of the nation, their indispensable labour is unacknowledged, unpaid-for and poorly taken into account in national development plans. Because of their educational and other social deprivations, the cycle of ignorance, poverty and oppression is kept recurrent. Most women are oppressed by their double workload which is unappreciated and un-remunerated. Their real and difficult situation is kept up by psychological oppression through the powerful forces of social propaganda by the populace, the media and the arts, all of which promote the ideology of patriarchy and its attendant myths of male superiority and female archetypes as the final chapter on the media shows.

It is our duty as human beings to fight for a just society and human liberation which cannot occur without the cessation of the oppression of women.

Long live WIN!

Long live the struggle for Development, Equality and Peace!

9. The Rights and Humanity of the Nigerian Woman

According to a United Nations release on its work on women, other international organizations had dealt with the question of equal rights before the United Nations was established. They are the Inter-American Commission of Women on the Organization of American States whose first meeting took place in 1930 and which continues to this day, and the League of Nations which considered the question of the status of women in all its aspects in 1935, after 10 Latin American Countries at the urging of women's organizations requested that the subject be placed on the Assembly's agenda. In 1937, the League resolved to publish a study on the legal status of women, but the only section completed before the Second World War was on private law. The mandate for United Nation's action to advance the status of women was contained in the U.N. Charter of 1945. The Charter's preamble declared that the people of the United Nations were determined to reaffirm faith in the fundamental human rights, in the dignity and worth of the human person, in the equal rights of men and women and of nations large and small.

The Charter of the United Nations makes the Economic and Social Council responsible for promoting universal respect for, and observance of, human rights and fundamental freedoms for all, without distinction as to race, sex, language or religion. (Article 55).[1] We could look at the various areas of rights wherein the U.N. conventions have set down principles in order to evaluate Nigeria's achievements in such areas.

Political Rights of Women

It is in this area that the most progress has been achieved for women of many countries since the U.N. was founded. In 1952, the General Assembly, on the recommendation of the Commission on the Status of Women, adopted the Convention on the Political Rights of Women, the first world-wide treaty in which states parties undertook a legal obligation concerning the exercise of political rights by their citizens. It was the first treaty in which the Charter principle of equal rights for men and women was applied to a specific problem. The convention set out three principles:

1. Women shall be entitled to vote in all elections on equal terms with men, without any discrimination;
2. Women shall be eligible for election to all publicly elected bodies, on equal terms with men, without discrimination;
3. Women shall be entitled to hold public office and to exercise all public functions on equal terms with men, without any discrimination.

By all appearances, it can be said that Nigeria has fulfilled these requirements, at least in theory. But, for a myriad of reasons, in our civilian experiences, women have only managed to win 7 seats out of almost 1,900.[2]

Nationality of Married Women

In many cases, in the past, the specific nationality laws of many countries, have discriminated against women by depriving them of their nationality upon marriage to, or divorce from, a foreigner, in addition to other kinds of discrimination.

In 1949, the Commission asked for an urgent preparation of a convention on the nationality of married women, that would assure women equality with men in the exercise of *their right to nationality* and prevent them from becoming stateless upon marriage or at its dissolution.

The Convention on the Nationality of Married Women

The Convention on the Nationality of Married Women, drafted by the Commission, was adopted by the General Assembly in

1957, and sets out the following commitments of each contracting state:

1. That neither the celebration nor the dissolution of a marriage between one of its nationals and an alien, nor the change of nationality by the husband during marriage, shall automatically affect the nationality of the wife;
2. That the wife of a national who changes his nationality may retain her nationality,
3. That the alien wife of a national may acquire her husband's nationality through special nationalization procedures.

Nigeria has laws respecting these various articles. Complaints may be made, however, in the area of the acquisition of Nigerian nationality by the alien husband of a national woman. The alien husband seems to have more difficulty than the alien wife in obtaining nationality or securing property. The Nigerian Citizenship Act of 1960 entitles the non-Nigerian wife of a Nigerian citizen to citizenship of Nigeria.[3] The same is not, however, the case for a non-Nigerian husband.

More unfair and basic in its significance is that Nigerian married women still need the written consent and approval of their husbands to acquire passports. This implies that the married woman's basic *rights to nationality* is not guaranteed since she can only gain or exercise it through another individual, that is, her husband. Correction is urgently needed in this area.

Consent to Marriage, Minimum Age for Marriage and Registration of Marriage

This convention, prepared by the U.N. Commission on the Status of Women, was adopted by the U.N. General Assembly in 1962.

Here, Nigeria still has severe problems due to national traditions of religious or secular and indigenous origins. Women's Organizations have been working on the issue of the consent to marriage and the minimum age for marriage.[4] Although it has to be dealt with, this has been a very sensitive issue in the nation's political experience, which must not be allowed to explode into religious confrontations. Women's Organizations are choosing to approach this problem through demanding a minimum age for marriage.

Civil Rights

In the area of civil rights, the U.N. Commission has studied questions relating to the property rights of women during marriage and during its dissolution; tax legislation affecting married women workers; right to rest and material security in old age; illness or loss of capacity to work; inheritance laws; parental rights and duties, including guardianship; discrimination against persons born out of wedlock; status of the married mother; action on recovery abroad of maintenance; and domicile of married women and family planning.

Many of the topics listed above still require adequate legislation protective of women's rights. The National Council of Women's Societies has been calling for legislation in the area concerning property rights during marriage and its dissolution. Tax legislation is still discriminatory as WIN (Women in Nigeria) and the International Federation of Women's Lawyers as well as other groups and individuals pointed out in the daily newspapers after the budget speech of January, 1987.

Early Retirement of Women

Women, in many institutions are still required to retire before men despite the fact that women live longer than men, and may have to support their families well after the demise of their husbands.

Inheritance Laws

Inheritance laws still require clarification particularly where constitutional law, the post-colonial marriage "ordinance" laws and the traditional or indigenous laws (called customary laws) conflict. The WIN Document of 1985 sums up the situation concerning women's inheritance rights as follows:

Inheritance Rights

Under customary law, generally, a woman cannot inherit her husband's property. She, however, has the legal right to remain in possession and make use of the matrimonial home. She is also entitled to make use of his farm land. These rights however cease as soon as she remarries or otherwise leaves the family.

In most bodies of customary law, no distinction is made between male and female under testamentary disposition (i.e. disposition by will). However, a particularly crucial issue, for peasant women who make up 70% of Nigeria's rural population, is that under most customary laws women do not inherit land.

Under Islamic law, the male heir is regarded as having greater responsibility than the female. A male child is thus entitled to a portion of the property equal to that of two females. The wife is also entitled to only one-quarter of the inheritance. Where the wife predeceases the husband, he is entitled to half of her property where there is no issue. Where there is an issue, the husband is entitled to one quarter.

Under statute law, parties to a statutory marriage are governed by the provisions of Statutes of Distribution of 1670 and 1685. Under these statutes, if a man dies intestate leaving a widow and issue(s), the widow is entitled to one-third of his personal estate and the remaining two-thirds goes to his issue in equal proportion. If, however, a man dies without an issue, the widow is entitled to one-half, the other half goes to the father of the deceased. Where there is no widow, but issue, the property is divided among the issue in equal proportions. No distinction is drawn between female and male issues. The only discrimination is in respect of making the father but not the mother succeed where there is no issue. Where the wife predeceases the husband, he is entitled to her estate absolutely, whether or not there are any surviving issues. Statute law is however, very seldom applied in the event of a husband dying intestate (or even where he does not), even in cases of statutory marriage between the couple.

There is also the tendency under all three forms of law to treat minor children as forms of property inheritable only by the husband's relatives. Thus a woman is likely to lose her husband and her children at the same time, as well as any family property.[5]

Persons born out of wedlock

In Chapter IV of the 1979 Constitution (section 39), it is stated that no citizen shall suffer discrimination merely by the circumstances of his or her birth.[6] A child born out of wedlock, we know, is the product of two consenting adults and is not responsible for the circumstances of his or her birth or the iniquities of those adults. The child should therefore not bear the brunt of their misdemeanour. On this kind of argument hinges the action of Nigeria in declaring illegitimacy non-existent in the country. It is said that to punish the illegitimate child would be to revert to the backward Judaic law of visiting the sins of the parents on the child.

But where does this leave the Nigerian legally married woman? Many Nigerian women see these arguments as specious efforts to protect patriarchal interests in the polygamous and flirtatious freedoms of the Nigerian male. The women argue that men must learn to respect the contract of marriage and its sanctity. They believe that this constitutional provision for the child, born out of wedlock, would condone the creation of alternative families which disrupt family life and constitute sources of terror and blackmail from husbands throughout the marriage. The existence of alternative homes does severe psychological damage to wives and constantly threatens their marriages. It creates instability in conjunction with the already existing tendency for men to discard their wives for other women after the legal wives have become spent within the marriages. Nonetheless, this writer feels that the humanity of the blameless child should come first at all times. Perhaps offended wives should be more willing to press the bigamy laws against their erring husbands than vent their rage on the child and its mother.

The status of persons born out of wedlock needs to be widely discussed by women at all levels. This problem is exercising the thoughts and energies of the Constitution Review Committee which is at present sitting in Abuja. This is the time for women to send memoranda.

The Unmarried Mother

The unmarried mother needs protection from the negative attitudes and legislation in society. The terms of her employment in many institutions often need to be made more just. At this point, we might do well to stop and consider more broadly the rights of women at work in Nigeria.

Women at Work

The United Nations on its part, reminds us that job opportunities for women are greatly affected by the economic situation of the community in which they live. When there is widespread unemployment and under-employment, women find it especially difficult to obtain work in competition with men, although their qualifications may be equal or better. Discrimination against women in these cases is often based on the assumption that women do not need work as much as men do; an assumption that has repeatedly proved false. The majority of women who work do so to support themselves and their children in the absence of a male member of the family, or to augment the wages of their husbands. Millions of women in the developing world work because it is essential for survival, and many of them are responsible for feeding their families on a day-to-day basis.

Women in Rural Areas

Women who live in rural areas make up, in most Third World countries, the majority of the female working force and the total rural labour force, male or female. Yet the mental habit in Africa, is still to think of farmers and rural workers as men. Women account for a substantial share of food production. They play the main role in procuring and preparing food for the family consumption. Where such women get paid at all, these women usually receive lower pay than male agricultural workers.

The U.N. Commission requested that the Food and Agriculture Organization report to it at each session beginning 1979. The FAO Conference in 1975 requested FAO to intensify its efforts to improve the role and status of rural women, and in 1976, FAO established an Inter-Divisional Working Group and Development to advise its Director-General on policies and programmes for the inclusion of women in on-going and future development activities of FAO. At the World Conference on Agrarian Reform and Rural Development held in 1979, a principal item on the agenda was the participation of women in agrarian reform and rural development.[7]

Directives Relevant to Rural Women in Nigeria

The Federal Military Government has set up two directorates: The Directorate of Food, Roads and Rural Infrastructure (DFFRI) and the Directorate for Social Mobilization (code-named MAMSER) to work in conjunction with relevant directorates and Ministries (of Employment, Labour and Productivity, Information and Culture, and Social Development, Youth, Sports and Culture) to plan strategies and projects for the amelioration of the lives of rural women. At the time of writing, "Better Life for Rural Women," schemes have been launched in many of the states. It can only be hoped that these top-down projects can begin to touch the phenomenally deplorable conditions of the rural Nigerian woman.

Women and Health

Women's right to life which encompasses the right to support in the event of sickness, disability or old age can be considered under the rubric of health which has been re-defined broadly by the WHO as "a state of complete, physical, mental and social well being and not merely the absence of disease or infirmity." While medical services are only nominally free in Nigeria, the most interesting event in the area of health has been the Primary Health Care Programme which is being strenuously championed by the Federal Ministry of Health to reach every village or local government community in the country.

The members of WIN have not only written on women and health, in Chapter IX of our document, they have also discussed women as producers and consumers of health care, cultural factors impeding effective health care for them, concluding as usual with recommendations. The organization has also published the proceedings of its conference on *Women and Family*

(1985)[8] with the assistance of CODESRIA in Senegal.

Women and Education

The rights to education is another fundamental human right which should be the natural right of every Nigerian. In this area in Nigeria, however, it has been observed that there are many constraints to female education in relation to male education. Those constraints are *falsely religious*, economic or cultural. In addition female education is generally biased towards the allegedly "feminine" subjects. Considerable changes have occurred since independence in 1960 in the attitude of men towards educating their daughters. Nonetheless, in the face of any economic squeeze, sons are preferred in a family's education plans.

WIN has recommended that:

1. Education should be free and compulsory for all children, female or male, at least at primary levels.
2. The curricula should be restructured to remove gender biases, and teachers given reorientation towards the same end.
3. More school places should be established for females especially in vocational and technical training, either by creating new schools or reserving a minimum quota for females, in existing schools and colleges.
4. The government and media should launch an active campaign to encourage females to take up science-related subjects.
5. A nationwide mass adult education programme designed specifically for rural women should be launched, with particular attention being paid to skills that will enable women to generate higher incomes, and to make classes accessible to women by timetabling and venue.
6. There should be a minimum age of marriage based on physical and emotional maturity.

The proceedings of the WIN conference on *Women and Education* has now been published by the Ahmadu Bello University Press. It will include our conclusion, communique and recommendations to the federal government.

The Forward Looking Strategies of the 1985 U.N. Decade Conference on Women in Kenya (FLS)

It remains for the Nigerian government to implement consciously and in detail the Forward Looking Strategies (FLS) to improve the economic, political, legal and social rights of women as identified at that vast and highly successful conference of representatives of women worldwide in Kenya in July of 1985. While not a compulsory document, the FLS was binding on all countries signatory to it, and Nigeria was one of them. The several new Directorates in Nigeria, in particular, the Directorate for Social Mobilization, would be appropriate organs to spearhead the implementation of the strategies.*

The Humanity of the Nigerian Woman

I would now like to say something about the humanity, the *personhood* of the Nigerian woman because I believe it is this basic fact which stands in her way of being given her rights and her recognition. It prevents her from being remembered or planned for when anything is being shared out in the Nigerian polity. This conception of her as a *person* first, and a person in herself, though seemingly obvious and unnecessary as a point to be made, is not taken for granted, even believed in, in a country where the woman is primarily seen in relation to someone else. She is often an appendage to someone else — a man — because most of our cultures are patrilineal and patriarchal even when those cultures have matrilineal property laws and rituals. She is primarily a man's daughter, sister, wife and mother, not a person in herself, with individual fundamental rights, *claimable by herself* and without reference to anybody else. This is why in most customary inheritance laws, she gets things through her children, not herself, who has slaved for years as a wife in the household.

---

* Since the first writing of this paper, the institution of a National Commission for Women has been announced in Lagos, September 1988, by the Federal Military Government. A national Constituent Assembly has also been set up to continue the work of the Constitution Drafting Committee.

The preamble to the U.N. Charter speaks of the dignity and worth of the human person. What is the worth of the Nigerian woman and what dignity accrues to her from this evaluation? The greatest obstacle to the improvement of the condition of the Nigerian woman, to her attainment of her fundamental human rights, is, in my view, that basic and primary societal attitude that the woman is *never* a person in herself. She is not always considered her own person but a laborer married to provide a source of descendants and unpaid labour whether domestic or public. On divorce, she has few rights to the products of her own body. The attitude towards the use-value of women within marriage,still very strong, even among the educated and the Westernized, corroborates my thesis. If the payment of bride wealth (or bride price) is somehow held responsible and justifying of this attitude, then such payment should be stopped. But you find men opposing the stoppage because it would subvert their authority in the home; women, in a false consciousness, also oppose it. As some women say, lack of payment diminishes their worth in their husband's eyes and affects the dignity they are later accorded by him in their marriage. This attitudinal situation indicates that a cash-value is being placed on the humanity and personhood of women; a condition which women themselves should resist, were they more politically and socially conscious.

Due to attitudes perhaps surviving from some of our pre-capitalist social formations, the woman is often in the status of a de-facto minor. It is considered most appropriate that she be under the legal and social guidance of a male; her father, brother, husband and later son. These attitudes affect traditional property and inheritance laws, to the chagrin of the women.

Therefore, it does not immediately solve the problems of the Nigerian woman to super-impose the fundamental human rights of the West. These human rights arose in the heat and struggle of the rising European bourgeoisie in their eighteenth century revolutions when burdgeoning capitalism was seeking progressively to empower the individual against the constraints of the Church and feudal polities. The continuities and vestiges from the indigenous cultures must first be confronted, removed or modernized to be harnessed to the present reality. This should be done only in the positive aspects which are pertinent to present day life, dignity and the modern personhood of the Nigerian woman as a full-fledged citizen of her own country.

Because of some obfuscating traditional and pre-1945 (U.N. Charter) attitudes, some of which are also traceable to British Victorian and anti-female prejudices introduced with the British administration, women still have to resist the patriarchal attitudes which are socialized into every Nigerian (African) boy at school and home, sometimes through specialized initiation rites. Women still have to persuade the society that they also have a "right to life, liberty and the pursuit of happiness," as proclaimed in the American constitution of 1776, an idea which has percolated down and influenced most modern governments in the world today, including our own. It needs to be pointed out though, that those ringing phrases of the American Constitution, as for the French Bill of the Rights of Man, were pealing out only for the European *man*. This is why progressives, male and female, and feminists all over the world had to institute struggles for the attainment of the fundamental human rights of everyone, in particular, the women. European activists, in particular, feminists, should therefore avoid a historically maternalistic attitude towards Africa in the struggle for human rights and humanity; less than a hundred years ago, a European man could exchange his wife for his debts or his pipe in an argument with his male buddies in a pub.

Nigerian women, on their part, must realize that they have very decisive roles to play to empower themselves since: one, no one else will, and two, they socialize male children from infancy into patriarchy. They also carry out many of the anti-woman family rites such as genital mutilation, initiation and widowhood observances.[9]

Nigerian women still have to overcome the subtle, covert and overt, oppositions in society to their primary rights such as: the right to free speech, to free movement and association (which would affect their ability to participate in politics or not; to attend meetings at what time or not), the right of choice of dress and of course freedom from molestation of any sort, which apart from the obvious and rising incidence of rape, takes many psychological and disabling forms in social interactions at home and at work.[10] The first thing, however, is to be regarded as people, not possessions to be distributed by fathers or husbands or considered only in relation to someone else.

To conclude, I would like to present some of the constraints which the U.N. Commission on the Status of Women identified as standing in the way of the implementation of the World Plan of Action adopted in 1975. They are:

1. Lack of involvement of men in efforts to change the position of women in society (very important);
2. Lack of political will in many countries to change the conditions of women;
3. Attitudes of both women and men concerning the role of women in society;
4. Lack of recognition of the value of women's work in both paid and unpaid sectors;
5. Lack of attention to the particular needs of women in planning;
6. Too few women in decision-making positions;
7. Insufficient services, such as cooperatives, training and day-care centers and credit facilities to support women's participation in national life;
8. Lack of financial resources;
9. Lack of communication between women in greatest need and policy makers;
10. Ignorance among women of opportunities available for their development;

We may as well add:

11. Lack of educational opportunities;
12. The effects of mass communication reinforcing traditional attitudes often portraying degrading and humiliating images of women.

References

1. "United Nations Work for Women" prepared by the Branch for

the Advancement of Women for Social Development and
Humanitarian Affairs, Department of International Economic
and Social Affairs, United Nations, Vienna, Austria. There are
copious quotes from this document for technical reasons.
2. Flora Nwapa, "Women in Politics", *Presence Africaine* No. 141,
1987, 117.
3. The WIN Document: Conditions of Women in Nigeria and Policy
Recommendations to the year 2000 A.D. *Women in Nigeria*
Organization, Nigeria submitted to the U.N. in Kenya, 1985.
4. The National Council of Women's Societies (NCWS) and WIN.
5. The WIN Document.
6. The WIN Document.
7. U.N. Work for Women, *op. cit.* above.
8. *Women and the Family* ed. WIN Collective (Senegal: Dakar,
Codesria & WIN, 1985).
9. Ogundipe-Leslie, Molara, "Nigeria; Not Spinned on the Axis of
Maleness" in *Sisterhood is Global*, ed., Morgan, R (New York:
Doubleday Publishers, 1984) or Ogundipe-Leslie, Molara,
"Women in Nigeria," *Women in Nigeria Today* (London, Zed
Press, 1985).
10. On the obstacles to the self-redemptive roles of the African
(Nigerian) woman, see Ogundipe-Leslie, Molara, "African
Women, Culture and Another Development" *Journal of African
Marxists* February 1984 or *Presence Africaine* No. 141, 1987.

This essay has benefited from conversation with Professor D.A.
Ijalaye now working on the National Constitution Review
Committee at Abuja. He is substantively at the Obafemi
Awolowo University, University of Ife-Ile Ife, and a professor of
Law.

10. African Marxists, Women And A Critique Of Everyday Life

I hope that the criticism here will be taken in the spirit in which it is being offered, and that people do not get defensive in the discussion of these issues, so that we can at least try to find solutions to some of the problems.

I begin with two quotes, the first:

> Marx himself had thoughts to unite theory and practice, to reconcile thought and feeling, to overcome the separation between the personal and the political. But his original emancipatory thrust has been abandoned or diluted by most of his followers, who have reduced the complexity of his thought to a crudely mechanistic, economical, sociological determinism.

The second:

> Revolution in the sense of the socialist transformation of economic life and social forms does not automatically entail changes in actual persons. Any revolutionary movement which simply aims at taking over the state apparatus and effective social changes in society, without liberating the *individual psyche* [that's my stress - without liberating the individual psyche] is at best a process of Marx-mystification, offering only a transient emotional catharsis to the masses without any permanent realization of liberation, or worse, simply an agency of newer and even more barbarous modes of repression masked by pseudo-populist mythology and rhetoric.

This essay is an effort to argue that any revolutionary project in any society must take account of what is happening inside people's heads and hearts at any historical moment in order to cohere the personal and the political to the end of creating a more genuinely and thoroughly liberated society. We may as well begin with ourselves. How liberated are our individual psyches for the process of revolutionary practice? How, as Marxists, do we cope with the problems of everyday life, including our relationships with the opposite sex? Africa needs new Fanons to do an analytic psychology within the framework of historical materialism on segments of African society, in addition to Fanon's great achievement with a set of the African intermediary bourgeoisie. (I speak about what analytical psychology should do.)

Erich Fromm once said that analytical psychology investigates one of the natural factors that is operating in the relationship between society and nature: the realm of human drive and the active or passive role they play within the social process. Analytic psychology enables us to understand fully the ideological superstructure in terms of the process that goes on between society and man's nature.

As a literary person, whose primary concern is humanism and human character, I find myself highly interested in the foregoing conjuncture. It is clear from the failures of socialist societies to make their populace interiorize the ethics of Marxism, to internalize the values of the revolution in the very structure of the individual personality, that people also have to be liberated from specific forms of psychological oppression, in addition to the economic and the political. It is well known how, in some societies, like the Soviet Union and other socialist experiments, authoritarian, patriarchal and other conservative prerevolutionary attitudes persist after the revolution.

In an anthology of contributions about the women's situation from women from 72 countries, (Nigeria, too, has an entry), we find that all entries from the socialist countries are united in the feeling of the survival of the old patriarchal attitudes, oppression and prejudices of those societies. Many of the societies have laws in the books guaranteeing women's rights, but these women's rights are not fully enacted in these societies, nor are they experienced in the lives and functioning of the people. So, we do not want to change society at the political and economic level only. We should also change society at the attitudinal, motivational levels, thereby changing the effective and psychic structures of persons.

So, look at the African Marxists first and ask what are their motivational impulses to become Marxists in the first place? Are they persuaded that Marxism is the most effective method of the scientific analysis of societies, which will yield the most appropriate facts and social results, or is it because Marxism is the newest fad, the most recent intellectual import from Europe since colonization closed doors to progressive ideas? Do we approach Marxist ideas in the way we have approached Islam and Christianity, as a body of ideas that we have learned by heart and quote religiously, substituting sloganeering for radical analysis; spontaneity for conscious criticism and political consciousness?

We cannot even contribute to the theoretical enterprise within Marxism worldwide, for many have not or will not read the original basic and important texts, nor will they situate the texts historically in their application. They will only quote excerpts, as from the Bible and the Koran. Such practice subjects us to the ridicule of our fellows, while it loses us audience amongst the African people, not to speak of the glee it arouses among the degenerate African ruling classes who hate any suggestion of change in the interests of the poor. Sometimes one wonders if African Marxists are attracted to Marxism for reasons of intellectual exhibitionism; offering them an opportunity to reel off other sets of specialized political and sociological jargon. For why can we not be intellectually clear in expression, for instance, when we speak? For example, why do we indulge in very turgid and obfuscating vocabulary and syntax when we write "Marxistically." For achieving such clarity, I would like to congratulate a person like Ngugi wa Thiong'o, who is able to write the most theoretically profound ideas in the most accessible English prose.

There are other issues of personality which interfere with revolutionary praxis among Marxists in Africa today. Related to manifestations of intellectual exhibitionism, is a trace of sheer egoism, ego-tripping, a desire for every male to be the leader of his group, or else no dice. The struggle over being the Mao of Kenya or the Lenin of Ghana, is put over and above the actual social struggle. The desire is to simply stay in power permanently within the group just like the bourgeois presidents for life. Is there anything in our socialization that impels Africans to monarchism or dictatorship? I believe that the exceptionally striking egoism of the African male is not unrelated to the strong patriarchal ideology in the culture. This is evident even when the society is matrilineal as in Ghana. Patriarchal ideology encompasses the strong sexual gender hierarchies, which springs therefrom. African Marxists very often do not show that they have dealt with and overcome the problematic of (what I call) the masculinity neurosis.

We are all subject to the psychological and above all, the sexual repression imposed on the individual during primary socialization, within the context of the patriarchal families. Within these families, for women, mental structures of dependency, servitude and masochism are built up. So you have the Amazonic woman who absorbs pain, deprivation and abuse on behalf of others, in particular her children and her husband — in that order. For males, it is to be raised to be a little king, the centre and navel of his little world. My daughter, Isis, calls it "the little prince" syndrome. Being male makes him very special and superior. He goes through life functioning thus, and demonstrating his virility and rulership. His sex has conferred on him the right to rule — in particular —women.

These forms of awareness unsuperceded in adulthood, prevent male Marxists from being successful in their revolutionary projects. They are always in disarray; however, we must analyze more closely elsewhere why the Left in Africa is always in disarray, though I heard from a German comrade that the Left in Germany is also in disarray. But, in Africa, it appears the masculinity neurosis with its attendant syndromes, prevents comrades from being able to cooperate or work as a team, a basic need for the collective enterprise of socialism and communism. Deriving from this neurosis also, is the desire to be significant in society by being different, by advocating new and revolutionary views, playing to the gallery, dressing the part by wearing rags and beards, black berets and jungle batiks. I believe we insult the masses when we pretend, as petty-bourgeois elements, that we are one of them. They certainly are not deceived, for they see us clearly.

At this point, we may also mention the alarming reality that some of us Marxists actually despise the masses; some hate them, even though the masses are seen as a means to realize egocentric ambition. Some Marxists feel arrogant because they are better educated and socially superior, while others confuse literacy (the ability to read or write) with intelligence and knowledge. What exactly am I saying? I am saying that Marxists themselves have to engage in a continuing process of criticism and self-criticism. That politicization has to commence at the level of the self in the dialectic of uniting the struggle for the creation of a new self with the creation of a new society.

So when you come to the issue of African Marxists and women, the enterprise for the creation of the new self hinges in a very significant way on one's relationship with the opposite sex and society. How much, for instance, do we, as Marxists, contribute to the perpetuation and survival of the patriarchal family which breeds psychic structures for the domination of women and children, by promoting the patrocentric paradise, the patriarchal figure of the male and the sexual repression and exploitation of women? All of these are interrelated. The egoism of most males will not let them abandon the patriarchal and the patrocentric family structure, where they, as men, are dominant. Some males will even resort to cultural justification of patriarchy while making racial declarations that the objection to sex and gender oppression is a European phenomenon, a factor belonging to the Western world, and of complete irrelevance within "our great African heritage". Most do not see how sexual oppression is related to social oppression. However, we need to point out that most male Marxists have not grappled successfully in their everyday life with the problematic of their African past and heritage.

Apart from the fear and dislike of intellectual and liberated women, which all men manifest in all cultures — particularly Africans — African Marxists sometimes manifest the generalized tendency for men to advocate that women should stay in the past as pots of culture, as defenders and custodians of outmoded modes of existence (as *Song of Lawino* by Okot p'Bitek) while the men move forward to grasp the future. Then follows the mystification of the past and the mystification of women, with all the psychological and emotional blackmail that the African women should be truly African and stay in the past, or stay within oppression. In their opposition to the liberation of women, which actually is the truth of the African male's position, it often occurs that in the revolutionary practice, some Marxists argue that their nations be liberated first, after which they will deal with the problem of women.

I have heard some African National Congress (ANC) men argue this at conferences, while some Southern women, SWAPO and ANC, have said that the liberation of women was a diversionary and divisive issue. However, it has always been the case that, after the revolutionary political changes in African societies, women are firmly put back in their places; in the kitchens, in the farm fields and other subordinate places where they labour unacknowledged as beasts of burden. The debate between class and gender oppression and their relative importance has produced a volume by a Nigerian Women's Group, *Women in Nigeria Today*, published by Zed Press, which is an anthology and account of a conference structured around the issue of sex and gender oppression in relation to class oppression, and which came first.

The theory that class oppression predominates and includes other forms of oppression is responsible for the view that class oppression also determines the existence and levels of other forms of oppression. This, however, is not true, as sex, gender and race are elements which compound class oppression, but exist independently and have to be fought independently. That psychic structure outlasts political and economic situations, brings us back to our initial thesis: that socialist transformation of economic life and social forms, does not automatically entail changes in actual persons. And so, revolutionaries who postpone the enterprise of the liberation of women until later, are making a mistake. I agree with the positions taken on this subject by Samora Machel and Thomas Sankara: sexual and gender oppression must be tackled as specific issues which are separate and yet related to oppression.

Some African male Marxists who are male feminists, have sometimes complained to me about the mental condition of the African woman herself. These male feminists are genuinely sympathetic to women and would like to relate in a new way to abjure male supremacy, but they very often despair when confronted with the reactionary, dependent and exploitative consciousness of most African women. But what strikes me is that they do not see the alienation of the African women themselves. They are, in the sense that Marx explains in the *Economic and Philosophic Manuscripts,* captives of ideas about themselves which are now reified and interiorized by them, by the women themselves. They are mastered by the view of themselves which patriarchal and class ideology has taught them. The male comrades soon turn on the women and blame the women for their level of consciousness. It appears to me that this impatient reaction of blaming the victim is not unrelated to political laziness. This is the same kind of political laziness, comrades manifest toward the business of the reform of the consciousness of the masses. Due to the conjunctures of traditionalism, colonialism, racialism, and class oppression, in any revolutionary practice in Africa, a great deal of political education and re-education has to be done. Women, like proletariats, have to be intellectually and emotionally emancipated from the existing system. So I find struggles for a reform of consciousness must accompany the struggles against political and economic power. Marxists must realize that it is part of their revolutionary task to advance the thinking of women by being supportive, while advancing their own, according to the ethics of Marxism.

On a more personal level, when the personal and the political should converge, female Marxists complain of several tendencies among male Marxists: that in the face of the breakdown of values in Africa, the breakdown of family systems, of sexual morality, and old cultural patterns, male Marxists respond by exploiting the female comrades. No longer bound by the responsibilities and structures of old Africa or the demands of capitalist monogamistic marriage, the male comrades seem to see the female comrades as free creatures to be exploited emotionally, sexually and sometimes financially! It is also said that male Marxists seem to want to put the onus of living up to the ethos of the revolution on women alone, as always. Marxist women must not relate to men of the enemy classes, while the men move freely, even marry imperialist agents, royalists, racists and other reactionary elements. The woman, however, is supposed to be true to the revolution and relate only to fellow comrades.

Finally, most important to the critique of everyday life, is the position we give to the aesthetic aspect of the revolution. The puritanism and joylessness that we find, the cultural dryness which you often encounter — this need not be a part of revolutionary practice. The celebration of life, which does not mean indulgence in various modes of social perversions, should be current. And I do believe we must also evolve strategies to express by cultural and aesthetic means, the ideal of the revolution.

Finally, I would like to emphasize the insensitivity of male Marxists to the issues of women. This is directly related and comparable to their insensitivity to the problems of the masses, and is, therefore, responsible for the frequent failure in their revolutionary projects. Alienated from the real problems of the masses and women, Marxists apply undigested theories which they do not live up to, to the society, and then despair quickly or fall into confusion when the masses refuse to either swallow this medicine, or be cured by it. We must liberate ourselves, men and women, from specific forms of oppression at a psychological level.

11. Mobilizing the Mobilizers: Sex and Gender Problems in Nigeria Today*

Defining Sex and Gender

It is necessary that we stop in our tracks to examine our attitudes in self-criticism regarding the all-important but often neglected area of sex and gender oppression in our society. "Sex," we are using here to mean "the biological, physical characteristics of male and female." Gender means "the socially defined capacities and attributes assigned to persons on the basis of these alleged sexual characteristics." Gender is therefore a *social* not a biological category. For example, in some cultures, farming is men's work and is associated with masculinity, in others, it is done by women, and has feminine connotations.[1] Weaving and sewing in some parts of Nigeria are traditionally women's work but in some, where they are highly lucrative, they are men's work. Since the colonial experience, weaving and sewing are more associated with women, home economics and inferior work in middle-class circles. What is crucial in the sex/gender distinction is that we must always differentiate between the actual biological differences between men and women (such as in the differences in reproductive capacity), and the socially defined roles ascribed to men and women supposedly on the basis of these differences.[2] Sex and gender conceptions are manipulated conveniently in patriarchal society to better assure the status quo of male domination. When women are successful or achieve the approval

* Original version first presented at the National Workshop for Mobilizers, in Jos, Nigeria, 1987, organized by the Directorate for Social Mobilisation.

of male society, they are praised as male or designated "male". When women reach menopause and are therefore freed for more action in public life because of their freedom from mothering and child care, they are again viewed as male because the reproductive characteristics and activities peculiar to women are not as valorized as the male's. They are considered inferior and obstructive to normal life (which is men's activities). Everything biologically female is considered inferior, though, what makes one human organ superior to another in the scheme of nature and the reproduction of the species, beats any imagination but the patriarchal ones.

Thus, in patriarchal society, women as daughters are co-opted and integrated into the male lineage, as daughters, to help effect the subjugation of women who are wives — affinal relations — people who marry into another lineage and remain women (mothers playing biological and biologically related roles), while daughters in their father's homesteads can play "male" roles of marrying wives or producing children to prolong their infertile father's life.[3] Thus in pre-colonial Nigerian society, there was an accepted distinction between sex and gender which was juggled to keep women where they should be — under the control of their fathers, husbands and sons, particularly within marriage.

Sex is used to exclude women from power and privilege and hijack material benefits from women. When the basic means of production is palm tree farming, the male-dominated ruling group decrees that women cannot climb palm trees or own them; when bureaucratic jobs are scarce and are in demand, it is pleaded that women get pregnant too often and have monthly periods, hence they cannot work well. The sexual characteristics of women which, at other times, are very useful in society and basic to its equilibrium and continuation are then used to deprive women of their legitimate rights in society. Sex is used to create gender roles and problems. Sexual taboos, rituals and cults are built around economically productive activities. Modern versions of cults are Rotary clubs, the Metropolitan club in Lagos etc. where men share information on power and wealth.

Sources of Gender Attitudes

The sources of gender attitudes are diverse and still under investigation by sociologists, psychologists, historians and other social scientists. Anthropologists attribute the theory of male superiority to the struggle against female power which was established when agriculture was first discovered by women; they were the first farmers, being sedentary while men hunted. Psychologists fall back on the theory of complexes — basic love and fear of the mother, in conflict, harking back to the days of infancy; others distort religious texts. Whatever the sources[4], it is tenable to say that the overruling attitude in Nigerian society is that the male is theorized as superior and comes first. Our pre-colonial societies take this thesis for granted though age, status and other variables often mediate.

From this basic assumption come many other attitudes which may affect our mobilization and nation-building negatively.

Gender Attitudes in Nigeria Today

It would be amazing, or perhaps not so, to reveal the existence of crudely sexist gender attitudes in seemingly educated, progressive and sophisticated Nigerians. I have discussed elsewhere the problems of integrating the ethos of the progressive and revolutionary world view in our everyday lives, in particular among declared socialists and Marxists.[5] History has shown that the establishment of a socialist society does not immediately wipe away the patriarchal attitudes and gender oppressive structures in society nor does it immediately transform the lives of its citizens in their daily and personal interactions with women.[6] The transformation of progressive theory into practice by progressives in their thought and action still remains a serious and basic task to be effected.

Even on the most basic level of conversation, many men are incapable of dialogue with women as equals. The immediate, spontaneous and ingrained attitude is to patronize the women; not to talk as equals, as person to person but as a superior and wiser intelligence. The tendency is to begin to calm the woman as if she is naturally less capable of calmness even though she may be a more stable character; or to offer advice even though the male is less experienced, less informed, less travelled, less intelligent or whatever. An illiterate male village petrol-seller of seventeen years will begin to give an educated, urban and well-travelled female permanent secretary of fifty-seven years, advice on how to handle herself, situation and people. The assumption is that the male "element" in him, whatever that is in sexist biology, gives him that advantage to "lead" any woman while he is in complete ignorance.

Such an assumption of the natural right of men to leadership affects the exclusion of women from leadership roles — one of the situations that the Directorate for Social Mobilization is set up to correct. If women are viewed as naturally second rate, the impulse to call on them to play leadership roles will not be there. Even in universities and other circles, women are not naturally called upon to play intellectual leadership roles. This happens constantly in our universities which we must target as a group for mobilization.

Surely, there are women academics, politicians, sociologists, anthropologists, historians, lawyers and scientists, etc. to participate at all levels. But perhaps, the natural impulse is to not think of female varieties when we make up lists — or not to think of women at all when we construct schemes of anything.

In this way, our gender attitudes affect planning and will definitely affect nation-building. When we think of who can contribute thought and action to anything, we do not naturally think of *men* and *women*, yet society is made up of both. The cultic stag, all-the-boys, old-boys' mentality predominates while most men only think of their token women friends and colleagues. Some even resent gender issues being brought up at all.

One bizarre or perhaps perverse and incorrigible attitude is to say one is avoiding discrimination by not thinking about gender problems. It is an assumption that the problem of gender discrimination is already solved; so it becomes solved. Such a thinker then goes on to construct so-called "gender-free" programmes in a society, ridden with gender problems. In such ways, the status quo is maintained and the deprived and disadvantaged continue in their suffering. We cannot also plead reverse discrimination in a situation where the givens are not the same; where the competitors do not start from the same point of take-off; when the attendant circumstances of their lives are differently disabling.

Finally, we may exemplify the issue of leadership attitudes with the everyday issue of "the chairman". The question of how to name that figure dramatizes the problematic of gender attitudes. So used are many people to male heads, so taken for granted, that they come out with Mr. Chairman, Mr. Chairlady, Mrs. Chairperson or perhaps they are simply too confused and unaware of the problem. The word "Chairperson" was coined by feminists to avoid naming the sex of the holder of the position in order to concentrate on the person's role as that of *the chair*. It need not matter that the Chair is a man or a woman. Nigeria has however, managed to bring us back to the same sexist position by calling only women "chairperson." Both men and women are "chairpersons;" failing to call them this, we could call them simply "the chair."

Recommendations for Mobilizers
1. Mobilizers must read and study the history and anthropology of Nigerian women to rid themselves of sexist assumptions.
2. A handbook should and will, be prepared for mobilizers on gender issues by the women's Division of MAMSER.
3. Workshops and seminars should be organized for mobilizers only, specifically on gender issues.
4. Workshops on women in religion in particular, Islam and Christianity should be held to study the position of women, using original and undiluted texts.
5. In planning, mobilizers should perhaps ask themselves certain basic questions always, when they are working, somewhat like the Rotary club:
   (i) Have I thought of both men and women in this project?
   (ii) Have I asked and looked for women to play leadership roles in this?
   (iii) Am I thinking and acting in terms of the truth about women?

(iv) Is this fair to all concerned i.e. to both men and women?

Conclusion:

This paper argues that in Nigeria, we, the mobilizers, also need mobilization to the right attitudes on sex and gender issues which are often obscured by false and dishonest positions. We need attitudes which guarantee the fundamental rights of women as fellow citizens who should have equal opportunities, recognition etc. Sex and gender attitudes, dating back to pre-colonial times and exacerbated by Islam and Christianity, often in their distorted forms, persist and predominate in modern Nigerian society even among so-called radicals, progressives and the educated. Sex and gender theories are manipulated to exclude women from power, privilege and wealth, all of which they have a natural right to share.

A conscious effort must be made to fight sexist gender attitudes as they affect speech and dialogue with women in every day life; these attitudes influence planning with and for women in society. The paper ends on recommendations on attitudinal and policy positions which mobilizers themselves should always take in their approach to the task of nation-building.

References

1. Women in Nigeria Today, (London: Zed Books, 1985), Introduction.
2. *Ibid.*
3. See Amadiume, Ifi, *Male Daughters, Female Husbands* (London: Zed Books,1986).
4. Many texts exist on this subject. Bibliographic references can be provided to any interested reader.
5. Ogundipe-Leslie, Molara, "African Marxists, Women and a Critique of Everyday Life" *The Journal of African Marxists*, 10, Spring, 1987.
6. See Morgan, Robin, ed., *Sisterhood is Global* (New York: Doubleday and Anchor Books, 1984) and (Pelican, 1985). An international feminist anthology on essay and data notes on seventy-six countries. Entries from the socialist countries show that even with the rights of women guaranteed in the books, the male-dominating attitudes persist in society.

12. Beyond the Women's Decade: A Message to Middle-Class Women*

What is Beyond the Women's Decade?

If one were to give an answer quickly to this question, one would say it is to consolidate the gains of the U. N. Decade for Women and to focus on special problem areas. In the world-wide women's movement and the struggle against discrimination in any form against women, the U.N. has revealed that certain factors have militated against the improvement of the status of women in all countries. They are:

1. Lack of involvement of men in efforts to change the position of women in society.
2. Lack of political will in many countries to change the condition of women.
3. Attitudes of both women and men concerning the role of women in society.
4. Lack of recognition of the value of women's work in both paid and unpaid sectors.
5. Lack of attention to the particular needs of women in planning.
6. Too few women in decision-making positions.
7. Insufficient services such as co-operatives, training and day-care centers and credit facilities to support women's participation in national life.
8. Lack of financial resources.

* Original version presented to the National Conference of the Nigerian Association of University Women, Zaria, Nigeria, in 1988.

9. Lack of communication between women in greatest need and policy makers.
10. Ignorance among women of opportunities available for their development.

I will add,

11. Lack of educational opportunities.
12. The effects of mass communication reinforcing traditional and modern culturally-distorted attitudes often portraying degrading and derisive images of women.[1]

Regarding the last point in particular, Nigerian cartoons are things against which a war must be waged.

What we are fighting is world-wide patriarchy, the ideology of male dominance.

The obstacles to women's progress need to be studied and worked upon by all of us — women of Nigeria. We must seek to remove these obstacles where they present themselves. Most of the described factors apply in Nigeria, some of them with relative gravity.

What Can be Done?

Middle-class women's groups, such as NAUW, have their own specialized roles to play, given the talents and opportunities which are afforded them as educational women in a continent which is largely illiterate. What should be our roles now as intellectuals, not academics; educated and concerned persons? We should be clear in our minds that being an intellectual involves more than having degrees and paper qualifications. It involves more than the mere academicism which is fast becoming the surrogate for intellectualism in Nigeria. An intellectual is interested in knowledge, seeks knowledge and *generates* it innovatively, while not parroting, preferably, European ideas. An intellectual engages in experimentation, mental and social. African women must become, and be recognized as, producers of *ideas* in addition to children. We, as women intellectuals, must generate knowledge and engage in inquiry and action regarding our interests *as women* in the context of the genuine liberation of women in Africa as the continent liberates itself economically. The liberation of

160

women, as Frelimo in Mozambique rightly said, is not an act of charity. It is not a game or hobby to be engaged in by bored or idle middle-class women in their spare time. The liberation of women is not a kindness to be granted to us by sympathetic men. It is not the result of humanitarian or compassionate attitudes. It is a "fundamental necessity for change, the guarantee of its continuity and precondition for its victory. The main objective of any meaningful change is the destruction of the system of exploitation and the building of a new society which releases the potentialities of human beings reconciling with labour and nature. This is the context within which the question of women's emancipation arises" (Frelimo).

African women activists have been criticized over and over again by people such as media practitioners, academics etc. as being elitist and not representing the interests of the rural poor, as if those critics are themselves concerned with the rural poor. Are they not themselves in particular concerned only with reporting what government is doing, their salaries and personal advancement? Though the intention of the criticism of elitism may be diversionary and divisive among women, as it is in most countries, we ourselves need to look at our functioning and mentality to see if criticism of us is in any way pertinent. One thinker has criticized the social concerns of middle-class women as being trapped within the preoccupations of their own narrow and ultimately elitist environment. Their quest is for equality, he says, within the elite rather than the liberation of the mass of women. "The day-to-day degradation of ordinary African women is an experience they look upon from the viewpoint of a charity worker or a missionary"[2]. Is this true? I am afraid his criticism is correct.

African elite activists must cease to see themselves as charity workers and missionaries among poor women. This means we must get rid of patronizing attitudes towards the poor and realize that we are not God-ordained leaders of disadvantaged women. The poor women will lead themselves, will articulate their own needs if invited to the forefront; also when they *come by their own will and struggle* to the forefront of nation-building. Because of the language problem in Africa, what we can do is to be interpreters perhaps, or conduits and conveyor-belts within the mass movement. We must see ourselves humbly as catalysts and energizers, not the souls or the natural leaders of the continental struggle for the liberation of Africa, unless we work for, gain, and earn that leadership.

In our particular situation in Nigeria, there are special tasks to be faced. One task is to refuse to be deluded by the tokenism of having individual women here and there as ambassador, MAMSER director or junior minister in government. We must not take this to mean that the women's problems are now solved, nor must we let the voices of carefully cultivated elite women, hand-picked by whoever, be used to drown the true and anguished voices of the women of Africa. We must choose our own leaders. Poorer women will choose their own leaders.

What then do we do? We must become more political. Political in several senses:

1. In being interested in the social and economic independence of Africa wherein the condition of the African woman in any country is situated. At the very primary level, it means reading newspapers, reading the serious sections of those newspapers, not just the fashion pages; knowing the social problems of Africa.

2. In informing ourselves always of political issues in a systematic way.

3. In helping to organize a broad network of women's action to influence decision-making and policy, rather than struggling for individual posts or women presidents who, at present, can only function in isolation in male-dominated cabinets.

4. In learning about power; learning to hold power, to organize, to administer; to take leadership positions; to work with groups, in particular with other women. To work collectively towards a common objective.

5. To abjure our usual divisiveness; petty competitiveness, the "co-wife" mentality; and destructive rumour mongering.

6. In short, to live on the level of history, not on the level of animal survival — of the search for food, shelter, sex and clothing only; although all these are important too.

These are enormous tasks. But we must keep on keeping on, as African Americans say. A scholar, male feminist and member of WIN (Women in Nigeria), Professor Olusanya of the NIIA (Nigerian Institute of Internal Affairs) has rightly said that women's position will not change until women lose the tendency of always seeking to make it through men — using men in one way or another.[3] Our dependency complex, built into us from early childhood socialization, is certainly one of our weaknesses to be combatted.

Women must begin to be self-reliant mentally, socially and economically in the context of our problems as underdeveloped nations. We can say to ourselves: Don't look for a man's money to spend. You are adult. Support yourself or think thusly. Raise your daughters to be the same way. Then men can respect you and relate to you as equals and responsible persons; not exploiters and dependents.

We know that men's own mentalities are also obstacles in the way of women's progress. As observed at the U.N., the Decade has been impeded by the lack of involvement of men in efforts to change the position of women in society. Many fall back on backward cultural attitudes and religious tenets, distorted from their original forms. Changing the attitudes of our men can be one of the tasks elite women set for themselves. This can be done through massive and detailed work through the various forms of media. It can be done through special campaigns. As a producer of ideas, NAUW can sit down to plan blue-prints of this kind of consciousness-raising . It can also help, with the educational talents of its members, to raise the consciousness of women generally, or at the elite level only. It can help to prepare women for participation in nation building.

NAUW can certainly help MAMSER in its massive programme for mass education and political education, the details of which can be disclosed to you later. I thank you for your attention.

Notes

1. *U.N. Work on Women*. Paper published by the U.N. Branch for the Advancement of Women, Vienna, Austria, 1985.

2. Hadjor, Kofi Buenor *On Transforming Africa: A Discourse with Africa's Leaders* (London: Third World Communication, 1987) 107-108. See in particular Ch. XII on the Emancipation of Women.
3. Gabriel Olusanya in *Nigerian Forum* Journal of the Nigerian Institute for International Affairs (NIIA). Special issue on Women.

13. Speech at a King's Palace*

Your Royal Highness, my distinguished colleagues from Abuja, the State Director of MAMSER,** ladies and gentlemen.

Good people of Okene, sons and daughters of Kwara State, MAMSER greets you. We apologize for any inconvenience and we thank you for your patience. In the name of our national chairman, Professor Jerry Gana, I greet you. We have brought you the message of MAMSER which is, for you, the people, to prepare for the political period; to prepare to seize the time in your hands; to organize in order to get the kind of leaders you, the people, want.

You, the people, can do it. It is your right to do it. It is your duty to do it; it is your time now to do it and we in MAMSER believe you can do it because Nigeria belongs to all of us and Nigeria belongs to you. You, the people, can decide the leaders you want. How? By using carefully and responsibly what you have, your vote. By not selling your votes. Do not sell your votes (they are your power). Don't sell them for small and short-term things — like some naira, some bags of rice or some promised offices or jobs which you may not even get once the briber gets into office. Use your votes to change your lives; to get the kind of leaders you want, those who will benefit your community.

* First presented at the Palace of the Attah of Okene in the former
  Kwara State of Nigeria, 1989, at a gathering of local communities.

** MAMSER is the difficult acronym for Mass Mobilization for
  Economic and Social Recovery. This writer was a national director.

You, the people, can determine the kind of leaders you get. They say a people deserves the leaders that it has. We want leadership by example, yes. We all want leadership by example. Everybody wants leadership by example; but in addition, we must also choose well. We must not practice or encourage corruption from cynicism and defeatism. We must help the National Electoral Commission (NEC) to succeed. We must be watchdogs against electoral malpractice.

We, the people, must insist on good leaders. We must make the new leaders accountable to us. Accountable to us, yes, because accountability is the new order that we want. Accountability is the new name of the game. Use your powers to make your leaders accountable. Use your powers of recall, of legal protest, of complaints to public complaints commissions, to MAMSER officials and we shall help you.

You, the people, must choose good leaders, I said, but who is a good leader? Some man or woman (notice I stress woman too), a man or woman who *cares;* a leader who cares for people; who cares for his or her community. A leader who has time to lead, who has time to listen to his or her people after elections; who will not, after elections, hide behind walls and ask you to telephone him or her; who will not put up a sign that you must beware of dogs and keep your distance; who will not put up a sign to say to you: "This gate is electrified. Keep away". This leader, a man or a woman, must care for you, the people. He or she must care for his or her community and wish to see the community improve.

Don't say a woman can't do it because a woman can. Our women have energy. Our mothers individually have the energies of ten people put together. Their work and energies made many of us possible, made us what we are today. But for our mothers, many of us would not be standing or sitting here today. Our mothers have made many of us. They have energy. They can do it. The physical safety of women in political campaigns can be planned for, organized and achieved.

We believe that politics now is politics for development. Politics is community development. It is not just sitting in Lagos, Abuja, state or local government capitals and driving around in big cars. It is getting good roads, good schools, good medical care and good jobs for your community. Politics is not finding a position or a place to steal officially. It is not taking the tax-payers' money and hiding it in personal accounts in Switzerland, in London or Spain or wherever they hide them. It is not rigging elections with violence. It is not monopolizing power or suppressing others. It is politics for unity, politics for peace, politics for quality life for you, the people.

And now you, my mothers and sisters, the great women of Nigeria, the great hardworking and long-suffering women of Nigeria, it is time to come out and be counted. It is time to organize, act and take part. Don't be indifferent. Don't be without hope. Don't say you will never do it. Never say never. Don't say you can't, because you can. Don't push it all on the men and then complain later.

Learn to politicize and organize. Give each other support. Don't fight or gossip. Get into the executives and important committees of your families, neighbourhoods, communities and political parties. Don't stay only in women's wings in order to dance, entertain and mobilize for others and then get forgotten when elections are over. Express and defend your own interests. Nothing will be handed to women on a platter of gold. You must struggle like everybody else. Don't wait to be nominated. Go for things. Work peacefully with men. Work charmingly with men (as we are wont to do). Don't think men should promote you because you women are adults. We must work at what we want.

So, we, the people of Nigeria, the men and the women together, shall win, if we try. We, the people, can win, if we seize the time in our hands. Nigeria belongs to all of us. Make Nigeria what you want.

And you, the youth of Nigeria, you have a role to play too. Help us to be watchdogs for justice, watchdogs for tolerance and watchdogs for peace. Tomorrow belongs to you, the young people.

God bless Nigeria.

14. The Image of Women and the Role of the Media in a New Political Culture*

As this is a period of using popular music and thinking for mass mobilization by MAMSER, I believe it is most apropos to use a thought kernel from the great Bob Marley — a thought which has great political (even social and personal) significance if we care to ruminate on it — "telling the children the truth". We know that "the children" in Rasta language means "the people, the masses, the wretched of the earth". Tell them the truth — the truth of their political realities, how they came to be so poor; what made them so poor and how they came to be "suffering and smiling," to quote our great Fela.

This is what I hope, all of us citizens and lovers of Nigeria want the press to do. Tell us the truth; tell the people the truth without the masks and taints of personal or corporate prejudice and interests. The need to tell the truth is nowhere keener than in the reporting of women's conditions, experience and interests.

The State of the Media and Women

The media in Nigeria has not given women the space they need, either structurally within the media administration, or psychologically in the representation of women's images. Despite the early presence of women like Theresa Ogunbiyi, Lara Morel etc. in the history of Nigerian media, despite their

* First presented to a workshop for all political correspondents in all Nigerian print media, Bauchi, Northern Nigeria, 1989.

courage, their sophistication and intelligence, such women still found themselves shunted on to women's pages.

Writing in the 1980's, a media specialist, Therese Nweke, an employee of NAN and National Secretary of the Nigerian Association of Media Women, observes that the statistics in media showed that there was no woman in the approximately one hundred chief executives of broadcasting stations constituting the top management. There were only three female editors and one acting editor among the 300 journalists of the *Daily Times*, a quarter of whom are women. There are only eight women out of 127 of (*the News Agency of Nigeria, NAN*) journalists, none of whom occupies a senior management position after four years of the inception of NAN. Only one woman sat on the ten-member board of directors of the agency. In the FRCN, the Federal Radio Corporation of Nigeria, despite women being 35% of the total workforce, of the six assistant directors in the senior management cadre, only one is a woman.[1]

In the print media, the story is not much different though we now have two or three very visible women in top management positions. Still, statistically, what is their proportion? Women are usually not seen as news editors, chief sub-editors or editors. Only the very rare management will consider women for these posts. Women are more likely found in positions of assistantship. Yet it is the positions of news editor, chief sub-editor and editor which can help, and succeed, in the reflection and projection of women's media, very importantly because news stories must pass through these officers to get to the masses, the people, "the children." A sexist news editor has the power to simply throw away the report, slant or suppress the news.

The structural oppression of women is one of the root causes of women's subordination in society. Women are constantly excluded from any participation or effective participation because they are absent from senior management positions and policy-making bodies. Conceiving of women in supportive and service roles only breeds structural asymmetry which then affects the art or science of government of the country, that is, the politics of the society.

It is in recognition of the basic urgency to correct structural discriminations that the U.N. General Assembly adopted, a resolution approving the draft convention on discrimination against women in 1979.

The articles of the draft include measures to be taken by member-nations to eliminate discrimination in various areas including political and public life; special attention was given to the rights of rural women and the elimination of stereotypes about women.

In "the Forward-Looking Strategies" for the integration of women compiled at the Nairobi UN Decade Women's Conference of 1985, a special section is devoted to the role of communication in the struggle for the upliftment of women world-wide. A copy is attached as appendix. Needless to say, the power of the media to make and unmake the image of women, to hasten or retard the progress of women in society, cannot be denied or underestimated.

Mental Oppression

The power of the media over minds argues that the media needs to act responsibly in the reporting of women's issues, particularly now, in the transition programme period when there is an undeniable national movement of women's awareness and a political period to commence soon in the second quarter.

At the moment, the press has created an atmosphere about women which is not exactly positive. The press seems to be reluctant to lend support to any attempts (superficial though they may be) to enhance the status of women.[2] The press will only be positive when glamorous and powerful women are concerned and that change has only been recent. The basic attitude toward the women's movement is still disapproving. It took the emergence of the First Lady, Mrs. M. Babangida and other first ladies, and perhaps the social success of Chief Mrs. Kuforiji-Olubi for our chameleon press to change their tune. Previously the NCWS and Mrs. Adefarasin had been embattled for years, fighting antipathy, derision and irrationality about women.

The Press pays much attention to negative issues about women. It is as if the news for women were "the ugly, the unusual, the odd, the negative, the conflictual" and the disastrous. The extent to which cases of apprehended female criminals were reported and sensationalized was unprecedented in the history of media activity.[3] More sympathetic media would want to get to the bottom of issues — how did and do the women get involved? What is the nature of their structural oppression here? Are they their own persons or agents? How can we protect such abused and misled women? Needless to say that our fearless press does not write on, or expose either the roots or the barons of the crime world in Nigeria.

The psychology behind such demonization of women through sensationalism in my view is that media practitioners decide from their own love of their mothers that women are saints, holy and perfect. The mother (not the wife) is, after all, the only female type who is respected and divinized in African culture. Once a woman falls from this grace of "the mother as the perfect woman", the journalists go at her with virulence for disappointing them and shattering their self-created icon. They make a straw woman and proceed to battle it. The truth of the matter is that women are neither saints nor devils; they are just human; capable of both good and evil. The question is, how does society contribute to their nature and behaviour?

Emphasis on the conflicts among women characterizes reportage on women and their activities. A salient example is the election crisis of the NCWS in 1988. It is as if election crises are not politically or humanly permissible and expected in a human, though women's, organization. It is as if the mace was not broken in 1965 in the Western House of Assembly; as if Constituent Assembly "wise men' were not fighting like cats and dogs in 1979 and almost recently at Abuja; as if women, like any other group, are not going to have disagreements and conflicts.

Any cold and objective analysis would show the political and human issues which produced that crisis, while the tactics of the women at the meeting were no different from the tactics of the men of the first and second republics. Nigerian women are also, after all, Nigerians, influenced by the life around them;

hence characterized by the behaviour patterns and values of their community. Who created the image that women are saints anyway? Women may commit less embezzlement in offices but they also disagree among themselves. But the reportage on women by media is hardly given a historical, sociological or scientific kind of analysis. The reportage is often simply a cover for derision.

The volume of positive coverage accorded women's achievements is not only smaller, but limited to only prominent women particularly in southern media. Our Fourth Estate, which constantly accuses women's organizations of being elitist, itself covers only elitist women. One can, in fact, list the four or five women who are written about and interviewed *ad nauseam* in the Nigerian media. Is this laziness on the part of the media or a class attitude which makes the media interest themselves only in what the elite and the government are doing. What is the rural person, man, or woman doing? Why is the rural person never covered, talked about or with, interviewed and brought into our national life? Why are their opinions on national issues never reflected? Why does the press represent the poor, Bob Marley's "children", as criminals, fools and psychotics in the tradition of the class-ridden British Press which was the mother or father of the Nigerian Press?

Abounding in Nigeria are stereotypes of women which are promoted by the media. Contrary to women's contributions to production such as farming, fishing, pastoralism, construction work and commerce, and despite their proven mental abilities in school, women are still generally considered weak, irrational, passive and inferior; therefore they are not to be trusted in positions of authority. If Bola Ige and Richard Akinjide were women leaders who lost their tempers on TV, as those gentlemen did in 1979, this would be used to discredit women. If a woman leader wept freely as did Sam Mbakwe, she would certainly be out of office. I have discovered in my press interviews and from commentary in the media, that stereotypes of women are beginning to affect the consideration of women in the politics of the coming political phase.

Women in Politics

A new political culture must be created which must see women's participation as normal, rather than abnormal or, only just "modern," since women's participation is in consonance with our traditional cultures and village organizations where the dual stratification of roles, political and social, was quite frequent.[4] Most village communities cannot think of organizing without consulting or including the women; but in our modern and Westernized planning and nation-building, we can.

The stereotypes which are beginning to affect the conception of women as political leaders and activists include the false assumptions that women cannot stand the rigours of politics, the campaigns, the machinations and the physical violence. Women who traditionally faced, and still are facing, the rigours of agricultural production, the hurly-burly of the market place and the customs posts and borders (including the hardships of poverty) are believed to be incapable of facing the rigours of politics. Can this be honest? Such a disqualifying assumption is being made when women do tour and participate in the violence of campaigns as entertainers, as entourage members of the women's wings of the parties or as loyal wives of male candidates. Why, then, can women not be candidates themselves? The issue is for Nigerians to be conscientized to accept that women, having great endurance and managerial abilities, can face the rigours of politics while their physical safety, as that of everyone else in politics, should be legally guaranteed. Women should be encouraged and supported to get into the executive positions of parties, into the decision-making bodies of community organizations and go for candidacies. Women should not only be mobilizers for others and party entertainers.

Another question frequently asked is whether a woman can be President. Personally, I feel this question is unnecessary sensationalism at this point because I do not think having a woman president is the most important factor in the integration of women into the political life of the nation. The creation of a broad network of conscious and active women in politics is infinitely more important and primary. A woman president could emerge from this broad context after the politicizing and educative involvement of the woman president herself, through party work and community organization. The media, however, constantly ask this diversionary and irrelevant question, perhaps to reduce the issue of women in politics to absurdity, as usual.

This is not to say that it is absurd for a woman to be President. I am saying that being President is not necessarily the first and most necessary political step for women. If, however, we are asking if women have the administrative, intellectual and authoritative ability to be a President, the answer is, "Yes," for I can name many women who can do as well, if not better, than some of our men who have been Presidents and Prime Ministers.

The Press must be fair and objective in reporting issues which affect women. They must therefore engage in interpretive journalism. More basically, they must report women in the first place because I have noticed a politics of exclusion and media blackout in the handling of events. Women's presence, speeches and photographs are often ignored or man-handled in the reporting of public events. What women say or think is not considered material for news or even considered, while men are quoted copiously. The press must do better in the new political culture.

Women in the media themselves must contribute to the creation of new roles for the media in the new political culture. Some print media women are in the forefront of the struggle for the positive re-creation of the women's image in our society. Still, we must change a situation where approximately 60% of women's articles and programmes are about women in the context of love and marriage.[5] Women readers consume much of the pulp and gossip literature and soft media programmes — *Vanguard, Prime People, Top News, Climax* and *"Behind the Clouds".* *Women in the media must help educate the tastes of women.* This last point is very important. Media women must find attractive ways of introducing women to social and political issues.

It was in recognition of the power of the media to eliminate stereotype images of women and provide women with easier access to information that paragraph 206 of the *Nairobi Forward*

Looking Strategies for the Advancement of Women called for "the participation of women at all levels of communication policy and decision-making, in programme design, implementation and monitoring."[6] We pray the Nigerian media will realize these nationally necessary objectives in their performance in the new political period to come.

Notes

1. Therese Nweke, "The Role of Women in Nigerian Society: The Media" *Women in Nigeria Today* (London, Zed Books, 1989) 203.
2. See also Idowu Sobowale, "News and the African Journalist", *New Nigerian*, January 31, 1989. Owens and Hannt, *Understanding Media* I (1985).
3. *The WIN Document*, (Women in Nigeria Editorial Collective, Ahmadu Bello University, Zaria, 1985) See the section on the media and women.
4. See Okonjo, Kamene on dual stratification; Ogundipe-Leslie, Molara, *Not Spinning on the Axis of Maleness: Women in Nigeria, Sisterhood is Global* (NY: Doubleday, 1985) and (Pelican Books,) See also Mba, Nina, *Nigerian Women Mobilized* (Berkeley:, South California Press, 1982).
5. *The WIN Document* (Zaria, 1985)
6. "The Forward Looking Strategies for the Advancement of Women" U.N. Decade Conference on Women, Nairobi, Kenya, July 1985.

Appendix:
Areas of Specific Action
Communications
Paragraph 206

In view of the critical role of this sector in eliminating stereo-typed images of women and providing women with easier access to information, the participation of women at all levels of communications policy and decision-making and in pro-gramme design, implementation and monitoring should be given high priority. The media's portrayal of stereotyped images of women and also that of the advertising industry can have a profoundly adverse effect on attitudes towards and among women. Women should be made an integral part of the decision-making concerning the choice and development of alternative forms of communication and should have equal say in determination of the content of all public information efforts. The cultural media, involving ritual, drama, dialogue, oral literature and music, should be integrated in all development efforts to enhance communication. Women's own cultural projects aimed at changing the traditional images of women and men should be promoted and women should have equal access to financial support. In the field of communication, there is ample scope for international co-operation regarding information related to the sharing of experience by women and to projecting activities concerning the role of women in development and peace in order to enhance the awareness of both accomplishments and the tasks that remain to be fulfilled.

PARAGRAPH 207

The enrollment of women in publicly operated mass communication networks and in education and training should be increased. The employment of women within the sector should be promoted and directed towards professional, advisory and decision-making positions.

PARAGRAPH 208

Organizations aimed at promoting the role of women in development as contributors and beneficiaries should be assisted in their efforts to establish effective communications and information networks.

This paper was prepared with the research assistance of Boniface Emenalo, NYSC media graduate and Mamser Mass Mobilization Officer.

15. Sisters are not Brothers in Christ: Global Women in Church and Society

The first session began with a meditation on sins against the Holy Spirit by a brother from Haiti. The gathering was a meeting in Razan, Japan, December 5–15, to monitor the gains of the Ecumenical Decade (1988-1998) declared by the World Council of Churches (WCC) in solidarity with women globally. The Decade is to further the work of the United Nations Decade for Women (1975-1985) which had climaxed with the massive conference of nearly twenty-five thousand of the world's women in Nairobi, Kenya in July, 1985. This editorial meeting in Japan in December of last year (1989) was held in the pleasing, provincial town of Razan which is one hour from Tokyo by train; a quiet town which houses museums and the National Women's Education Center (NWEC). These were the buildings in which the WCC monitoring group convened to write up a progress report on the WCC's Decade. [A point of information: the Roman Catholic Church is not a member of the WCC].

The NWEC deserves our attention because its existence should be exemplary for other nations and communities. Its declared objective is to contribute to the promotion of women's learning activities by providing a place for women to study; by encouraging women to continue their educational activities; by providing a place for exchange among people concerned with women and family issues, both in Japan and abroad; by pursuing specialized research on women and family education; and by collecting and disseminating information concerning women and the family. A possible critique of these objectives is that women are again linked inextricably with the family as if women had no identity outside the family and as if the family were the responsibility of women only. But then, this is Japan, a proud mixture, they say, of tradition and modernity.

The official brochure says that the center was opened to promote women's life-long learning through the practical training of leaders of women's groups and the conduction of specialized research on women and the family. The establishment of the center which falls under the jurisdiction of the Ministry of Education, Science, and Culture was an important item in the United Nations Decade for Women, which started in 1975. It was also the result of demands from women's groups throughout Japan for a national institution to raise women's consciousness. Since its founding, the NWEC has developed into a focal point for women's education in Japan and a major meeting place for women from all parts of the world. More than a million people have used its extensive facilities including over 5,500 non-Japanese from 111 countries. Its extensive facilities, include a main building of 8 rooms, cafeteria, snackbar and shop, a seminar hall with an auditorium of 600 seats, three conference rooms; and 26 other different size medium, small and studio size seminar and waiting rooms. The residence halls have Western-style and Japanese- style rooms, nine meeting rooms and two Japanese communal baths and include other beauties such as a gymnasium, an indoor swimming pool, tennis courts, volleyball courts and an athletic field; there is also a Japanese house for cultural activities and a tea ceremony house with a parking lot for two hundred cars. I briefly used the beautiful modern library which holds a respectable stock of international books and journals, some of them from Africa. "International" or even "Third World" does not always include Africa, alas! So it was pleasing to see Africa in Japan.

The Center is a typically practical and tasteful Japanese mixture of the old and the new where the grounds include a picturesque Japanese garden, straight out of any beautiful and serious Japanese movie you have ever seen. We in the AALA countries (Africa, Asia, and Latin America - my acronym), and Africa in particular may find manifold lessons to be learned from my deliberately long description of the Japanese National

Women's Educational Center. We could do with such investments in the upliftment of women's awareness as much as we could invest in armaments and other more destructive and secondary priorities. The mothers of the nation need to know, because they produce, raise and mainly socialize the citizenry. We could also, from the Japanese example, learn to respect our past in a critical way, proudly blending our traditional aesthetics with modern necessities. We should have African hotels built on modernized African architectural ideas of space usage, bedrooms, ventilation; with cuisine, games, storytellers and other artists for instance, instead of pornographic entertainment.

In one of the typically and technologically up-to-date seminar rooms of the NWEC, the brother from Haiti, a former Minister of Education, poeticized on the sins against the Holy Spirit. The sins included men preventing women from reaching God directly, monopolizing in the Churches, ordination, decision-making and worship. This, he called, the monopoly of God-action-whenever and wherever there is an insistence that the Holy Spirit should pass through one channel only (here, through men), where there is a denial of other channels or their authenticity; for example, the Pope versus the priesthood as channels, the priesthood versus the laity, men versus women, the West versus the other nations of the world, whites versus the people of colour world-wide. The deep question I ask is who controls and monopolizes reality? Who enforces what is considered true?

There were three sins against the Holy Spirit, our speaker postulated. The second sin, in particular, fascinated me as an intellectual and a writer because it is committed when people who know and should know — people in positions of authority — stand against the truth, hide or distort it; people such as the Pharisees, priests, ruling classes, elites, intellectuals and (my addition) artists.

It was an inspiring way to begin a convention of fifteen experts who were to consult on and write a document on the issues, the trends, and the challenges of the declared solidarity of the World Council of Churches with women world-wide. The members of this Decade monitoring group had come from

Haiti, Brazil, Oceania (Tahiti), USA, Sweden, Australia, Japan, South Africa, India, Germany, the Philippines, Uruguay, Canada and Nigeria. Though the members from Ireland, USSR, Cameroon, France and Germany could not be present, the group had written reports on their countries from which to work. We may pause here for background information.

The World Council of Churches, in deciding in January 1987 to initiate an Ecumenical Decade of Churches in solidarity with women (1988-1998), had the following aims:

1. Empowering women to challenge oppressive structures in the global community, their country and their church.
2. Affirming through shared leadership and decision-making, theologically and spiritually — the decisive contributions of women in churches and communities.
3. Giving visibility to women's perspectives and actions in the work and struggle for justice, peace and integrity of creation.
4. Enabling the churches to free themselves from racism, sexism and classism; from teachings and practices that discriminate against women.
5. Encouraging the churches to take actions in solidarity with women.

The Ecumenical Decade is not limited to the WCC. National and regional ecumenical councils are sharing information about the Decade. National gatherings and consultations, we are told, are coordinating activities in different countries. National Christian Councils and WCC member churches' women's departments will be providing more information. To achieve the Decade goals, the knowledge and experience of a broad spectrum of women and men will need to be gathered. In particular, the WCC has invited the participation of (1) local parishes, church women's groups and associations, theologians, church leaders, decision makers and church workers; (2) ecumenical women's organizations; local, national, regional and international ecumenical councils; (3) women's movements; women in youth groups and student movements; unions and action groups; women for different religious backgrounds (i.e. interfaith outreaches). This WCC initiative has a prehistory that goes back to 1948.

A recurrent question in all social spheres has been: do we really need to pay so much attention to women, particularly since the UN Decade for Women (1975-1985)? Wasn't the Decade enough, some people ask? Experience has revealed, however, that the radical improvement of women's conditions, hoped for through the UN Decade, did not take place. In fact, instead, the WCC finds that most women today face more difficult conditions than they did fifteen or twenty years ago. Increased military spending and injustices in the economic system (seen, for example, in the so-called debt crisis and in activities of transnational corporations) have worsened the situation. The globally dominant patriarchal culture is still accepted as "natural" by most people; men and women.

An African voice from the WCC Secretariat reminds us that the UN Decade has impacted negatively on African women. They were co-opted into development efforts which they had not been called upon to plan in collaboration with authorities. There was no women's development because women's ideas and views, thinking, hopes, and yearnings for the human community had not been included in the planning. Religion and culture were excluded from development only to become obstacles in the paths of women's development in Africa and other countries of Asia and Latin America. Finally, development often led to a distortion of women's realities; their statuses and roles, like the exclusion of women from agricultural labour and technical aid; or the distortion of their culture and even religion such as the super-imposition of male-headed nuclear families on ownership structures by development agents.

The churches are now challenged to engage in world-wide struggle alongside women at the grassroots, both urban and rural to find solutions to the problems which the WCC identified for governments, churches and movements in its message to the UN Conference in Nairobi in 1985, namely:
- In times of economic difficulties, women are among the first to lose their jobs.
- Women industrial workers are often without protection and are paid the lowest wages by local and multinational industries which exploit their vulnerable position.

- Women in rural areas receive attention in development plans and are not consulted about their basic needs.
- Among the victims of nuclear testing are women who bear the burden of increased miscarriages.
- Apartheid and other forms of racism oppress women differently, often subjecting them to double and triple oppression — as women, as belonging to a discriminated race, and as poor people.
- Famine and war strike women hardest because they carry the heaviest responsibility for their families.
- As socio-economic conditions deteriorate, and men's frustration grows, the level of sexual abuse and violence against women rises correspondingly.
- Growing poverty, the spread of military bases and sex-tourism have encouraged the growth of prostitution, involving even younger women.

To solve these problems, every individual and community is enjoined to find and set their own priorities while the WCC has suggested the following priorities for consideration:

1. Women's full participation in church and community.
2. Women's perspectives and commitments to justice, peace and the integrity of creation, that is, social justice and the protection of the environment, the planet and nature.

The Ecumenical Decade has been on the move since 1988 along these stated priorities. Together with Brigalia Bam, an Anglican, and Secretary of the South African Council of Churches, who works closely with Archbishop Desmond Tutu, this writer prepared a report in Japan on issues, trends and challenges in Africa. We began with a brief statement on some of the problematics of any kind of mobilization in Africa: the challenges of coordination and communication as determined by Africa's size (five times the size of the USA, as many do not know); her multilingualism; the illiteracy of the majority of the women to be reached (which demands innovative oral and traditional media techniques) and necessary translations into local languages; the need for the close monitoring of projects and the implication of the tendency of people to think of Africa, vast as she is, as one country.

The Africa report highlighted salient points such as the popularity of the Decade with African church women whose great enthusiasm deserves praise for having registered significant achievements in the context of limited resources; launchings in many countries accompanied by interfaith action, dialogues, workshops, and consultations; the linking of social change to theology, scripture and ministry; the initiatives to do theology from African and feminist African perspectives on scripture and liberational theology particularly in the area of political resistance and struggle in Africa (as in South Africa); and the desire for more inter-regional outreach in Africa.

African Church women have challenged themselves to critique customs, rituals, and taboos to see where they are negative or positive for women's conditions; to combat their own internalized oppression which takes the form of living out stereotypes, low self-esteem, lack of confidence, over-aggressiveness, apathy, and servile attitudes to men, social structures and life itself; plus the economic development of women in its relation to practical realities like the working conditions of women at work, the debt crisis and IMF policies; to interpret the Bible from women's perspectives and the strong need for the training and education of women in church and society. Needless to say the institutionalized sexism of the Church, like the suppression of women through theology, their exclusion from ministry, the exclusive language of the liturgy and religious texts, and the exclusion of women from leadership and decision-making must engage African women in the churches while the churches themselves must come to own the Decade, which is still mainly a women's Decade.

Personally, the most inspiring aspect of the WCC action on women has been the issue of women doing theology and sharing spiritually. For me, the importance of struggle for social change at the level of ideas cannot be gainsaid. Needless to say, the ideational control of minds in particular through religion is one of Africa's imperative problematic, as it is an important variable in whatever happens or can happen in Africa.

These considerations activate my involvement with all actions which influence and concern the conditions of African women in society, even when the modalities of change are through structures of faith. In most societies, as we all know, people are best reached through their faiths. In many parts of the world, according to the WCC, women are re-reading the Bible in the light of their own oppression and hope. Christian women are re-interpreting symbols and icons; creating new symbols, reflecting on Mary's role in church history, doctrine, and the world's liberation, researching the roles of Mary and the suppressed women apostles of Christ, and generally challenging and questioning the patriarchal traditions from within their faiths. Most gratifying, women theologians all over the world, in particular in Asia, are utilizing the intellectual and social gains of the secular women's movements.

Most encouragingly, in particular, African women have set up a Circle of Concerned African Women Theologians (of which this writer is a founding member) to embark on Biennial Institutes on women in Religion and Culture. Its first meeting took place in Accra, Ghana in September 1989. With a theme of "Daughters of Africa, Arise! — A Convocation of African Women in Theology" it set itself the following goals:

1. to create a forum for women interested in the area of religion and culture in the lives of women.
2. to publish documents for the academic study of religion and culture.
3. to contribute to research that leads to policies affecting African women's development, their participation in religion and society.
4. to work towards the inclusion of women's studies in religion and culture in the research carried out by institutions of African studies in African universities and other tertiary institutions.
5. to enable African women in religious and cultural studies to contribute to cross-cultural studies of contemporary women's issues.
6. to establish a network of women to monitor women's interests in the area and to serve as advocates for the inclusion of women in all deliberations in the field of religion and culture.
7. to promote inclusion of specific women's concerns in the

theory and practice of evangelism. Who controls the story controls the reality, says a Southern African proverb. (All enquiries about the institute should be directed to Mercy Oduyoye, Deputy General Secretary of the World Council of Churches). There were African diasporal joys at the meeting. The black brother from Rio de Janeiro (Brazil) embraced me when I told him that I was a Yoruba who had noticed that he was wearing some Santeria Ogun beads. The brother from Haiti rejoiced pridefully that he had just completed a tour of West Africa. These greetings were soothing home coming from a country where people were debating their African derivation and heritage, claiming to be Afrindeurs. I became as "thick as thieves" with the lady from South Africa who did grassroots skills training with women in Soweto. Others soon began to wonder what we were always laughing about*. Oh, the importance of laughter! How do we survive our crazy, bedeviled continent without laughter! (No stereotypes intended, please).

South African church women said in their report that the challenge for women was to work for the transformation of society; for women to move from passivity to action; from servitude to service, from aggressiveness to assertiveness, in order to change the traditional structures of the church and society for the good of all. Women must give movement and "vibration" they say, to the Ecumenical Decade which is their Decade and their challenge.

I shall leave you with the Twelve Theses on Feminist Theology put together by women at a liberation theology meeting in Strasbourg in July, 1986, for you to ruminate on continually and relate to your work and experience.
1. Sisters are not brothers in Christ.
2. Patriarchy is a multinational corporation of the churches.
3. Women are not honorary men.
4. God is beyond God the Father.
5. Priesthood is for people, not for men.
6. To recognize sexism as sin is the beginning of change.
7. Women are not in the church to justify themselves but, rather, to put it in order.

8. It is through feelings and tears that God speaks.
9. The body of a woman is her inherent property.
10. To listen to each other is a way to hear God.
11. That women keep silent does not mean that men speak for them.
12. Feminist theology is a breakthrough from death to life.

* The Soweto woman told me they were taught in South African schools that George Washington founded and ran "the underground railway" historically operated by Harriet Tubman. The wonders of apartheid and Bantu Education! Nat King Cole records reportedly also had photos of a white man on their covers. A black man could not possibly have such a beautiful, velvety voice!

Note: Since the writing of this essay, a vast center for women has been built in Abuja, Nigeria.

Afrindeur means "of African, Indian and European descent."

16. Stories of Structural Adjustment (SOSA): The Human Cost of Structural Adjustment Policy (SAP) for Women

Stories of Structural Adjustment (SOSA). I am starting with this acronym SOSA to demonstrate that it is a Nigerian national sport to make acronyms of everything. NEC (Nigerian Electoral Commission) MAMSER — one difficult to handle — (WAI) War Against Indiscipline. Structural Adjustment Policy (SAP). What we do not have is WAC (War Against the Citizenry) which is what structural adjustment has turned out to be.

I am going to speak to you here as a creative writer and an Africa-centered nationalist intellectual. I leave the rest to you as social scientists to accept or reject, to disprove, research and document statistically or paper over with theory in Greek and Latinate words, percentages and graphs.

To my knowledge, how has structural adjustment affected women in Nigeria. What has been the human cost of it, particularly for women?

I have personal and reported testimonies of the impact of structural adjustment on rural and urban Nigerians. To begin with, my landlord where I was living in rural Nigeria, was a lace maker. I rented his apartment because I was teaching at a new Nigerian state university which is experimenting with non-residential campuses for faculty and students. The colonial tradition has been that faculty and students were housed on the campus at the expense of the university. My landlord, the lacemaker, owned a modern computerized factory which produced lace for the local bourgeoisie and their imitators — lace being the chic and ceremonial material to wear for naming ceremonies, weddings, state occasions, church festivals like harvest, any big celebration, and most of all, funerals. The material for producing the lace, the thread, I believe was imported, there not being sufficient cotton or silk plantations to back up the industrial production any longer.

The factory was run by a team of Austrian workers (called experts) who worked with local employees to whom they were allegedly unwilling to reveal the secrets of the machines and production. The local hands, however, being highly intelligent, had private schemes to crack their codes (which they did), in their hope and conviction, quite well placed, that they should take over the running of the factory in due time. The Nigerian owner had educated his own son in lacemaking in Austria for eventual takeover by the young man.

The first effect of structural adjustment through the devaluation of the Nigerian currency, the naira, was that the salaries of the expatriate managers could not be paid. This led slowly to their exodus as also happened in the universities, research institutes and businesses leading to the impoverishment of the cosmopolitan quality of Nigerian intellectual life and performance in general. The devaluation of the naira was in this consequence a blow struck at the development of local human resources in terms of person power, as it was the attrition of the local bourgeoisie which should necessarily be the producer of certain types of knowledge and industry in the country. Yet the structural adjustment policy (SAP) claimed to have as one of its objectives, the eventual development of a local class which would produce export goods which would compete with the imports coming freely into the country through trade liberalization. What sweet deception! My landlord was to be one such competitor.

Very soon, all the managers in this factory had to go. Many of the local workers were sacked because the factory had to function at a reduced production level. The majority of the workers were women who worked on the threading and the sewing machines. These women were therefore income earners and breadwinners for their families. Among a sub-ethnic group of the Yoruba (the Ijebu), these women had long standing traditions of being economic producers. With SAP, men who were associated with the factory, lost the ability to support their families at the level to which they were accustomed. Being polygamists in general and Muslims, many of the men had large families whose members, including the women, suffered from the impact of the subversion of this factory. Other examples existed in this rural town. Modern mechanized farmers in agro-business had to close down their businesses. Others almost declared bankruptcies. Several private and small businesses had to close down.

These cases were only in one part of the country. Other examples existed to the East and to the North. The moral of these stories is that the SAP has contributed seriously to, if not caused, the destruction of the entrepreneurial middle class in that town and in Nigeria in general. Yet the beguiling song of the policy was that trade would be liberalized so that local producers would compete in the import and export trade, producing goods for export. How can the local industrialists produce goods to compete with goods from Britain, Japan, France, Germany and the U.S. when these local industrialists could not fund the production of raw material, pay for the fuel and electricity needs for their machines, pay their workers a decent wage, etc. Even simple local industries manufacturing writing paper, toilet paper, feminine hygiene products, soap and cosmetics had to close down. How could the local bourgeoisie compete, given their devalued naira?

So it appears to the layperson and the commonsensical person that there was a ruse somewhere. Who is fooling whom? Who, Nigerians say in pidgin: noh know go know! (Who does not know, will know). In education, boys were simply kept back from going to school since parents could not afford to pay their fees and the various development levies which went along with schooling. Some fathers told me that their solution was to apprentice their sons to trades like car repairing, blacksmithing, printing (if they could find a printing house still in business), tailoring and haircutting, etc., in the hope that these boys would learn a gainful mode of existence without going to formal school. The girls often just married in primary school, and went into trading without leaving the schools. There were, therefore, pregnant school girls walking around campuses. If boys were being kept back from school, you can imagine what is happening with the girls who are felt to be potential lost assets since they would marry into other families. This was in Ogun State.

In Imo and Anambra states, for instance, those of us who were involved in literacy campaigns found that we did not need to argue for women to be in school. Only girls were in the schools, in the first place. The boys were being trained as apprentice marketmen in Aba, Owerri and Onitsha — in city centres. It was felt that schooling was an unsafe and expensive venture for a boy who was a potential head of a household, in a social context which did not promise jobs for his certificates. Sending boys to school which parents could ill-afford was felt to be an unwise investment. Education itself seemed to be under siege. It appeared that education was being made inaccessible to all but a small class of people who could afford it. And certainly the military class could afford it. In fact, it appears that the only surviving schooling system with respectable standards and equipment are the various military schools for children and young adults. The condition of schools, including the universities themselves, in particular the great old Ibadan, is a matter too deep for tears.

The universities and the intellectual middle class (i.e. members of the schooling systems, the media and members of the bureaucracy and business) also appear to be under siege. Academics can no longer live on what they earn; a full professor's salary is the equivalent of $2,200 a year at the highest calculation. In their bid to pay their bills and meet their responsibilities as parents and family supporters, some academics had to resort to all kinds of extracurricula work. Many, in conjunction with their wives are becoming part-time petty traders, selling beer and groceries in their garages. The academic as a petty trader.

Clientism with the political class has become the order of the day. Days are spent by academics in trying to provide themselves with the infrastructure which the state cannot provide, in a country where everything — water, electricity, postal communications and fuelling, has broken down. The African scholar spends his or her day running after tap water, food, petrol (gas) in what I call a plastics culture, while his or her peers are at their computer screens in the countries of the IMF and World Bank planners. (Plastic cans are needed to fetch everything by car for home use.) These plastic-can carrying intelligentsia of the post-IMF culture, are the shining elite who are conceived in false development theories as potential vanguards to lead the structurally adjusted countries into the millennium of growth and market competition in a free world of market forces and trade liberalization.

This intellectual bourgeoisie is so harassed by hunger and repressions that many of its members are escaping to places where they can live at a decent modicum and practice their skills in peace while meeting their human responsibilities. This intellectual class, after all, is so malnourished, due to poor or insufficient protein consumption, that it cannot engage in sustained intellectual activity. For foregoing reasons, a new phenomenon has arisen in contemporary Nigeria — that of *the intellectual as migrant labourer* abroad. His or her departure has been so marked that the government set up a Brain Drain Committee to investigate the causes of the loss of academics and intellectuals to foreign countries. Indeed! Let's look for the causes. How did the academics get lost? Who does not know the trick of putting a piece of meat in your mouth and looking for that piece of meat after it is lost down your throat?

The departure of middle class elements has led to the subversion, shattering or restructuring of immediate families. Spouses have to live apart; parents are separated from their children as they have gone abroad to forage for those children. Families are moved suddenly to strange settings; children's educations are disrupted while women, the constant steady points of crisis pendulums, bear and withstand most of these economic, social and psychological stresses.

You may ask why all this is allowed to happen in our countries. Why are we playing victims? We must remember that the

IMF packages are negotiated by national groups who may wish, for reasons of their own, to subvert the intellectual class. Local national groups, we find, are fighting their own local battles of self-interest which may include hegemonic struggles of ethnicity or political power — e.g., who becomes the post-colonial ruling political class? Who controls the economy? Who represents the national interests in the international economic order? Shortsightedly but perhaps self-interestedly, these groups who negotiate the IMF packages are conniving with the destruction of certain classes and power groups at home.

In this tragicomic world where the citizenry is reeling from what it does not quite understand, (from the incomprehensible economic virus which has hit it), gender roles have been forced to change. Salaries have been rendered inutile by devaluation without wage increases or by slashing. Many workers have been retrenched. A new World Bank agreement for funding the universities has raised the ire of the local academics. Students have protested the agreement. More and more, women are becoming household heads. Male household heads find that they have to acknowledge more the contributory financial roles of their wives. Women have always contributed as wives, but theirs is the unrecorded and uncompensated contribution of buying family food, children's clothes and the family homes (of which they are sometimes dispossessed by recalcitrant husbands, when marital conflicts occur).

A professor friend said to me privately and quietly, almost sadly: "you know, my wife, Lydia, feeds us now". His tone was very affectionate; it was as if he were just discovering a new value and goodness to Lydia. Lydia is one of the women who did not take the academic path but became a self-employed business woman soon after her marriage. When the IMF struck, following the decline of the Gowon national economy which has been declining since Gowon in 1978, Lydia was able to take the whole family on her back financially where she had previously been perhaps only supporting arms.

What is happening with non-middle class families — with the peasants, the urban industrial and lumpen proletariat classes? Peasants in the countryside were finding farming very hard to do. Shortages have, in a positive way, forced everyone to re-appreciate the value of farming and producing one's food in addition to cash crops. (Cash crop farmers were simply smuggling their produce across the border to sell in neighbouring countries since they could not get good prices at home. Some food crops were also being sold). Food farmers found it hard to produce much from soils now unproductive from the farming neglect of the oil-boom years; soils had been eroded from the use of imported fertilizers in the days of "Feed the Nation" gimmicks, when destructive fertilizers were being dumped into Nigeria from elsewhere in fertilizer deals with foreign business sharks.

Peasant life was itself eroded as peasants tried to glean food from an unyielding and abused soil. What they are able to plant were subject to the greed and appropriation of middlemen who carted the produce to town at exaggeratedly expensive rates. Poor farmers, men and women, were not able to transport their own produce to towns and thus to consumers. The transportation of produce and solutions to that need were leitmotifs in the plaints of rural women whenever they discussed with me their needs from any "development scheme". What food was not transported simply rotted.

The provision of storage facilities and methods was another pressing need. These rural farming women and men could hardly be expected to possess, find or afford motor transportation, (considering the sky-high cost of motor vehicles, spare parts and fuel), thanks to the friendly SAP. These farmers in Nigeria were not organized into cooperatives which could, in time, organize their group finances around the renting of vehicles to transport produce to towns or marketing rural spots, as you have in Zimbabwe. Some peasants just gave up trying to fare independently. They became wage labourers on other people's farms or on company farms. Traditional dignity and autonomy were put under attack, sometimes lost, and women were the most preferred wage labourers since they could be paid less, sometimes next to nothing.

So, irony of ironies, it is this local peasant class under siege which sometimes has to absorb the stress from the cities and the middle class. Those with middle class relatives sometimes find they have to be the haven and back-up systems for relatives who have been retrenched or impoverished in their wage labour elsewhere. Children are sent back to poor and struggling rural relatives; sometimes to grandparents who themselves are trying to piece together a life. Children return to rural schools without books or sometimes without teachers. Mothers have to temporarily give up the nurturing and socializing of their own children because they are first opting for the physical survival of those children.

From the northern states, there was news on the grapevine (the alternative media system) that working class families could hardly feed themselves. We heard that peasants were pounding the husks of corn and millet to resourcefully make a new kind of staple, where they could no longer afford the grains themselves. Beans (thankfully more nutritious) had to replace meat where people could afford the soaring prices of beans in the first place. The ingestion of protein was the privilege of those blessed with the ability to buy a chicken for (Naira)35, when the daily wage is only 1.75 (one naira seventy-five kobo).

What do you imagine the health situation to be in such a setting? Mothers have to continue to breastfeed, to pass on the milk they themselves do not have. Of course, many had to stop breastfeeding and resort to cow's milk, unhygienically used in rural areas and markets; cow's milk was condemned as not the best for children in the international market. While these women struggle to keep their children alive, they are berated with media noise about family planning and the need to not have children at all. (Deprovera, a condemned birth control drug circulates still). Among the Gwari of Abuja State, peasant women began to campaign among themselves that the family planning clinics should be avoided because their children were being injected with dangerous drugs which may kill. Some spoke of genocide. The point is that they did not see the agencies as addressing their own most pressing reproductive needs. Some feared their babies were being sterilized permanently while still others felt the children were being injected with the AIDS virus. The moral of this is the need for better communication between the state and its citizenry; the need for greater attention to local needs, particularly in the working class.

A strong gender solidarity exists between the men and the women of the working classes because in my view, both genders see themselves as victims together in a world they do not understand or control, a world which unprovokedly subjects both men and women to existential hardship whose purposes are beyond their comprehension. The role of middle class women in the SAP drama will be material for future stories of structural adjustment.

In a country of the hidden agenda, as I describe Nigeria, a country which is certainly not open or an ideal bourgeois state (which does not exist anywhere anyway); in this our Nigeria where nobody knows what is really going on and many hidden agenda are being pursued, not before our very eyes but behind our very backs, what can be said to relieve this grim picture? Is it all bad with no relieving goodness?

So grim is the economic life that the whole country, particularly the South, is held hostage by armed robbers. The country is under siege from armed robbers who now strike most boldly in the day, not just in the night. Sometimes such actions take on the appearance of a class vengeance. The thieves break in your house, rape your female relatives and deplete the food and drink in your refrigerator. Some thieves practically hold a party on your living room floor, before they leave. Some are known to have made statements of class bitterness before they depart. Women are sometimes members of these armed gangs; they have been known to be used as decoys by the groups. Some women members of drug gangs have died inexplicably. Conversely, women have been at the greater receiving end of these violences of armed robbers. Thieves now find it easier to attack women than other men. In the past, they feared to violate women. Women have jewelery snatched from their necks in cities. This has happened to me in Lagos. One of the thieves once said to an attacked woman: "I snatch something from your neck and you scream. Suppose I take off your underpants". Some armed robbers drove off with school children who were being taken home from a nursery in their mother's car. What happened to those children? Child slavery? Or charms for money?

Single women or women alone are often subjected to robberies; accessible and unprotected. My Peugeot 505 car was driven away by an applicant who wanted to be my chauffeur. Women in one state were being hunted and killed because their body parts are highly valued for charms, to make money in an economic situation where people are desperate. The local spiritual belief tells them that women's parts are specially sacred and powerful.

Against this background of horrors, we may find some good: the effects of the expression of the irrepressible human spirit, the great sense of humour, the resilience and the natural intelligence of the Nigerian peoples. There is now an outburst of various creative activities geared towards survival. Farming is now highly valued. The textile trade and trade in clothing have bloomed while local production has become imaginative and accessible given the prohibitiveness of everything else needed for survival. Proletarian music and the arts have surged; for instance reggae music and drama in traditional languages and English, express the commentary and the resistance of the citizenry. Writing has also flowered, leading to the daily production of new magazines, newspapers, popular novels and performed and written poetry. This creative efflorescence is the nightmare of the secret police and those who would gag the freedom of expression.

The citizenry in Nigeria, enduring WAC (War Against the Citizenry), is being sucked into one hidden agendum; perhaps only hidden in Nigeria and not so in the international centres where policies for the Third World are constructed. It is at this level of conceptual planning for Africa that humanists need to intervene. Nigeria is simply being sucked into an international industrial system to take her pre-planned and imposed place of primary producer of raw materials for capitalist industries. To be producers of oil, coffee, cocoa, mineral resources, etc., we are advised that tertiary education, even a secondary one, is not needed. You need just enough education to count the bags of produce. So batter the universities, break the intellectuals, shatter the local entrepreneurial and burgeoning middle classes. Deal only with local reactionaries in whatever forms they come; support their tyrannies while talking democracy; distract their citizenry with political games in the context of religious and ethnic rivalries.

We are being distracted in Africa with issues which are not our own, in language and discourses which we do not generate. Mirages are set before our eyes, like a seeming search for democracy, while local dictators are propped up militarily; family planning and genital mutilation are made priority issues, where women are bereft of basics like food, shelter, health care and education. Over these false and macabre games hangs the pall of AIDS, a ravaging disease which has mysteriously hit certain parts of Africa more than others. The scourge of this disease is discussed with a peculiar glee by foreign commentators, many of whom predict, with almost salacious delight that most people in Africa will have died out in ten years anyway— do we have longer? Noticing their glee, one thinks of diseased blankets and Native Americans, a new biological warfare perhaps. We hear that there will be a population hole in the area of Uganda, the Central African republic, Kenya, Tanzania and Ethiopia — oh —by the year 2000; a population hole which can then be filled supposedly by foreign immigrants. In the AIDS epidemic, women occupy the predictable victim role as they also suffer decimation.

What are the prospects for peace in this turbulent and complex scenario? A great deal certainly has to be done before peace can be achieved. On the level of description and analysis, Africa's crisis has to be understood, not as something mystical and endemic to Africa, essentialist as it were, but something flowing from Africa's situation in a world economic order. Nigeria's leaders are not functioning in a vacuum while both internal and external factors cause and influence these events. Democracy should not be fetishized outside the political economy of the state and its impact on the people. Democracy itself needs to be adapted to meet and represent local needs and perceptions of justice within global humanist standards.

We must tell our story — our story of Africa — wherever we are, whenever we can. Perhaps somebody responsible and humanistic somewhere will hear. Perhaps somebody intelligent somewhere will see and hear through the inhumanity and deceptive jargon of monetary economics to look for the human faces in the results of these policies. Perhaps someone will look for what is wrong with SAP and remember to plan for the people and children of Africa, not genocide or a mortgaged continent, but a dignified future as fellow caretakers of the Mother Earth, not part of the flora and fauna to be exploited or laid waste at will. The citizenry in Africa know what is happening to them. Understanding and transforming their knowledge into positive governmental actions are, at this crucial historical moment, necessary parts of the search for genuine development and true peace.

Notes

1. See the Progress Report on the World Bank Federal Universities Sector Adjustment Operation.
2. See also Ogundipe-Leslie, M. "African Women, Culture and Another Development," *Presence Africaine* No. 141, 1987.

AAWORD papers on the African Crisis and Women (Association of African Women for Research and Development) Dakar, Senegal.

Ogundipe-Leslie, M. "Women in Nigeria" in *Women in Nigeria Today* (London: Zed Press, 1985).

Sen G., Grown C., *Development, Crisis and Alternative Visions*, Third World Women's Perspectives (New York: Monthly Review Press, 1987).

WIN Collective, eds., *Women and the Family* (Dakar: Codesria, 1986).

17. Mandela, Decolonization and the Rest of Us

There is a text which, I believe, has been neglected by us when the world rocked with the furor over *Spycatcher*, a book by Peter Wright, former Assistant Director of MI5 of Great Britain writing the title described as "a candid autobiography of a senior intelligence officer." It seemed we were so concerned with the unprecedented appearance of bald censorship in welfarist Britain, the alleged home of all the sacred "freedoms" like those of free speech, the press, and publishing that we perhaps ignored the details of the revelations in *Spycatcher*.

We did not, therefore, notice the following text which I think is of the utmost significance for the so-called Third World (or AALA countries, my acronym for Africa, Asia and Latin America) and of all decolonizing peoples. Here comes the crucial passage:

> The entire Cyprus episode left a lasting impression on British colonial policy. Britain decolonized most successfully when we defeated the military insurgency first, using intelligence rather than force of arms, before negotiating a political solution based on the political leadership of the defeated insurgency movement, and with British force of arms to maintain the installed government. This is basically what happened in Malaya and Kenya and both these countries have survived intact.
>
> The fundamental problem was how to remove the colonial power while ensuring that the local military forces did not fill the vacuum. How, in other words, can you create a stable local political class? The Colonial Office was well versed in complicated, academic, democratic models — a constitution here, a parliament there — very few

of which stood the remotest chance of success. After the Cyprus experience I wrote a paper and submitted it to Hollis, giving my views. I said that we ought to adopt the Bolshevik model, since it was the only one to have worked successfully. Lenin understood better than anyone how to gain control of a country and, just as important, how to keep it. Lenin believed that the political class had to control the men with the guns, and the intelligence service, and by these means could ensure that neither the Army nor the other political class could challenge - for power (Viking, 1987, Ch.ll, p. 158).

This text becomes most pertinent again with the release of Mandela which, we hope, is simply not an extension of the boundaries of his jail, as one cynical South African brother put it, laughing bitterly and knowingly. The "release" of Mandela and the initiation of a process towards a negotiated peace are, however, historic not only as important political landmarks, they are also imperative as a time for black African political actors and activists to pause in the political whirl to reflect on the lessons to be learned from us, the rest of Africa, their predecessors in the debacle of decolonization and political manipulation by former colonizers. Certainly, we are their predecessors in the business of eating from the same dish with Esu, the Yoruba god of chance, outwitting and trickery or, better still, with the python who invites you to eat from his own dish as he proceeds to surround it with his fat and threatening body .

Clearly the Peter Wright passage contains a significant and complacently described tip from the "master's" bag of decolonizing tricks. For this reason, the passage needs to be applied to the South African and other situations in their relevance, bearing in mind that Peter Wright was writing recently (he was published in 1987), and the test cases of British decolonization still lie before and around us.

Britain decolonized most successfully wherever she defeated (read also disarmed or subverted) the military insurgency first, using intelligence rather than force of arms, says Peter Wright, before negotiating a political solution based on the political leadership of the defeated insurgency movement; thereafter, using British force of arms to maintain "the installed government" (his own words). Wright approvingly names Kenya and Malaya as two cases of successful decolonization which he says have "survived intact" - perhaps meaning where British economic power and political influence have survived intact.

The passage suggests that the Mau-Mau movement was subverted by intelligence first and then replaced by the political leadership of the defeated insurgency movement which was probably hand-picked and then supported in power by British force of arms which maintained "the installed government" . We may ask here, a ' la Hollywood, whatever happened to the revolutionary Jomo Kenyatta? Notice Peter Wright's phrase, "the installed government." Parallel procedures could occur in South Africa where an insurgency movement is being asked to call a military truce even before apartheid has been structurally dismantled. Meanwhile, leaders are being released for a negotiated solution in a context where foreign force of arms will not be needed, this time, to maintain "the installed government" considering that there is a South African army and other law enforcement agencies, fully controlled perhaps by nonprogressive forces.

The fundamental problem according to the cold colonialist in Peter Wright, was how to remove the colonial power while ensuring that the local military forces did not fill the vacuum. How, in other words, can you create a stable local political class? All these considerations are being made about other people's countries. Apartheid, as we know, is colonialism on the spot. How do you remove the obvious, dominating power, at least, remove its detectable face while ensuring that local forces do not fill the vacuum? How do you construct papier-mache masks of power and fit them on the faces of hand-chosen Africans?

To solve this problem, Peter Wright says they turned to Lenin; to what he called the Bolshevik model. And this recourse should be a lesson to us Africans who sing of home-grown ideas, or, are wont and quick to condemn sources, without looking for the usefulness or relevance of their ideas to our conditions. Here we have a cold, British colonialist borrowing from Lenin whom he probably otherwise hates. Here, however, cold and self-interested practicality prevails, as is typical of any would-be successful Machiavellian imperialist. He uses Lenin's idea that "the political class had to control the men with the guns, and the intelligence service, and by these means could ensure that neither the army nor another political class could challenge for power."

Many relevant questions rush to the fore. Is this what did not happen with many neo-colonial governments in Africa? Can Lenin's axiom be the root of our problems? What actually happened in Kenya? And with Kenyatta? Who controls the army in Kenya today? What happened in Nigeria in 1966? Did the political class lose control of the Army in 1966? Kole Omotoso's *Just Before Dawn* implies that the political class did lose control of the Army with the connivance of the British in Nigeria. Is the loss of power over the Army by the political class in 1966, followed by the transformation of the Army itself into a political class, manipulated by internal and external forces, the hidden text of Nigeria's political history since 1966? Here we have ample room for interventions by our political experts and analysts. Certainly the African scene is more complex than can be explained by the facile diagnosis of "corruption."

Back to South Africa, we could put forward certain caveats: that a window-case political class not be installed while the real political class controls the Army, the intelligence service and, of course, the local economy as the installed Africans play out a charade of democracy and government for the consumption of international media and their watchers; that the local political groups not be divided and ruled in the good old colonial style.

Already working in the shadows are wraiths of the aged, tried and tested ways of dealing with black and suppressed peoples. Already in the air are cries and reiterations of "divisions among blacks," "irreconcilable factionalization," "tribalism" and "black-on-black-violence" — blaming the victim for the crime, as ever. Why is it only the victim and the disempowered who are required to be monolithic in their views? Failing to be, they deserve to be imposed upon by outsiders; ruled and exploited. Is there any group of humans which does not (even should not) have differing interest groups with different opinions and objectives? Why the constant blackmail that blacks or the oppressed or the disempowered be "one" to deserve their just desserts? Of course, it is a recurrent argument of abusers about the abused — of the colonizer about the colonized; of so-called whites about people of color; of men about women. Women do not speak with one voice hence others should appropriate their voices.

The world should be tired of this cliched ploy by now; but it is not. The point is that people be left alone to work out their objectives, options and differences as adults without their abusers throwing fat on the fire. Let the blacks in South Africa work out their problems without external machinations, and that includes the media. The funding and support of war-lords should stop, as Alistair Sparks courageously pointed out on the ABC Nightline show of Town Meeting on February 15, 1990.

The same goes for black-on-black-violence. The culprits should stop promoting and funding violence in order to use it as a justification for the continuing domination of blacks. Put simply, that people are fighting each other is not a reason to have a master come in to sit on them. The argument that the master should do this is one of the most naked and appalling admissions of an imperialist consciousness which is often expressed only towards people of color. Europe and America have had some of the bloodiest and warridden of human histories yet their nationals would not for one moment think that this justifies Mexicans, Nigerians, Australians or Martians coming in to take them over and govern their lives and their properties. It is therefore amazing, yet familiar, to hear the comment that the most important problem in South Africa today is not the dismantling of apartheid, but the ending of black-on-black-violence. This comment is what the Yorubas of Nigeria would describe as neglecting leprosy while struggling to eradicate ringworm.

The revelation in Peter Wright's *Spycatcher* should stand in our mind's eye, always, when we think about South Africa and other forms of decolonization. Needless to say, power mongers and brokers borrow from each other's notebooks. The rest of us should learn from each other too. Importantly, South Africans should learn from the rest of us, the rest of Africa and the rest of the colonized globe. The case of Zimbabwe should be studied carefully. Decolonization comes in many forms and coming out of prison, however stage-managed, is just one small step in the direction of avoiding a manipulated peace and becoming an installed political class.

February, 1990.

18. Stiwanism: Feminism in an African Context

Preamble

There is a difficulty in having a feminist discourse in Africa today because of the context and backgrounds of certain issues, for instance, the issue of racism in the social sciences and scholarship on Africa in general, and in white feminist movements which want to see all other human social organizations as less developed and less evolved in the linear and social Darwinian scale often constructed in order to have a hierarchical superiority.[1] The African woman feminist has to be careful that she is not buying into this kind of racist discourse. Some white female feminist racial supremacists want to claim that the white woman is inherently ahead of all the women of the world in all areas of social being and social organization. This is, certainly, not the case.[2]

Then there is the difficulty of speaking against a background of Africans who think that race and class issues are more important than gender issues. They claim that black men and women need to unite against white hegemony, male and female. But, in my view, black men and black women cannot unite around conflicting interests and across antagonistic classes.[3] To think that this is possible is to be either romantic, hypocritical or dishonest, or perhaps just unintelligent. The same men who argue unity of black male and female against white hegemony will blithely relate to the white world in other contexts. I have written in another essay that even African male revolutionaries and social practitioners freely marry or date apolitical and conservative white women. They marry CIA agents and RCMP (Royal Canadian Mounted Police) workers.[4]

Some black men say to us that we should not read white feminists because this is a sign of domination and mental colonization, but they gladly and proudly read Hegel, Marx, Foucault, Bakhtin, Terry Eagleton, Frederick Jameson and other less distinguished theorists. They may argue that the reason they read them is not racial, but perspectual. Nonetheless, they read liberal humanists and other Western scholars who are as estranged from African cultures, if that is the argument, and as misrepresentational as any white feminist to whom they may care to point. I think as international scholars and sophisticated cosmopolitans, African women must read white feminists, but with discrimination, and with a critical sensitivity to their relevance or non-relevance, to the complexity and differences in our history, sociology and experience as different peoples. In the final analysis though, African women, I think, must theorize their own feminisms.[5]

Racism in the women's movement is often cited to discourage African women from talking about feminism. They say, "how can you work with racists who want to be new cultural imperialists." It is true that there is racism, but that has to be confronted differently. African women must still organize and confront the problems of gender in their own cultures, despite the racism in the international movement. I think that white feminists will continue to have to work on their own endemic and insidious racism which seems to be ever-present. It not only occurs when it is brutally obvious, as with events like lynching, but racism also exists in patterns of exclusivity, monopolization of resources, patronization, the exploitation of Third World women, physically, emotionally and intellectually. Racism exists in self-interested politicking and so on. These points have been made by other feminists before me like bell hooks in the U.S. and Sherona Hall in Canada.

There are, however, African men who see the positive aspects of the complex and paradoxical construction of the African woman in all our societies. Professor George Dei spoke on Afrocentricity and I think he noted this complexity in his talk. He speaks of the centrality of the African woman in many of our social patterns, in particular the matrilineal organization of society.[6] We cannot repeat enough that there is matrilinearity in Africa, not matriarchy. Matrilinearity refers to descent through the men in the mother's line. Also, Ali Mazrui has made an interesting distinction between being centered, being empowered and being liberated. I do not think, however, that Mazrui has a full and correct appreciation of the role and place of the African woman in traditional societies or even of traditional society in general.[7] I think, though, that the distinction which he makes is significant and helpful. Another male example is Thomas Sankara, the assassinated president of Burkina Faso, who was perhaps one of the most articulate speakers on the position of African women and her importance to African liberation. He comes in the tradition of African political leaders like Neto, Machel, and Cabral; that is, in the tradition of political thinkers who appreciate that there can be no liberation of African society without the liberation of African women. Contemporaneous liberation is not something that comes after the struggle has been won, as some others like to say.

At home, on the continent, African men seem to be often riled by the idea of equality between men and women. They are not opposed to equal opportunity, equal pay for equal work, or equal education, but with equality between men and women, they are uncomfortable. They say, "how can men and women be equal?" and look flabbergasted. Many love the parable about the five unequal fingers of the hand; an appeal to Nature, I guess. They think that men and women are not equal *essentially*. This is an issue on the continent— whether it is a matrilineal or patrilineal society. It seems that the woman *is seen* as subordinated in her very essence, to the man; in quality and specifically in marriage, which is a major site of women's subordination; her status and roles being multifaceted and varied outside marriage.

I think that this is also because African men seem to be locked into gender roles which they want to keep. They say, "a father cannot be equal to his daughter" or, "a husband cannot be equal to his wife." A Senegalese sociologist, Malick Ndiaye, said at the CAAS (Canadian Association of African Studies, 1990) conference that it is the tyranny of gender roles which hampers the women's movement in Africa. He says that men do not wish to change these roles. He goes on to say something controversial: that the tyranny of gender roles is one of the causes of the African man's incapacity to express tenderness in intimate relationships. Most African men are paralyzed by their gender roles. "A husband behaves this way toward a wife". A "father" does this; a "man" does that. Even in intimate relationships there are certain things "a husband" does and certain things "a woman" does. A husband cannot be spoken to in a certain way.

All theoreticians of African liberation have failed to confront the issue of gender within the family or to confront the family as a site for social transformation. They will talk about changing society, mobilizing Africa, but not about the issue of the relationship of men to women; gender relations. With the modernization of Africa, however, in my view, there has to be a new reordering of society, particularly at the level of family, because of erosions and changes within the indigenous family patterns stemming from new developments which have to be interrogated.

African women themselves have to re-examine those gender roles and not be opportunistic about them. African women sometimes accept those male gender roles which soften life for women. They must cease to want to exploit men financially or to burden the men within the family while talking about equality. African women need to educate themselves about the rights and responsibilities of liberal democracy in a modern nation-state for the woman as an independent individual and not as a dependent. If a woman thinks that she has the right to be independent and to earn her own money etc., then when she gets her paycheck and she is in a marital relationship, she must think of contributing to the home and family. We cannot speak of a liberation without responsibility in which a man pays the rent, the food for the home, expenses for the woman, and the woman keeps her paycheck. There is therefore, the question of accepting responsibility, particularly financial responsibility, if one is wholly committed to attaining equality with men.

One of the greatest opponents to the feminist movement in Africa is the group of women I will call "The Married Women

Incorporated". These married women are afraid to shake the status quo; they are afraid and want security through men; they are harsher on other women than men are; they cling to the vanishing respectability of being married. Some conservative men manipulate the situation by saying that if you are not married, you are not really a woman, and if you do not have children, you are not human. Privileging child-bearing in Africa is a matter of human ecology, the survival of the group and the species. The childless woman is emotionally protected in the concept of "mother in the community" and the practice of adoption and care-giving to other people's children. By accepting polygamy, the modern, middle class and Westernized woman often victimizes herself.

One finds that there are African women who want to keep the bridewealth, who want to keep what is called the "lobola" in Southern Africa. The bridewealth formerly called the "brideprice", was not a price, until the colonials tried to set prices in order to be able to do their books, making marriage gifts a kind of taxation, rationalizing the system that "a man must pay ten pounds or so many hundred francs." The colonialists introduced commercialization. Usually, the bridewealth was a kind of material benefits compensation to the family of the wife from the family of the groom. This is very different from the dowry, as in India, which goes from the bride's family to the groom's family to compensate the groom for taking on the responsibility of a woman. The dowry is a very different, in fact, opposite, concept. Bridewealth was a symbolic expression of the respect and valuation of a woman. There are African married women, African middle class and westernized women, who will argue that they want to have their bridewealth no matter how corrupted and commercialized it is; if they do not, their husbands will not respect them and treat them with the appropriate recognition that their family had officially and ceremonially handed them over. Yet, we in the feminist movement are saying that this attitude is an indication of lack of self-respect and independence because the modern corruption promotes the commodification of women.

Now—the issue of polygyny. There are modern, middle class

and westernized African women who collude with the institution of polygyny. These women want to be married at all costs and if they cannot find a single man, they will attach themselves to a married man. They also want to have children at all costs. At least they want a man who admits to the paternity of their children and helps with their care. Concepts of illegitimacy differ in Africa; in many societies, you are not illegitimate if your birth parents claim you. In Nigeria, single women speak of the benefits and comforts of having "a male umbrella". They say that it is better than being a single woman, living by herself. There is single parenthood in Africa, but very often the father of the children is around also. He is often acknowledged socially. I think women collude with polygamy because very often they are afraid they will not find a monogamous relationship and do not want to "be left growing fungi on their bodies in the house"; as they say in my language (ilemosu).

On the continent too, there is the paradox associated with the power of the female body as a sacred vessel. People still regard the woman's body as sacred. She can even use it for political action. She can threaten to curse while touching her breasts or her reproductive parts. If she threatens to strip and go naked, even government will back down. Recently, however, military governments are not backing down. In fact, some just round up the women and jail them.[8] But, if a woman threatens to strip and show a man her nakedness, he is scared and will do what she asks to avoid seeing the kind of breasts from which he fed. He will also avoid seeing the passage that he came through to enter the world. A woman's vagina is sacred. It is the passage through which all of us came into the world. In fact, the restraint against incest with one's mother, is that one does not go back into the passage through which one came headfirst. It is supposed to be a great abomination to want to insert yourself into a passage from which you came into the world. Some women want this power of the body and want to use it. For example, when they get angry with their children, they may threaten "unless I did not feed you with these breasts". With such talk, the men, particularly the sons, usually back off. This is one way to control a son. The enjoyment of pornography is mostly a newly acquired taste in Africa. The mutilation of women, as on American TV, is not yet a cultural pleasure.

The sacredness of women's bodies sometimes restrains men from abusing women, although violence against women is common and in some societies battery against women is even taken for granted. It was reported that in Kenya, the issue of women-beating was raised in parliament. One of the parliamentarians represented the view of many African men when he said, "But, how can you control women if you don't beat them." On the other hand, in even highly patrilineal societies, it is still often maintained that women's bodies are sacred to the point that you may not beat a woman because her body has produced children. A visitor to Nigeria, will often notice in public areas that the Nigerian woman is very quick to start fights; to grab men by the throat or by the robe (agbada) and shake them, wanting to fight. She somehow knows that the man fears condemnation if he beats her back; and people will say, "don't you have a mother? How dare you strike a woman who is a mother?" Women are only mostly beaten as wives.

The terror of women's bodies has been used effectively in Nigeria, with armed robbers who sometimes capture and threaten to shoot people. There are cases in which they have not shot the women because the robbers were scared. On the other hand, there are hardened armed robbers who are now part of the modern world, and have watched many videos and mafia films. Many of the scenes of armed robberies resemble mafia films and Hollywood situations; for example, robbers may shoot into a car and leave corpses around.[9] Some armed robbers even rape the women before they shoot them. In fact, rape has become common now in urban settings as a way to affront. The final affront you can give to a man is to come into the house and rape his wife and possibly his daughters in his presence. These are changes. Of course, the final affront is to the woman herself. In a patriarchal society, however, the affront to the woman is less emphasized or understood than the affront to the husband.

The sacredness of the woman's body and its products such as milk or menses, also has to be understood for there is a tendency to homogenize all women's histories and experiences.[10] It is not misogyny that causes African men especially, to fear women's menses, but a conceptualization of the female reproductive system and excretions and body parts as powerful and potent. Menstrual blood is believed to have the power to disrupt, interfere with, or cause to happen. Thus women's monthly blood is also considered very effective in making potions.

Finally, and unfortunately, lesbian and gay discourses have not yet received earnest attention in African thought. Same-sex sexuality in Africa is only beginning to be discussed. Some African feminists have argued that Africa does not know enough about her own sexuality, while there is still too much silence and silencing.

Feminism in an African Context

This very appropriate title was provided by Fatima Haidara and the African students at Virginia Technical Institute, Blacksburg, U.S.A. It opens up the issue of feminism at a very problematic and controversial point in African discourse on gender. People always want to know whether feminism is relevant to Africa. In thinking of Africa, one wonders, "what is an African context?" "What can feminism be in Africa?"

A broad range of attitudes about feminism in Africa today is being expressed by different kinds of persons and groups at different levels. For example, currently in Nigeria, right-wing women, most men, and apolitical women, like to quip that African women do not need liberation or feminism because they have never been in bondage. Progressive, political, and left-wing women, however, are saying that African women suffer subordination on two levels: as women, and as members of impoverished and oppressed classes where women are in the majority. That is the official position of Women in Nigeria (WIN), the organization with which I was involved in the founding.[11] The public position of the Federation of Muslim Women of Nigeria (FOMWAN) is that the woman has been liberated for thousands of years under the Shari'a law, never mind that Islam itself, a religion which demands our respect in its own right, has not been around for thousands of years. The point that the Federation of Muslim Women makes is that feminism is influenced by Western white feminists. They say things like, "it breeds pervasive traits like lesbianism.", (I don't know what is meant by that; "pervasive traits".) "...abstracting the individuals from all concrete and collective bonds; pitting the individuals against institutions, relativising and trivializing the family..."[12]

The point to note is that religious fundamentalisms in Africa, and fundamentalism as a worldwide movement, are issues to be looked into as they affect attitudes towards women, and the struggle for progressive conditions for women all over the world.

Our title, "Feminism in an African Context," also necessitates an interrogation of itself. We could ask, "what is feminism?" and "what is it in an African context?" What is the reality for African women?

When they think of Africa, most Africans think only of Black Africa or more correctly, if they would be honest, of their own little ethnic groups. When we say, "Africa," we mean "the Yorubas," "the Ibos," "the Kikuyu," "the Luo," "the Toucoulour," "the Serer," or "the Fulani," and so forth. We generalize from the characteristics of our own ethnic groups to describe the whole of the continent.

Some social scientists like to speak of "Black Africa" or "Africa south of the Sahara," but, what does "Black" mean in relation to, say, Libyans, or Egyptians or Moroccans who are white in Africa but are as black as people designated "black" in the United States. Again, North Africans who are considered white in America are darker than some high-colored African-Americans who can pass for white but are considered black in affirmative action forms. Obviously, being "black" is a political metaphor and importantly, skin color is not a useful, necessary and sufficient way to taxonomize Africans.

In view of the history of Africa and cross-cultural links across the Sahara, the reality of cultures and acculturations in Africa, and in view of countries like Chad and North Mali, which have an expanse into the Sahara, what does "sub-Saharan" mean? The term "sub-Saharan" itself is political. To repeat, Africa cannot be taxonomized in terms of color, which extends above the Sahara. Euro-American color notions cannot be easily transferred to a global context. North Africans are Africans. Africans think North Africans are black, but they are often considered white in the United States. Racism is a messy and unhealthy subject.

We must all avoid simplistic statements about Africa's reality, in particular, the reality of her political and social complexity. Therefore, when we speak of an "African context", do we mean all the countries of the geographical continent of Africa? This is what I like to mean when I use the term "Africa". This is a large piece to take on one's analytical plate, I admit. Our question then becomes: What is feminism in the context of Africa as I have defined it? We must define specificities. Again we cannot generalize Africa. Do we mean: a Christian or a Muslim Africa; Africa with indigenous religions; the Lusophone African countries which underwent liberation struggles; South Africa still under siege; independent African countries; Arab Africans; Black or White South Africans; the right-wing Inkatha elements, or white liberals; are the white leftists in the South African Communist Party included; Africans who adhere to pre-colonial values; or westernized Africans, by which we mean Africans with syncretized values?

With regard to color, and the following fact is particularly important for Africans of the diaspora, there are no color purities in Africa; if there ever were since the beginning of time. Everything, biology and culture, has been mixed or shall we say, "dynamized", by Africa's historical movements of peoples. These movements are not only the result of Western influence, as hegemonic Euro-Americans like to think. They have been going on since the beginning of time. Africa has been open to the world since the dawn of history.

In fact, history began with her, as archaeologists are saying. Some Western historiographers and other social scientists like to think and state that indigenous Africans were isolated from each other. In fact, Africa has not been isolated but has been at the heart of human concourse and interactions in those early times when so much was going on, and from which events

Europe was isolated. The interactions were between the then civilized peoples of the world: China, India, South America (the Incas, Mayans and Aztecs), Southeast Asia, the Middle East, the countries of the Mediterranean and Africa. Much later Europe emerged from her Middle Ages to learn science (e.g. mathematics), technology, and many arts from the rest of the world. Europe enriched herself from the world of people of color to have her Renaissance. Europe's triumph after the 1400's was not due to superior intellect or courage but to the capacity for acts of unbelievable cruelty and political treachery such as the world had perhaps never known before. It was Europe, not Africa, which was isolated from the world before the 1400's.

We tend to think of Egypt as being outside of Africa. Some of us have been socialized to think of Egypt as in the Middle East. That is the result of political scholarship. Egypt is within Africa and gives to and was influenced by the Sudan. Egypt is also connected to and influenced by, African countries farther South and West. From North Africa, it is only across the Sahara to West Africa. On the other hand, the world connects with, did and still does influence East Africa and South Africa from across the Indian Ocean. These are some of the currents of movements and cultures in which Africa has been the central point in both receiving and giving.

How complex it is to speak of an African context! Africa or Africans cannot be generalized. We must always be aware of specifics while we describe our criteria for taxonomies. We must acknowledge our delimitations and realize always that there are many kinds of Africans. We cannot essentialize blackness, even on the African continent itself. Race, class and gender, among other variables must mediate our discourses as they mediate our understanding of ourselves and each other. Race and class also mediate gender for the three categories intersect each other at points. Let us simplify our task by thinking of the continent of Africa, rather than our own familiar home cultures, and let us try to identify patterns on that continent. Needless to say, such a discussion will not be exhaustive. We can only identify patterns and themes, but we will be extrapolating from the whole continent.

What is my own location in this epistemological cartography? I am speaking as a middle-aged African woman of Yoruba descent; now middle-class but from traditional aristocratic origins, alas; born by Christian and of a color, "black," which is devalued. Yet I do not think of myself as "black" nor do I refer to myself as "a black woman." This is not because I do not love my color or the idea of being black, but because I was not socialized to describe myself physically and in terms of color. Africans do not suffer from "colorism," to use Alice Walker's phrase; they do not suffer from the colorism of the Western world that Gayatri Spivak calls "chromatism."[13] We do not have a mentality of animal husbandry; of classing or grading people in terms of how they look: the color of their eyes or hair as if we were running kennels.

Africans, in Africa's non-racially organized countries, that is, outside the settler territories, tend to see themselves in terms of culture; how people think and behave. You are the culture that you carry, despite your color. Hence, a black person in color could be white mentally. It is not that Africans do not recognize racial difference. They see it but they do not assume that a person is necessarily African from the way that he/she looks. They do not privilege one kind of a color over another. They do not privilege whiteness over blackness, nor do they essentialize. I am talking now of the peasant majority Africans, not middle-class Africans. Peasant Africans attribute superiority to whites in the realm of technology. They do not, however, think that the white person is inherently and essentially superior to them as a human being. They know that s/he has certain cultural things which they admire and which they want—the automobiles and airplanes, blenders, to minimize the labor of grinding, yam pounding machines—but they do not think that these gadgets make her/him intrinsically superior. The problem of accepting superiority is usually one of middle class Africans who have undergone colonial education. The middle-class African may tend to think that whites are superior. In any case, problems of identity and issues of negritude are issues of the middle-class. The level of the colonial mentality of the African will dictate the level of a sense of inferiority that he or she has. Usually, you will find that the less Westernized a person, the more self-assured that person is.

Because culture, not color, determines identity, most Africans, use many terms such as: h/she is white or Oyinbo or Mzungu or toubab or brofo, to describe a person who is physiognomically black but "white" in behavior and mentality.

In the West, I am a "woman of color." Personally, I do not know what that phrase means. It sounds like some rare bird or creature of Nature. I am Molara Ogundipe-Leslie, a middle-aged Yoruba and Nigerian woman. I have included middle-aged because among my people as among many African peoples, a woman's status is mediated and improved by age, economics, kinship roles and by the class she comes from as well as birth and her achievements in her lived experience. Therefore, it is in my interest to emphasize my middle-agedness, in fact, my oldness, and not try to compete with teenagers. In the West, however, I find that the first and constant variable for me is race: a "woman of color," a "black woman," a "brown woman," a "chocolate woman."

The subject of feminism is no less complex to define than the phrase, "an African context." The chosen title of this talk is good for another reason: that it raises very common but important controversies in Africa today, namely, "Does feminism exist in Africa?" Should it exist in Africa? What are the definitions of feminism? For us? For me? Perhaps I can reverse this definitional task by naming what feminism is not, in order to confront the notion embedded in the counter-discourses to feminism in Africa today.

In answer to the usual reactions of most African men, right-wing and apolitical women:

1. Feminism is not a cry for any one kind of sexual orientation and I am not homophobic or heterosexist. Sexual practice in Africa tends to *be* private and *considered* private. Same-sex sexuality still awaits more attention and research.

    Homosexuals are not persecuted by the State in West Africa.

2. Feminism is not the reversal of gender roles, "gender" being defined simply as socially constructed identities and roles. It is not only the doing of dishes or the washing of napkins

as my Malawian poet friend thinks. I shall share a part of the poem which he addressed to me. I should note that we used to have many arguments and an intertextual intellectual life in Nigeria.
The poem is called:

Letter to a Feminist Friend (an excerpt)

My world has been raped
looted
and squeezed
by Europe and America...
AND NOW
the women of Europe and America
after drinking and carousing
on my sweat
rise up to castigate
 and castrate
their menfolk
from the cushions of a world
I have built!

Why should they be allowed
to come between us?
You and I were slaves together
uprooted and humiliated together
Rapes and lynchings...

do your friends "in the movement"
understand these things?...

No, no, my sister,
 my love,
first things first!
Too many gangsters
still stalk this continent...

When Africa
at home and across the seas

is truly free
there will be time for me
and time for you
to share the cooking
and change the nappies—
till then,
first things first![14]

I use this poem at the beginning of my essay on women in Nigeria which is published in *Sisterhood is Global* (edited by Robin Morgan), a collection of essays by women of different countries. Again, I want to draw your attention to the use of the first person in his poem. It is his world that has been raped, that endured the slave trade, colonialism, imperialism, and neo-colonialism. He is the Prometheus figure. He does not yet have time for women's rights. The world has been built by him and he must attend to those pressing issues. His position is the usual one of "divide and rule" strategists. Divide and rule the women of the world who are perhaps united around gender oppressions. Women may differ about strategies and methods, but they do not differ on basic assumptions: that women are oppressed as women and they are oppressed as the majority members of subordinate classes which are also in the majority. But his position is almost typical of most of the men of the continent.

3. Feminism is not penis envy or gender envy; wanting to be a man as they like to say to us. "Well, do you want to be a man? You can join us if you want to." Or, "Whatever you do, you can never have a penis." A car mechanic once told me that I could not fix my car because I did not have a penis.
4. Feminism is not necessarily oppositional to men. It argues, rather, that a woman's body is her inherent property,[15] "not to be owned, used, and dumped by men," as radical theology feminists are saying.
5. Feminism is not, "dividing the genders," as they say to us in Africa. It is not dividing the race or "the struggle," — whatever that overused word means.
6. It is not parrotism of Western women's rhetoric.

7. It is not opposed to African culture and heritage, but argues that culture is dynamically evolving and certainly not static; that culture should not be immobilized in time to the advantage of men as most men in Africa want it to be.

8. Feminism is not a choice between extreme patriarchy on the one hand or hateful separatism from men on the other.

What then is this feminism? I have made these rejoinders because they touch on the points that some African men make to counter our feminist discourses in Africa. We are accused of the attributes implied by their criticism. Often the argument is that feminism is not necessary in Africa because gender was balanced in an idyllic African past, which is their own creation. African feminists are said to be merely the parrots of Western women. Race and nationalism are used in bad faith to attack gender. Sometimes race, nationalism, and class are brought together to attack gender politics. Feminist concerns are said to be the predilections of Westernized women like myself or Ifi Amadiume or Filomina Steady, for example.[16] Feminist concerns are, then, not those of the great rural and faithful African women who are "the true African women" who are happy as they are and have always been. But what do research and analysis tell us about these newly discovered and glamorized creatures; "the rural women of Africa?" Certainly not that "rural," poor women are happy with the status quo and desire no change.

Feminism can be defined by its etymological roots. Femina is "woman" in Latin. Feminism, an ideology of woman; any body of social philosophy about women. This definition of feminism gives us enough leeway to encompass various types of feminisms: right-wing, left-wing, centrist, left of center, right of center, reformist, separatist, liberal, socialist, Marxist, nonaligned, Islamic, indigenous, etc. Believe me, all these feminisms exist. Nawal el Saadawi is an Islamic socialist feminist. So, one question could be, "What is feminism for you." What is your feminism? Do you, in fact, have an ideology of women in society and life? Is your feminism about the rights of women in society? What is the total conception of women as agents in human society— her conditions, roles and statuses—her recognition and acknowledgement? Generally, feminism, however, must always have a political and activist spine to its form. If we take feminism to imply all these, is the African woman on the African continent, in an African context without problems in all these areas?

For those who say that feminism is not relevant to Africa, can they truthfully say that the African woman is all right in all these areas of her being and therefore does not need an ideology that addresses her reality, hopefully and preferably, to ameliorate that reality? When they argue that feminism is foreign, are these opponents able to support the idea that African women or cultures did not have ideologies which propounded or theorized woman's being and provided avenues and channels for women's oppositions and resistance to injustice within their societies? Certainly, these channels existed. Are the opponents of feminism willing to argue that indigenous African societies did not have avenues and strategies for correcting gender imbalance and injustice? Will they argue that these aspects of social engineering could only have come from white or Euro-American women? Are they saying that African women cannot see their own situations and demand change without guidance from white women? Nationalism and race pride, I know, will make our men beat a retreat at this question and they had better beat that retreat. The issue is that there were indigenous feminisms. There were indigenous patterns within traditional African societies for addressing the oppressions and injustices to women.

So, what kind of feminism exists in an African context? In view of all I have said above, in view of all that I have argued as well as the realities of Africa, we should more correctly say: What *feminisms* exist in Africa? Indeed, there are many feminisms, depending on the center from which one is speaking or theorizing. These feminisms have to be theorized around the junctures of race, class, caste and gender; nation, culture and ethnicity; age, status, role and sexual orientation. Certainly more research is needed to discover what African women themselves, particularly, the working classes and the peasantry think about themselves as women, what ideology they possess and what agenda they have for themselves, daily and historically.

Once we agree that an ideology of women and about women is necessary and has always existed in Africa, we can proceed to ask if these existent ideologies remain relevant or need to be changed. Our opportunistic and irredentist compatriots who argue culture and heritage when it serves their interests, should consider whether our inherited cultures should be taken hook, line and sinker, or should be subjected to change where necessary. Should we, when necessary, change the notion that man is always superior to woman, hence, boys should go to school and girls should only go when they can, when there is money to "waste" and no work to be done at home or in the farms and markets? Should we apply the sexist ideas in the Bible, without criticism, with preference for Old Testament ideas and the Pauline section of the New Testament, stressing only the verses on male dominance? Should we adapt Koranic ideas to modern times or continue to beat the recalcitrant woman lightly as said in the fourth Sura of the Koran. (If your woman does not listen, first admonish her then, sexually withdraw from her and finally beat her "lightly.") How light is light? Is not the issue the proprietary right to beat her in the first place? Should culture be placed in a museum of minds or should we take authority over culture as a product of human intelligence and consciousness to be used to improve our existential conditions? Should we preach cultural fidelity only when it does not affect us negatively, which is usually the position of African men who wish to keep only those aspects of culture which keep them dominant?

For the rest of this essay, I shall try to indicate what some of the outspoken African women are saying about feminism in Africa. Some quite outstanding women like Buchi Emecheta, say they are not feminists without saying why. Others like the Nigerian writer, Flora Nwapa, say that they are not feminists, but they are "womanists". There are still other views: the great and late South African writer, Bessie Head, says in her posthumous essays collected under the title *A Woman Alone*, that in the world of the intellect where she functions as a writer and an intellectual, feminism is not necessary because the world of the intellect is neither male nor female.[17] I think she is deceived or perhaps deluded on this point by the post-romantic and Victorian patriarchal notion and myth about the world of the intellect being sexless. This, women know to be a myth, although it has been sold to all the women of the world. We know how male sexism actually functions in the world of the intellect or in the world of "the life of the mind" as they say. Bessie Head, in my view, expresses a false consciousness often expressed by successful middle-class women of all cultures (including African women who proudly and aggressively announce that their achievement has taken place outside of their identity as women). "I am just a writer, not a woman writer," "I am a professor of physics," "an astronaut," "a prime minister, not a woman" and I wonder what is that? What is that neuter thing? But notice that only women engage in that kind of rhetoric. It speaks volumes that only women make that kind of statement. Have you ever heard a man say, "I'm just a professor, not a man." "I'm just a professor," "a mathematician," "a tycoon," "a president of the United States, but not a man, not a man at all." Perhaps we need to deconstruct that formulation elsewhere.

Let us now, however, consider the theories of some of the most visible African women who hold that feminism is relevant to the African context. A summary of their positions indicates some common denominators:

1. That feminism need not be oppositional to men. It is not about adversarial gender politics.
2. That women need not neglect their biological roles.
3. That motherhood is idealized and claimed as a strength by African women and seen as having a special manifestation in Africa. Davies has asked whether African women have specially cornered motherhood.[18]
4. That the total configuration of the conditions of women should be addressed rather than obsessing with sexual issues.
5. That certain aspects of women's reproductive rights take priority over others.
6. That women's conditions in Africa need to be addressed in

the context of the total production and reproduction of their society and that scenario also involves men and children. Hence, there has always been an emphasis on economic fulfillment and independence in African feminist thinking.

7. That the ideology of women has to be cast in the context of the race and class struggles which bedevil the continent of Africa today; that is, in the context of the liberation of the total continent.

It is this generally holistic attitude of African women to feminism which often separates them from their Western sisters.

Organizationally, women in AAWORD,[19] our pan-African Organization of women, Women in Nigeria (WIN), in ZARD, in Zambia,[20] the Arab Solidarity Front organized from Egypt for the Arab world,[21] African members of DAWN[22] and African Women in the World Council of Churches working on the Ecumenical Decade have expressed such holistic perspectives. Individual women in their writings have also theorized holistically in a way, not necessarily disruptive of their insertions into their own cultures and their identities as African women. Fatima Mernissi, for instance, of Morocco, as early as the sixties underscored the patriarchal undergirding of Islam.[23] Mercy Oduyoye of Ghana and Nigeria does radical theology in Christianity and is one of the foremost African theologians[24]. Nawal el Saadawi of Egypt, in her book *The Hidden Face of Eve,*[25] theorizes a feminism within the parameters of Islam, socialism and social justice for the poor. Filomina Steady of Sierra Leone in her introduction to *The Black Woman: Cross-Culturally,*[26] and her chapter in *Women in Africa and the African Diaspora,* edited by Terborg-Penn, Rushing, et. al,(1987) identifies the peasant woman as the original feminist in her self-assertive and empowering roles of producer and reproducer. She concludes by calling for a humanistic feminism that encompasses men, women and children. Ama Ata Aidoo of Ghana, a writer, Micere Mugo, professor of literature from Kenya, writer, playwright and poet and Molara Ogundipe-Leslie locate their feminisms within race, class and the international economic order. Bilikusu Yusuf and Ayesha Imam write about Hausa society in Nigeria while Achola Pala Okeyo writes about Kenya. Other voices exist like Ifi Amadiume and theorize our feminisms. Miriam Tlali's long answer to the question, "how do people feel about feminism in South Africa," is quite informative:

> As you know, up to this moment I'm still the only black woman who has ventured to write about feminism. There is no equality. If you do something out of the ordinary men are more inclined to see you as a kind of 'fellow man' than to acknowledge that you have accomplished something important as a woman. That would present too much of a threat. In South Africa white women have more rights now than they used to. Their legal status has been improved to the extent that their husbands no longer have to sign for the purchase of a refrigerator, or a car or for a contract. But that's still the case for us. I wasn't allowed to sign my own contract with the publisher. My husband has had to sign, even though it was my book! Even though we're both fighting against white male domination, there is no real solidarity between black women and white women, because we're fighting on different levels. Apartheid stands in the way of true sisterhood in South Africa. This was the conclusion reached by an English journalist who came here to study the question. She asked white women why they didn't fight alongside their black sisters to help improve the position of black women, who lag so far behind. The answer was, "Our men wouldn't be pleased if we were to stand up to the authorities for that sort of reason." Which means that in the end white men decide which activities 'their' women are permitted to take part in. We try to set up our own women's organizations but, as I said in the beginning, it's an uphill struggle. Just trying to keep your head above water seems to take up all your time. Black men don't give their wives much encouragement either. A lot of men don't want their wives to read things they don't know anything about.[27]

Mamphela Rampele of South Africa[28] and Dangaremba of Zimbabwe[29] locate feminism within the complexities of race, class and gender, geographical location and the collusion of women with the oppression of women within patriarchy. Dangarembga argues like other writers that women's silence needs to be broken, that women need to "transform silence into language and action," in the words of the eloquent African-American poet, Audre Lorde.[30]

All over Africa, African feminists are theorizing our feminisms and we will do well to listen to them. Coming home to me, what do I say about African feminism? In one essay from *Presence Africaine* published in 1987 in a special edition on *Images of African Women*,[31] an essay which I had written as a conference address to the Association of African Women for Research and Development in Dakar, Senegal in 1981, I implied that feminism is relevant to Africa because African women are oppressed as women by race, class and other realities. I discuss how the African woman has more than the four mountains that Mao Tse Tung theorized as resting on the backs of Chinese women: namely, colonization, feudalism, backwardness and the Chinese man. In her case, the African woman has six mountains on her back: one, oppression from outside in the form of colonialism and neo-colonialism; two, oppression from traditional structures: Feudal, communal, slave-based, etc.; three, her own backwardness; four, the African man; five, her color or her race and six, the woman herself because she has internalized all these oppressions. African feminism for me, therefore, must include issues around the woman's body, her person, her immediate family, her society, her nation, her continent and their locations within the international economic order because those realities in the international economic order determine African politics and impact on the women. There is no way we can discuss the situation of the African woman today without considering what the IMF policies and the World Bank are doing to her status and her conditions.

Later, in another essay, a discussion of women in Nigeria in *Sisterhood is Global*,[32] I concluded that it would seem (to those who are not good listeners) that I am arguing that men are the enemy. I say that individual men are not the enemy, but that the subordination and oppressions of women are systemic, hence we need to look at structural patterns which distribute social justice between the two sexes. I said, "No, men are not the enemy. The enemy is the total system in Nigeria which is a jumble of neo-colonialist and feudalist, even slave-holding structures, and social attitudes. As women's liberation is but an aspect of the need to liberate the total society from dehumanization, it is the social system which must change. Men, however, do become enemies when they seek to retard or even block these necessary historical changes; when, for selfish power interests, they claim as their excuse "culture and heritage," as if human societies are not constructed by human beings; when they plead and laugh derisively about the natural enduring inferiority of women; when they argue that change is impossible because history is static which it is not.

I have since advocated the word "Stiwanism," instead of feminism, to bypass these concerns and to bypass the combative discourses that ensue whenever one raises the issue of feminism in Africa.

The creation of the new word is to deflect energies from constantly having to respond to charges of imitating Western feminism and, in this way, conserve those energies, to avoid being distracted from the real issue of the conditions of women in Africa. The new word describes what similarly minded women and myself would like to see in Africa. The word "feminism" itself seems to be a kind of red rag to the bull of African men. Some say the word is by its very nature hegemonic, or implicitly so. Others find the focus on women in themselves somehow threatening. Still others say it is limiting to their perspectives, whatever those are. Some, who are genuinely concerned with ameliorating women's lives sometimes feel embarrassed to be described as "feminist," unless they are particularly strong in character. The embarrassment springs from being described by a word which encodes women (in "femina") so directly. So effective are the years of phallocratic socialization! Be a Stiwanist. I am a Stiwanist.

"Stiwa" is my acronymn for *Social Transformation Including Women in Africa*. This new term describes my agenda for women in Africa without having to answer charges of imitativeness or having to constantly define our agenda on the African continent in relation to other feminisms, in particular, white Euro-American feminisms which are unfortunately, under siege by everyone. This new term "STIWA" allows me to discuss the needs of African women today in the tradition of the spaces and strategies provided in our indigenous cultures for the social being of women. My thesis has always been that indigenous feminisms also existed in Africa and we are busy researching them and bringing them to the fore now. "STIWA" is about the inclusion of African women in the contemporary social and political transformation of Africa. Be a "Stiwanist."

I am sure there will be few African men who will oppose the concept of including women in the social transformation of Africa, which is really the issue. Women have to participate as co-partners in social transformation. I think that feminism is the business of both men and women anywhere, *and* in Africa. I think that all men need to be progressive feminists, committed to a socially just society, wherein a woman can realize herself to her fullest potential, if she so chooses. The right to choose, for me, is the definition of liberation, "freedom," if you like. The right to have options and to choose. All black men in Africa or in the diaspora need to be liberatory feminists to ensure a fuller life for their mothers, daughters and sisters. I am saying this because it is very often said that feminism is not relevant to Africa or relevant to African men or to the diaspora. It is this belief that makes the organization WIN (Women in Nigeria), of which I am a founding member, advocate the membership of men in its constitution, and men do participate in the organization. There are male feminists who are members of WIN. The feminist agenda everywhere in the world must include men and mobilize men in order for us to attain a more successful completion of the work of humanizing society.

I ended my essay on women in Nigeria with a stanza from one of my poems which says:

How long shall we speak to them
Of the goldness of mother, of difference without bane
How long shall we say, another world lives
Not spinned on the axis of maleness
But rounded and wholed, charting through
Its many runnels, its justice distributive.[33]

Finally, I shall share with you some of my poetry. What does my poetry say? It generally expresses some of my emotions and thoughts about being a woman, a mother, an intellectual and a creative artist in Africa, inserted into a global economic order which marginalizes my country and my people and the realization of our full potential as human beings. A world order which makes everything harder, even hardest for an African to do, a world order which considers us as sources of cheap labor, not deserving of even compensation for that labor and a sharing of the resources, not to speak of respect and dignity. I say in some of my poems how we must understand our past so that we can understand our present. How the African middle-class must be responsible to its peoples. How the ruling class must be responsible to its citizenry or they will betray their historic mission and certainly not fulfill it, to paraphrase Fanon. Many Africans feel that the middle-classes have already betrayed their historic mission.

I write about how women, in particular, women of the middle-class must overcome their false consciousness, demystify their minds, and take an interest to understand their societies. That is, get political, get interested in things around them. Don't just read fashion magazines. Don't read only the soft part of the newspapers, the "human angle" stories, the gossip, the scandal. Take an interest in society, not only in your immediate family. Get out. Get involved.

The first poem in my book of poems is entitled "To a Jane Austen Class."[34] At Ibadan University in Nigeria I taught Literature in English. I make a point of calling it "Literature in English" as opposed to "English Literature." "Literature in English" means literature written by any people in English, not literature from Beowulf to Eliot or Ted Hughes. The students, because of the kinds of mystifications, the kind of colonial education based on hidden information, the kind of epistemological experience one gets as a colonialized person, do not always see how what they are studying relates to their lives. They do not see how the wealth and the leisure of the people in Jane Austen are somehow related to the poverty of the people in Africa in that period of history. How the jewels and the emeralds in the crown of the queen of England which people admire, for instance, are the result of the colonial plundering of India and other parts of the so-called Empire of the British, including Nigeria for that matter. It is hard for them to see how we have anything to do with the Royal Family whose pictures are on everybody's walls at home, and whose personal lives everybody used to follow and still follow with great interest.

To A "Jane Austen" Class at
Ibadan University

> "Sew the old days for us, our fathers
> that we may wear them." — Kofi Awoonor

I greet you in your innocence
protected quite from time's insults
the agonies of flogged races, the
blood debt tumultuous floods our lands
our souths and hearts across the seas
where hatreds stalk like cougars

I salute the hope in your eyes
the faith between your brows as words
untried fall out
your gleaming teeth like touch of
nails on glass

sons of farmers - descendants of slavers - born of traders
in oil and liberty - offspring of riverain folk who plied to
horror ships with eyes quick white in hope - ask why the
Austen folk carouse all day and do no work - play cards
at noon and dance the while - the while the land vanished

behind closures - mothers' seeds into holds or marts -
and pliant life into pits - and in the south our souths, the
sorrow songs rake the skies - while death the autocrat
stalks both bond and free?

Have you heard of the fastnesses
- the fastnesses of human refusal?

Celebrate life, not death!

Do you ask why India grieves?
From whence the much-loved stones
in your much-loved crowns in London?
Do you tie your rote-learned tales of
the Navigator's men, Clive's antics,
routes traced and gained to time spent
and time stolen in Mansfield Park?
The gracious receivings, promenades
and tea-soaked evenings to mother's
hard palms, her meatless dishes,
grandfather's goitre and our madness
at history's noon-time?

Sew the old days
Sew the old days that we may wear them
to dance through coming storms
our steps detoning.

My good friend, Felix Mnthali read that poem and wrote a
reply. I think I should do him this favor by at least mentioning
a good poem of his. When I saw him again years later in
Zimbabwe he said, "you have done me a great deal of harm"
because everywhere he goes in the world, from Sweden to New
Zealand, the feminists always come up to him and say, "I don't
agree with your poem. We read your poem in Molara
Ogundipe's essay." So I said to him, "Well, I warned you. You
don't just jump into feminist discourses without knowing what
the arguments are." However, in this poem he writes a reply to
"To a Jane Austen Class" and the poem is entitled "The

Strangle-Hold of English Lit. (for Molara Ogundipe-Leslie)"[35]
Another poem of mine about the African elite is entitled
"Song at the African Middle-Class". It is very popular and
much anthologized. I wish they would anthologize other ones.
"Song at the African Middle-Class" was written for Augustine
Neto, the first prime minister of Angola.

we charge through the skies of disillusion,
seeking the widening of eyes, we gaze at chaos,
speak to deadened hearts and ears stopped with
commerce. We drift around our region of clowns,
walking on air as dreams fly behind our eyes.
we forage among broken bodies, fractured minds
to find just ways retraced and new like beaten cloth.

and if they come again
will they come again?
and if they come again
will they dance this time?
will the new egungun dance once more
resplendent in rich-glassed cloth?
will they be of their people's needs,
rise to those needs, settle whirling rifts
salve, O, festering hearts?
will they say when they come
O my people, O my people, how to love you delicately?

Finally, I have a long poem for the middle-class African
woman who is sitting on a keg of gunpowder, a casualty of history and as confused as most middle-class women in the world
who usually have a lot of problems. The poem was inspired by
a class reunion of middle-class women who, after years, had
come together. You know what happens at those reunions
where men or women come back years later, pretending to celebrate the school, but they are really more interested to see how
far each person has gone since school; they wonder who is a
political president's wife and who is president of a company,
who now rides a Mercedes-Benz and who is riding a BMW. As

they say in East Africa, "who has become a 'Wabenzie', the people of the Mercedes-Benz," and in Ghana, "who drives a Be My Wife (BMW)," a most popular gift that men allegedly give their female lovers.

When Father Experience Hits
With His Hammer (Song for the
Middle Class African Woman)

Lead in cry:

This is but a part, a first part only,
of the story of the woman bourgeoise.

.....
So we meet and infrequently
trading sorrows, stories, myths,
exchanging our marks of Cain,
our scarlet letters and dreams
aborted...

So many years ago...
So many years when we gamboled
as children and hoped for Eden,
in our various glorious prisons
named boarding schools, hoping for
Eden...

There we dreamt about
the tall, black and handsome
like Heathcliff. Was he
African to us? Did he look
like the men we knew?
like our fathers and brothers?

Or we thrilled to blonde
blue-eyed dreams, identified
with white winner-masters,
who strode through Edgar Wallace,

Rider Haggard, and Joseph Conrad.

There would be no more polygamy
in our world, no more pain,
for we were special...
Polygamy was for natives, illiterates
and all such creatures. Our men would
come a-gliding, clouds of snow behind them,
moving phantomly to the sounds of violins,
looking like Tony Curtis, Fred Astaire and
the Duke of Edinburgh!

They will lead us away, they will;
To monogamous havens
And True Romance Bliss.

So thirty years after, we stare at
each other with unbelieving eyes,
casualties of wars we know not,
children of Mother Experience
(or Father Experience)
Who hits with a hammer.
And we smile bleakly, defiant,
heroic, trading our mutual griefs,
thirty years after, while our
eyes shine with mutually integrated
woe or mutually integrated strength,
indentured to pain,
gay in heroic suffering which we think
is our fate inalienable and our mother's fates.

Or we hide our mutual griefs
While strange lights glint in our eyes
and suffering moves like egg-yolk,
And we smile and we fantasize and lie
And strut away to accept more...
perhaps...tomorrow, perhaps.

Or we cling to the children

And we lie about them; weave
ourselves and reasons round
their blameless necks,
claiming motherhood
where only fear lurks.

More truly we seek the space
our mothers had, the space within
and space without,
spaces emotional and spaces economic,
not confoundable with charades...
we confound the spaces sought
with charades of Western chivalry,
and monogamy, ignorant as we are
of the binds, the shackles,
the chattel life of the envied
Western woman, of middle class living
her hidden humiliations, emotional and legal
before this time and only some time ago;
housekeeper, cook and nurse,
secretary, chattel and whore
to *Mr. Husband*
swoppable and indentured for life,
till recently; the human, walking
Rent-A-Girl.

We knew not this for
the teachers of empire and
people of the church
conspired as always
to bend the truth and

flash their lies:
"all Western constructs
social, intellectual
religious, political
are by nature superior
to anything dreamt
or done by

people of colour...

So we envied the chattels
their rituals in bondage
who owned not their time,
not to speak of themselves.

And thirty years after,
we meet and we boast
and we giggle like babies
and scuttle back home
to our fancy class prisons
to please more the masters,
to win by cajoling,
to seduce oppressors
and demeaning systems
with our best, best behavior.

But when was the master
ever seduced from power?
When was a system ever broken
by acceptance?
When will the BOSS
hand you power with love?
At Jo'burg, at Cancun or the U.N?

No, we seek not to know
and seek not to act,
we avoid the political;
astounded or dancing,
we flower or fatten
in general un-knowing
or worry the supernatural
when Father Experience...
he hits with a hammer.[36]

Notes

1. I use "social Darwinism" in a sense that includes Karen Sacks's

definition in *Sisters and Wives : The Past and Future of Social Equality* (Urbana & Chicago: University of Illinois Press, 1982), 3, but I also include and emphasize the sense of a social evolution, imagined as reaching towards Euro-American ideals.

2. Some of the most pungent and fulsome critiques of Euro-American feminism are to be found in Chandra Talpade Mohanty's "Under Western Eyes & Feminist Scholarship and Colonial Discourses," *Third World Women and the Politics of Feminism* (Bloomington: Indiana University Press, 1991), 51–80. Reprinted from *Feminist Review* (Autumn 1988) 30 and Valerie Amos and Pratibha Parmar, "Challenging Imperial Feminism," *Feminist Review* 17, Special Issue: *Many Voices, One Chant: Black Feminist Perspectives.* (Autumn, 1984), 3–19.

3. See the position of some Nigerian leftist and socialist feminists in *Women in Nigeria Today* (London: Zed Press, 1985) Introduction.

4. See part II, ch. 3 in this volume, "African Marxists, Women and a Critique of Everyday Life."

5. A group of us, black feminists, are expressing such an effort in a text, *Theorizing Black Feminisms*, eds., James and Busia (N.Y. : Routledge and Kegan Paul, 1993).

6. George Dei, "Afrocentricity and Critical Pedagogy," Unpublished Paper of OISE (Ontario Institute of Studies in Education), Seminar on Critical Pedagogy, February 1992. To appear as "Afrocentricity: A Cornerstone of Pedagogy," in *Anthropology and Education Quarterly* (September, 1993).

7. See the debate between Mazrui and Ogundipe-Leslie on African women and gender studies published back to back in *Research in African Literatures* 24.1 (Spring, 1993). A longer version will appear in the Proceedings of the African Literature Association Conference (Seattle, Washington: 1992).

8. Nigerian women have used this threat effectively with military governments. Reports were that the threats did not work in the May riots of 1989.

9. In 1992, a certain criminal who named himself SHINA RAMBO for months terrorized Lagos, her environs and the police force allegedly with modern weaponry like sub-machine guns.

10. There have been attempts to equalize African attitudes to women's menses and reproductive parts or excretions to Judaic or Islamic attitudes. African attitudes, however, spring from attaching mystic *power* to women's emissions, not contempt or hatred.

11. *Women in Nigeria Today*, ed., WIN Collective (London: Zed Press, 1985) Introduction.

12. Bilikisu Yusuf, "Hausa-Fulani Women: The State of the Struggle," *Hausa Women in the Twentieth Century*, eds. Catherine Coles and Beverly Mack (Madison: University of Wisconsin Press, 1991) 90–108. Gives a history of FOMWAM in Nigeria. See also Murad Khurram, "On the Family" *Muslim World Book Review* 5 (1984) for some Muslim positions.
13. Gayatri Spivak, *The Post-Colonial Critic: Interviews, Strategies and Dialogues* (N.Y. & London: Routledge and Kegan Paul, 1990), 62.
14. Felix Mnthali, "Letter to a Feminist Friend," the poem will appear in an as yet unpublished volume entitled *Beyond the Echoes*.
15. See brochure of the World Council of Churches, on the Ecumenical Decade Solidarity with Women.
16. Ifi Amadiume, *Male Daughters, Female Husbands* (London: Zed Press, 1987) and Filomena Steady, *The Black Woman Cross-Culturally* (Cambridge, MA: Schenkman, 1981) see Bibliography. Steady "African Feminism, a Worldwide Perspective," *Women in Africa and the African Diaspora*, eds., Harley, Rushing and Terbog-Penn (Washington, D.C.: Howard University Press, 1987).
17. Bessie Head, *A Woman Alone: Autobiographical Writings* (London: Heinemann, 1990) 95.
18. Carole Boyce Davies, "Motherhood in the Works of Male and Female Igbo Writers," *Ngambika: Studies of Women in African Literature* (Trenton, NJ: Africa World Press, 1986), 241–256. See also the introduction to the book.
19. AAWORD/AFARD - Association of African Women for Research and Development/ Association des Femmes Africaines pour les Researches et Development founded by some us finally in 1977 with the initial headquarters in Dakar, Senegal. We had founding planning meetings at Wellesley College, U.S.A. and Lusaka, Zambia before the 1977 planning meeting in Dakar.
20. ZARD - Zambian Association for Research and Development. National branches of AAWORD were constitutionally empowered to name their own groups.
21. Arab Solidarity Front was founded by Nawal el Sadaawi who has been a founding member of AAWORD and a Vice-President.
22. DAWN - Development Alternatives for Women in a New Era, a third world network of women founded by women including Devaki Jain, my colleague in *Sisterhood is Global* and the initial *Women for a Meaningful Summit*. Nigeria has a branch of DAWN of which I am also a founding member.
23. Fatima Mernissi, *Beyond the Veil: Male-Female Dynamics in*

Modern Muslim Society (Bloomington & Indianapolis: Indiana University Press, 1987).
24. M.A. Oduyoye, *Hearing and Knowing: Theological Reflections on Christianity in Africa* (New York: Orbis, 1986).
25. Nawal el Saadawi, *The Hidden Face: Women in the Arab World* (London: Zed Books, 1980).
26. Steady, *The Black Woman Cross-Culturally.* Introduction. Also Terborg-Penn et al., *op. cit.,* see note 16 above
27. Miriam Thali, Interview in *Unheard Words*, ed., Mineke Schipper (London: Allison & Bushy, 1984), 66-67.
28. Mamphela Ramphele, "Do Women Help Perpetuate Sexism: A Bird's Eye View From South Africa," *Africa Today* 37.1 (First Quarter, 1990), 7–18.
29. Tsitsi Dangarembga, *Black Women's Writing: Crossing the Boundaries Davies*, ed. Carole Boyce (Frankfurt A.M. Ehling: Matatu, H.G. Jg.3g 1989), Interview.
30. Audre Lorde, "The Transformation of Silence into Language And Action" *Sister Outsider* (Freedom, Ca. : The Crossing P, 1984), 40–44.
31. *Presence Africaine* (1987) no. 141.
32. *Sisterhood is Global,* ed., Robin Morgan (London and N.Y.: Doubleday, 1984) included a shortened version of *Women in Nigeria*, ch. 4 in Part II in this volume as "Not Spinned on the Axis of Maleness."
33. Molara Ogundipe-Leslie, "On Reading an Archaeological Article" *Sew the Old Days and Other Poems* (Ibadan: Evans P, 1985), 19.
34. Ogundipe-Leslie, *Sew the Old Days*, 2–3.
35. Felix Mnthali, "The Stranglehold of English Lit. (for Molara Ogundipe-Leslie)," *The Penguin Book of Modern African Poetry.*
36. Ogundipe-Leslie, *Sew the Old Days*, 30-33.

19. In Search of Citizenship: African Women and the Myth of Democracy

What is democracy to her
Or she to democracy
That she should weep for it?
— Molara Ogundipe-Leslie
adapting from Shakespeare's *Hamlet*

In these portentous and unpredictable times, following the collapse of the Soviet Union, the fall into disrepute of the idea of the nation state contemporaneously with the planned re-organisation of nations into larger comities like the EEC in 1992; in these days of the "new world order" and the questioning of most social and political boundaries, it seems ironic, if not anachronistic, that African countries are being forced to re-organise themselves through parliamentary democracy into nation states. As the world is wracked by world-wide recession and teethers on the edge of economic doom, in AALA (African, Asian and Latin American) countries, and as world powers pursue miasmic democracies, even into Kuwait, Africa is being constrained to construct nineteenth century-type nations out of post-feudal, post-stateless, post-IMF societies, which are sometimes synchronic impactions of all the aforementioned formations. Virtual re-colonisation is taking place behind monetary economics in Africa. A political scientist, Professor Oyeleye Oyediran, has noted in his James Coleman Lecture: "Background to Nationalism: Thirty Years After" (UCLA, 1989) that "in Nigeria and at least in twenty-five other countries in Africa, the International Monetary Fund and the World Bank are the major policy makers." In the whirlwind of economic, political and social crises in which Africa is embroiled, what is the place of her women? If African nations were to seek parliamentary democracy, what would be the conditions of the women?

Notions of Democracy in Africa

There seems to be an almost superstitious (or perhaps just constructed) belief that multiparty systems will lead Africa to the political utopia that she needs. This belief appears implicit in the tying of aid to political stability of the parliamentary type. The populations in Africa themselves seem tired of the proliferation of military rule on the continent as they claim to be tired of the particular forms of governance handed down by soldiers. Between November 1958 and April 1984, 56 successful military coups were counted by one political scientist. Since then, more successful military coups have taken place in several countries, including Nigeria. While there is some general hope placed on democratic rule under civilians, even as marionettes, some voices are already warning that weak political parties can impede the installation and consolidation of democracy. One voice has warned in Africa Demos (vol. 1. no. 1. Nov. 1990) of "the danger that multipartyism will reflect, in the end, merely a consensus among the "elites" on the re-allocation of prebends." I feel that care needs to be taken that multipartyism does not promote ethnic division and hatreds while it ensures a further balkanisation of the continent.

Several heads of state have enunciated ideas of home-grown forms of governance including democracy. Museveni has been quoted to say that "development is actually linked to democracy but democracy as understood by our people not as dictated by other people." (Africa Demos, ibid.) His cultural nationalist stance comes in the tradition of other precursors in the theorizing of African nationalist struggles.

Very often too, on the continent, other nationalists, thinkers and political adventurers have harked back to our indigenous forms of government which some of us would argue guaranteed true democracy (if democracy is understood as the representation of the will of all the people who are encompassed by a political organism). Care has to be taken, however, to identify truly democratic procedures and structures in indigenous African governmental practice.

The term, "democracy," which is sometimes defined as "the assembly of the citizenry for the conduct of public affairs" should not, in this day and age, be applied to village gatherings and assemblies which exclude women and slaves, which recognise only adult men, men with wives, and the freeborn only, or male elders exclusively. Such gatherings should not be panegyrised, as some of us are doing, as fine examples of democracy.

By this token then, the village assemblies in *Things Fall Apart*, beautiful as their world was, are far from democratic; neither are the village or elders' gatherings in Ali Mazrui's film series *The Africans*. Modern democracies must do better than the Greeks (who also excluded women and slaves) and eighteenth century Europe which, for the most part, was not thinking of women.

An analysis of African democracy must look into the fine, unusual and quite un-Western processes and their interstices by which the reflection of the will of *all* members of the society, male and female, was achieved. I tend to agree with Achille Mbembe who says in *Africa Demos* (op. cit.) that "we risk reducing democracy to mimickry; or worse, to a convenient way of becoming more "presentable" in the eyes of the world . . . In Africa, as elsewhere, democracy will either be a historical construction or it will fail. Put another way, the forms democracy takes will derive from the underlying social struggles. . ."

Citizenship and Women in Africa

Fundamental questions first need to be posed, in my view, before we can even begin to discuss women and democracy in Africa. To get down to brass tacks, is the African woman, in fact, a national of her own country? In how many countries does she have legal citizenship? Research shows that some countries have not still re-written their inherited colonial or settler constitutions (and not only in Southern Africa) wherein and whereby women were legal minors. Ruling classes who are now enjoying the benefits of total control of their female counterparts may be loth to change these outmoded laws. Do not internationally accepted laws and human rights conventions support the idea of a woman's adulthood (like that of any man) at eighteen or twenty-one when she is considered able to be responsible for herself? Some countries employ other social and religious traditions to keep women in a state of legal and social minority. Imagine the trauma and the confusion for African women, who are considered adult at puberty within indigenous laws and who have been adult in their social comportment in traditional realms within the dictates of their cultures, suddenly finding themselves incredibly handicapped by legal minority in the modern state?

In how many countries can a woman sign her own forms to attain her own passport as a bona fide member and national of her own country of birth? The ability to acquire a passport is not a simplistic right, considering that a passport is one of the basic proofs of one's nationality. The woman's right to acquire her own passport without passing through a husband, father or male relative is often dismissed as a distractive and unnecessary introduction of foreign avant-garde ideas into Nigerian civil discourses. But if some African women are not, in fact, basic citizens of their countries through their own recognised will, how can we speak of democracy with regard to them?

Following right on the heels of the issue of citizenship are the rights of liberal democracy to which the African woman is supposed to be heiress. Does she have rights which the power classes in her country feel they are *bound* to respect? Is she considered an inalienable participant in the project of building democracy in the modern nation state or simply a means to an end, "a tool to democracy", an instrument for the mobilization of resources and rights to the male population? These are not idle questions as the experience of women demonstrate and the theories of development experts corroborate. Being instrumentalized has been the fate of African women in many countries. Established rights like freedom of movement or freedom of association are not so guaranteed as to make the African woman everywhere a free political actor.

Women as Instruments

Experience in several African countries has demonstrated that women are not only included as tokens and sops to the demands by women for representation and participation in national projects, they are also basically conceived of as instruments to galvanise their husbands and children. Women are not in themselves conceived of as subjects in political discourse and action or direct recipients of the benefits of both. In general, women are seen to exist as instruments to be used for the political purposes of men. The woman in herself is not thought of as a citizen to be mobilized to attain political rights, benefits and advantages *for herself*. This reductive attitude to women is to be found, strangely enough, even among the most verbally progressive of the menfolk.

The attitude toward women's claim to liberal democratic rights is often one of charity couched in benign patronization. "We shall *confer* some rights on you if you behave yourselves, and certainly do not talk feminist" sums up the attitude. In some circles, the saying: "Women do not have rights that we as men are bound to respect" is often laughingly interchanged with: "The poor do not have political rights that we are bound to respect." The institutionalization of the habit of appointing one token woman to cabinets, commissions and committees to represent 60% of the populace confirms the attitude of patronisation that men are being "kind" to women by including women at all.

The Politics of Exclusion and Silencing

Throughout Africa, a natural tendency seems to be towards the exclusion of women from national events, institutions and exercises, including *the writing out of her contributions* to the modern efforts at nation building, whenever these contributions are given space to occur at all. In addition, women are frequently not acknowledged for their ideas nor recognised as intellectual producers of ideas. When they have ideas, these are often pirated, appropriated and used without acknowledgement, recognition, or compensation. These politics of exclusion, unacknowledgement and appropriation help to ensure the silencing of women needed to shore up the hegemony certain men in the power classes derive from knowledge or the affectation of epistemic superiority.

Erasing the African Woman

Not only are African women sometimes not citizens or not considered as citizens in *themselves* (i.e., not as wives and mothers only), in the modern sociogony, planning is often not made with women in mind, neither are they called upon to participate in planning and policy. Some marginal spaces have been created by certain women in some countries where we also see an urgent haste for the usually phallocratic governments to coopt these women's spaces and activities. Sometimes women's energies and organizations are used to work against women's interests, as in the story (possibly not apocryphal) of the country where the President who wanted to stop a woman environmentalist only had to shout: "Where are the women?" for right-wing and establishment-oriented women to rush out to vilify the activist.

African women are not only written out of constitutions, commissions and committee reports, they are often erased out of the national canvas of power broking and resource-sharing. Middle class women are often excluded and vilified because they are said to be too Westernised to represent the "true African woman," that is, the romanticised, rural and unlettered African woman. At the same time, this rural and unlettered woman is naturally excluded and derided (in private, when the middle class woman is not being opposed) because she is too rural and too unlettered. So by this clever manouver of excluding both the lettered and unlettered African woman, African women remain unconsulted and erased from the realm of events while African men maintain hegemony. The contemporary African nation state sails happily ahead as the exclusive preserve of middle class, lettered and Westernized men. This, in my view, is one of the clever tactics by which women are defeated in the power politics of the modernization process while men in the ruling classes monopolise the political arena where democracy, in its ideal form, is supposed to reign.

In politics, however, women are supposed to participate fully as "instruments to power" for men; as entertainers, campaigners, and party workers. They are not naturally accepted as candidates or considered candidates of the calibre of men. Most men still somehow resent women in a position of authority over them. Sometimes Christianity and Islam are evoked to support these attitudes. Meanwhile, modern democracy is supposed ideally, to function irrespective of gender and other variables.

Women and the IMF

Nonetheless, in the national context, women carry economic burdens as heavy as those of most men; burdens which are now rendered heavier in our post-IMF cultures. The debt crisis, the structural adjustment policies and the resultant devaluation of our currencies; the loss of jobs, the immiseration of the African countries (including the pauperisation and proleterianisation of their middle classes, leading to resource flight and a continent-wide attrition) are all impacting the most on women: firstly, as mothers, wives and economic producers who now have new dependencies thrust upon them; secondly, as dependents within patriarchal or other family structures. Gender roles are being reversed, while some are being cancelled out or restructured to the detriment of women's conditions when social services, such as health, education, transport and communications, are cut in the IMF packages. Women become the most affected as homemakers, nurturers of children, and economic workers in town and country, in fields and markets.

Women, we know, need more personal and continuing health care throughout their lives. With the new restructuring of gender roles, it will be fair to say, however, that some men are developing a new respect for the resilience and resourcefulness of women as they counter the economic blitz.

In such desperate times, political rights become less prioritized by the women. An added effort may therefore be needed to make the majority of women, particularly in the peasant and working-classes, take any kind of interest in their national political cultures. Most women might now need to be strongly persuaded to the view that political participation could be any way out of the dark woods of the IMF in which their loved ones are now trapped.

Finally, to problematize from Claude Ake's elegant essay on "Democracy and Development" (*West Africa*, 26 March-April 1990), if multinationals bluntly acknowledge their preference for strong governments that maintain order, discourage nationalism and implement structural adjustment policies, can we have true democracy in Africa as defined earlier in this essay? And if capitalism is dissociated from its political correlate of liberalism, particularly for women in Africa, can women have democracy?

Afterword

Looking To the Future Through the Past

"Ti omode ba subu, a wo waju; ti agba ba subu, a bojuwo ehin." - Yoruba proverb. (When a young one falls down, s/he looks ahead; when an elder falls down, s/he looks behind.) The rain has been beating the vulture, oh, for so many years. It is not, therefore, surprising that my vulture has many stories to tell. Yet as soon as you finish telling some stories, you are inmediately faced with gaps, points left undeveloped, other narratives left untold. They all strain to be given life to make the seeing more complete. Yet no text is ever complete. This knowledge allows us to move forward as we look backwards. The bush-hen must see with her eyes and her feathers.

More narratives of African women's identities and lives, roles and statuses remain to be told. The dignity of African women will not be found, for now, in their coital and conjugal sites, though it should be. They, however, have dignity in other areas. All African women have multiple identities, evolving and accreting over time, enmeshed in one individual. Yet African women continue to be looked at and looked for in their coital and conjugal sites which seem to be a preoccupation of many Western analysts and feminists.

Africa herself needs more of her contemporary narratives told - her transitions, the arrangement of her own re-colonization by her own sons (and daughters?), the unleashing of unfinished nineteenth century conflicts, hatreds and political movements after independence in her various countries by their citizens. Nineteenth century realities had been unceremoniously interrupted by colonial experience. Today, they are still hermetically sealed into our consciousness, behavior and political fates. Unresolved, Africa will not find peace, in my opinion. Africans and other concerned analysts on the continent need to engage in deliberative and other activist actions to try to understand the many currents which form the undertow of Africa's present dilemma as some of us tried to do in the 70s and 80s, through platforms like the Ibadan-Ife Group, Positive Review, WIN, AAWORD, etc. For instance, a conference on "Radical Perspectives on African Literature and Society" which I initiated, found funds for and co-organized with the Ibadan-Ife Group at the University of Ibadan, Nigeria, yielded many insights. Such analytical ventures are even more needed in Africa today.

I think, more than ever, Africa needs to cope with her ethnicities. There is no way we can move forward without integrating the undeniable reality that most Africans have a four - tiered personality - the ethnic, the national, the continental and the diasporal. We must embrace and recuperate our ethnic cultures as we disinfect them. The ethnic defines the individual at the most primary, important and emotional level of health and historical identity. We are being asked to move into the future without our past and present by those who deny or misunderstand the value of ethnicity. Having ethnic cultures is not in itself shameful. The question is how we use them. Can we set up democracies of Western varieties on the psyches of people who have other heritages without taking those heritages into consideration? Do we move into the twentieth century as tabulae rasae? The need to air our inherited and sealed - in 19th century contentions and engagements coupled with the emergence of the military as a political class remain, in my view the most serious problematic of Africa's critical transformations today, in addition to the conundrum of South's Africa's historical development.

They say your true friends are those who, in a hunt in the fields, chase edible rats, not vipers, in your direction. How can I thank all my hunting friends, fellow travelers and students who, in many ways, have chased many edible and succulent rats in my direction? They know themselves and they are to be found all over the world, but particularly, in the last four years, in Canada and the United States where I have been, for a while,

a nomadic professor as migrant laborer. I thank you, all my unnamed friends as, I also thank my foes, for the wise Yorubas say: "Adaniloro f'agbara ko'ni." (The tormentor teaches you strength.)
Major among my friends of the edible rats are Kassahun Checole and the house of Africa World Press. I salute them all for their patience, dignity and steadfast dedication to issues of great moment for Africa, her diaspora and the world.
Kudos to my student friends in Canada and the U.S. who helped with the production of this manuscript. I also acknowledge thankfully all those who have, at one time or another, printed any of these essays wherever. I say "wherever" because my writings get published without my knowledge, permission or approval as happens with other AALA writers. It seems to be a special experience of (AALA) "Third World" intellectual production that we get used differently. Excuses are later given; but, true or not, I thank every pirate/friend for making my work accessible to any audience he or she has chosen.
Finally, my warm appreciation goes to Isis Olumeye Leslie, my daughter, the most tireless and fastest transcriber of my tapes I know. Thank you very much et je t'embrasse tres fort. This is a small offering to you and your generation in the hope that you may live in a better world of greater peace and harmonious collaboration between women and men.

—Molara Ogundipe-Leslie

INDEX